SURVIVOR FROM AN UNKNOWN WAR

The Life of Isakjan Narzikul

By Stephen Lee Crane

DIANE PUBLISHING CO.

UPLAND, PA

Published by Diane Publishing, Upland, PA.

ISBN 0-7881-7730-3

Library of Congress Cataloging-in-Publication Data

99-94704
Survivor From an Unknown War / by Stephen Lee Crane

Includes bibliography and index

1. Narzikul, Isakjan 2. World War II 3. Uzbekistan
4. USSR - Ethnic Groups 5. Czechoslovakia

To

MARY NARZIKUL

whose love, support and dedication

are felt by so many

CONTENTS

ACKNOWLEDGEMENTS

To the many people whose time and encouragement have made this book possible, I must extend the most heartfelt thanks. These supporters contributed generously and in a very timely manner. The man who made the work possible and spent two years in long interviews was Isakjan Narzikul. He introduced me to Dr. Ergash Shermat, whose knowledge and assistance were exceeded only by his warm friendship. Shelly Baum aided the effort with a continuous review of the text from the initial drafts onward and extensive use of her editorial skills. Jacqueline Silver also lent editorial talents. Dr. Mark Stolarik played a special role, as did my wife Marci, and Herman Baron. Jeffrey Crane served as graphics consultant. Additional help came from many friends, relatives and the resources of the University of Pennsylvania Library.

PREFACE

Isakjan Narzikul was born during the spring of 1923 in the small city of Jizzakh, in the middle of Central Asia, an area historically known as Turkistan. Turkistan stretches from mainland China, across the southern portion of the Soviet Union, and into Afghanistan. The Soviet portion consisted of five Soviet republics and one autonomous republic. Jizzakh sat in the center of the Uzbek Soviet Socialist Republic.

Turkistan occupies a large part of the immense plain covering a land mass that extends from Siberia clear into Europe and as far as the Mediterranean Sea. Except for small valleys, the grass vegetation never permitted intensive cultivation of the sort found in Egypt, India and the Tigris-Euphrates valleys. The steppes, therefore, developed a tradition of nomadic pasture in the midst of extreme climatic swings.

Lying between the "cradle of civilization" river valleys and their productive societies, Turkistan became a crossroads of trade along the many branches of the famous Silk Road. Fabulous wealth accumulated as a result of the business conducted in places like Samarkand and Bukhara, and this wealth attracted many conquerors including Alexander the Great, who took Roxanne as his wife in the area of Turkistan called Bactria.

For most of the peoples of the region, existence did not include visits to glimmering cities, but a harsh life on the plains. At certain times in the history of Turkistan, the inhabitants established an extraordinary unity which combined with unsurpassed skill in horsemanship to produce empires that ruled much of the world using terror against enemies, but peace and law for their own population.

Empires founded by Turkistani khans and sultans

vanished into dust after ruling for centuries, and most of the region was conquered by the Tsar of Russia. The Communist successors to the Tsar defeated attempts by Turkistan to gain independence after the revolution of 1917, and hence the majority of Turkistani people became subjects of the USSR. A smaller number live in North Afghanistan and Chinese Turkistan (Sinkiang).

The people of Turkistan staged a number of revolts throughout the years of Russian rule and during World War II established a government-in-exile with an army of over 200,000, but these efforts came to naught.

Today, after the breakup of the Soviet Union, Soviet Turkistan has become the countries of Uzbekistan, Turkmenistan, Kazakhstan, Kirgiz Republic, and Tadzhikstan.

A more detailed summary of Turkistani history appears in the postscript chapter entitled "Notes from Turkistan."

Two names in this biography have been changed. These are the Czechoslovak family named the Clepeks and Safi Oraz. The conversations and quotations are reconstructions and accurate in general content but not word by word detail.

The book is based on interviews and research. Its main source is a series of discussions with Isakjan Narzikul that he represented as true. As much as possible, his comments were verified by independent sources, but in many areas those comments are the only reference.

CAST OF PEOPLE

(Several are mentioned but not identified by name.)

CHAPTER 1 - WHO IS ISAKJAN?

Jurabay	Childhood friend of Isakjan
Isakjan Narzikul	Subject of the book, also Ilja or Jay
Isakjan's mother	Ougulay Narzikul
Makhmud Narzikul	Father of Isakjan

CHAPTER 2 - MILK AND GOLD

Tura Narzikul	Half brother of Isakjan
Rashid	Head, Tenth Anniversay of the October Revolution kolkhoz
Saraf Rashidov	Rashidov's son, Isakjan's mentor,

CHAPTER 4 - THE RED ARMY ALWAYS WINS

Admissions officer	Colonel Karpov (not named)
Nora Melkakze	Girlfriend of Isakjan

CHAPTER 5 - THE PROFESSOR IS DRAFTED

Ergash Shermat	Law professor, Isakjan's friend
Chokay	Turkistani nationalist leader
Kazakh judge	Buran Bayev (not named)

CHAPTER 6 – HOW LONG DOES IT TAKE TO DIE?

School commander	General Petrov (not named)

CHAPTER 7 - MEDICS WITH CLUBS

Nuriddin Qari	Anti-Soviet mullah

CHAPTER 8 - PROMOTIONS FOR POW'S

Meyer Mader	Wehrmacht officer
Veli Kayum-Kahn	Liberation Committee President
Baymirza Hayit	Turkistani military leader
Prussian trainer	Franz Helmut (not named)

CHAPTER 9 - ALLAH BIZ BILEN

Sergeant Schneider	Wehrmacht officer, advisor
Kamal Alimov	Turkistani Legion officer
Sattarov	Turkistani medical officer

CHAPTER 10 - THE HAY WAGON WITH MACHINE GUNS

Mrs. Rogozinski	German citizen, landlady
2nd tour advisor	Lieut. Laudenslager (not named)
2nd tour leader	Major Horst (not named)

CHAPTER 11 - EXILE GOVERNMENTS IN BERLIN

Dr. Karimi	Turkistani member of Committee
Safi Oraz	Intelligence (not correct name)
Prof. von Mende	German political liaison
Richard Oder	German broadcast chief
Luderzin	Wehrmacht liason

CHAPTER 13 - MONGOLS INVADE SLOVAKIA

El Rashid	German SS Colonel

CHAPTER 14 - BULLETS IN THE DESSERT

Colonel Boshinski	Red partisan

CHAPTER 15 - PARTISAN ACTIVITY

Mrs. Fridreich	mother-in-law
Eva Fridreich	Slovak wife
Frank Fridreich	father-in-law

CHAPTER 17 - DON'T RETURN TO PRISON IF YOU CATCH COLD

Parish priest	Father Vaclan Strecko (not named)
Neighbor lumberman	(not named)
Chief Stefanic	Hlinik police head

CHAPTER 18 - DOES CITIZENSHIP PREVENT ARREST?

Martin Suezz	Lumber broker

CHAPTER 19 - ESCAPE

Clepaks	Friends (not correct name)
Andre	Social friend and refugee

CHAPTER 21 - GYPSY BLOOD

Captain Jones	American supply officer

CHAPTER 22 - I AM STILL ALIVE

Sponsor	Alexander Kobasa (not named)
Mary	Wife of Isakjan (Jay)

EPILOGUE

V.P. Uzbek Society	Jurayev (not named)
Pres.Uzbek Society	Ramz Babajan (not named)

PROLOGUE

In 1954, a janitor for a Pennsylvania manufacturing company needed to see a doctor for a severe cold. The man had recently immigrated and spoke broken English. After finishing dinner he walked three blocks from his home outside of Philadelphia to the office of Dr. Crane. The physician routinely examined the patient and prescribed medication.

The man's humble manner drew no special attention, but as he began to speak, an irrepressible determination and intelligence caught the medical practitioner by surprise. The doctor invited the janitor to return the next evening after office hours for tea. A snack and ensuing conversation initiated a continuing friendship between the physician and the sweeper, Isakjan Narzikul.

As the two men came to meet the families and learn about the backgrounds of one another, it became obvious that Narzikul had lived through events not dreamed of by most people of the world and knew secrets suppressed by entire nations. One nephew who became especially interested in those secrets was Stephen L. Crane. Stephen Crane asked Isakjan Narzikul whether he was ready to tell the full details of his life. Narzikul was ready.

PART I

SOVIET PROMISES

For thousands of years humankind's finest minds have been struggling with the theoretical problem of finding the forms that would give peoples the possibility, without the greatest of torment, without internecine strife, of living side by side in friendship and brotherhood. Practically speaking, the first step in this direction is only being taken now, today.

Closing speech by Mikhail Kalinin
after the formation of the USSR
by the Unification Congress, and
reiterated by (later) General Secretary
Andropov in 1977. [1]

CHAPTER 1

WHERE IS ISAKJAN?

It is better to eat communist weeds than capitalist grain.

---Jiang Qing, wife of Mao Tse-tung

Jurabay struggled to raise his fallen body from the dust in the road. His solitary figure, old and bent, reeled drunkenly as he crossed the little canal bridge. As the only path serving the ancient Central Asian neighborhood, the dirt cartway needed no name, and delivered its largely pedestrian traffic with quiet anonymity.

He trembled from the alcohol, the years in Siberia, and the ostracism of officialdom after they proclaimed him an enemy of the people. Despite his confession and rehabilitation, the one-time rising star of the Communist Party merited no more than a position as assistant sweeper for the miller and, on weekends, town drunk.

This conclusion to life deprived his once brilliant mind of respect and faith. Perhaps he had invited the debasement when he crawled back to beg forgiveness, exposing those who sided against the regime and foolishly believing he could expose friends in exchange for exoneration. His deeds of infamy were no different from those of others, and yet some had avoided the traps set for them and escaped. Did they suffer also, wherever they sought refuge, or did a convolution of history single out only his life, tormenting him alone? What of his friend Isakjan (ee·Sak·'jon) Narzikul, who had disappeared so long ago?

Jurabay arrived at the door of the Narzikul house, his mouth thick with the odor of alcohol and his thoughts confused from long years in Siberia. He no longer stood as a man did, but as a former personality stripped by the abyss of terror and humiliation. He pounded his fists on the door, crying, "Where is Isakjan? Where is Isakjan?"

No one answered. Inside, Isakjan's mother sat motionless on one of the mats inside the sun-dried mud walls of the house. A dark solid door and windowless facade designed by a mind bent towards privacy faced the ancient dirt street, empty except for a boy and his donkey. Hidden behind the wall and house, hens scratched for scraps beside the family cow in a small enclosed yard.

She had last seen her son as a teenager, early in 1941, when peace reigned and he prepared for a career. A savage war had come with no forewarning and suddenly he was gone. She never even received a letter. She stared at a fading picture of him.

"Presumed dead," the authorities had said.

She didn't accept that conclusion so readily. What mother can ever presume a son dead? Over the decades, hope fueled by rumors yielded to the hollow realities of absence. And yet, the insistent inquiry of Jurabay stirred cobwebs that shrouded the past. She remained silent, also wondering, "Where is Isakjan?"

The other citizens of Jizzakh [2] knew better than to ask such forbidden questions. The little city scratched out a place on the edges of the desert in the Soviet Socialist Republic of Uzbekistan, one of five socialist republics and one autonomous republic in Soviet Central Asia, historically known as Turkistan. The people of Jizzakh followed the lead of the Uzbek government and put the question aside.

Others, in powerful positions, still wished to find out, and a few did know about Isakjan Narzikul, from the beginning. The beginning was long before, in Uzbekistan during the 1930's, when the Bolshevik Revolution and the boy shared a youth dominated by the all-consuming drive of hunger. The boy's hunger came from an empty plate; the revolution's, from an insatiable appetite for power.

Isakjan, son of Makhmud Narzikul, was named after the prophet <u>Isa</u> (Isaac) and looked to his father for guidance in the art of survival, only vaguely comprehending that a tremendous revolution had upset the balance of life in the dusty city. Makhmud

Narzikul remained aloof and distant from the boy, exceeding even the restrained familial relationship common in the strict society. He had reason to fear companionship, even with his seven-year-old son, because a casual word from the lips of the boy to the wrong person could place the father in great difficulty.

A mere lad could not be expected to understand why his father, a simple uneducated son of a policeman, insisted on continuing his trade of tanning hides long after his little business was nationalized, nor why he silently prayed to Allah in spite of official prohibitions. But nevertheless the boy did understand, at least partially, as he watched his father surreptitiously collect hides from some of the townspeople, and pile them on his donkey for a trip to hidden alcoves in the country where he dipped them into acidic fluids. His hands accumulated scars and yellow streaks, eventually looking like leather boots and emitting the noxious fumes which, together with the handling of dead animal skins, marked him and his trade with a low social status.

After nationalizing his trifling business, the government had assigned Narzikul a position as stable hand at the local collective farm, or *kolkhoz* (kɵl·Khɵz'). With this new position came a lower salary and less food on the family table, so Narzikul continued his old tanning business in secret competition with the government during his evenings and weekends.

Every time Makhmud Narzikul extended his hands for a "salaam" (sa̵a̵·Lɵm' a·la̵y·Kʉm' is the traditional greeting) or turned in his credit slips at the kolkhoz store, the undeniable polish and acrid odor reserved for those who work with the chemicals of leather emanated from his still yellow hands and tainted fingernails. Kolkhoz authorities noticed those cured hands. Narzikul's attempts to hide his illegal handiwork were too simple, too straightforward, like the man himself.

After the revolution, the status of the tanner had changed more unremittingly than just a loss of income and profession. Unsuited to conducting his life partly in shadows, he became a man afraid, and the fear reduced his Moslem religion to incomprehensible mumbles at the dinner table, and his fatherly guidance to pointers on the merits of melon skins in the diet of the family cow. Only in the ear of his donkey did Narzikul feel comfortable in pouring out his soul. When the aged beast lay down in the street to die, the man wept and hugged the animal's neck, nuzzling its mane with his bearded face and crying out to his "old friend," begging him not to leave in such terrible times. The religious and trade secrets the elder Narzikul imparted to his donkey were withheld from his son for fear of retribution from authorities. The donkey could not stay to comfort his friend, however, and passed away. Thereafter the men in the neighborhood referred to Narzikul as the "sentimental one."

Following his father on his daily work routine, Isakjan unsuccessfully sought the emotion that lay enmeshed within his father's heart. The child bounded with uncommon energy and could work a full day. As the youth trailed, the father passed down the street calling out to the neighbors, who brought their cows out to their front gates. On weekend mornings, he collected over a hundred, driving them to pasture and supervising Isakjan, who acted as round-up dog. In the afternoon, with the cows bawling and kicking up dust, customers dropped a piece of old bread, as payment for the grazing, into a large burlap bag held out by Isakjan. The begging shamed the boy and he wished to hide his face from the other children who played while he dragged his satchel of crumbs home to dinner

In the spring of 1930, Narzikul walked several steps in the lead while the young boy traipsed behind with the new donkey, Eshak. Isakjan dashed around the animal, prodding him with a small nail at the end of a stick.

Eshak reacted to the excited lad with insouciance, displaying the rudeness common to pack animals and insisting on frequent breaks. The boy and donkey carried on a battle for leadership, a struggle ignored by his father. When the opportunity presented itself, Eshak was not above launching a sudden hoof into Isakjan's bony bottom, while snorting uproariously at the resulting sprawl of legs, bare feet and rags. The donkey did not discourage the lad with his antics, but instead produced renewed determination and energy. Isakjan redoubled his efforts to conquer the beast.

Narzikul's destination required the troupe to pass the hill on the outskirts of Jizzakh where thousands of men in white embroidered garments gathered to celebrate Ramadan, the fast in commemoration of the prophet Muhammed's revelation from God. They assembled on the hill because Jizzakh no longer possessed a mosque. The crowd listened to three mullahs who had avoided arrest by the authorities. Many clerics had been imprisoned by the government for practicing religion.

Makhmud Narzikul never broke his pace. Fear of exposure settled upon his eyes like blinders, and he lowered his head and marched past the throng. Isakjan and Eshak paused, full of curiosity rather than apprehension, to wonder that so many people existed in the world. The mullahs chanted in the forbidden Arabic tongue as the mesmerized faithful swayed in a field of white cotton robes, all bowing in poetic rhythm to Allah. The excitement reverberated through Isakjan's body and he longed to belong, to melt into the mystery and unity of something sublime rather than the grit of his everyday drudgery.

The Narzikuls proceeded past the hill and then flat fields of young cotton plants with their emerging bolls of "white gold." As they walked, Narzikul's furrowed face looked beyond the cotton, to the rolling fields of wheat and hay while the boy glanced over his shoulder for a last longing view of the Ramadan assembly.

Father and son walked for a good portion of the day, to the farthest lands of the Tenth Anniversary of the October Revolution Kolkhoz, which extended for some ten miles. Here the cotton fields turned to waves of grain. Narzikul traded some of his leather products and received additional hides, which he loaded on the donkey while his son watched a dirty cow circle a rural milling stone. Eshak appeared eager to respond to the elder Narzikul, who never went to school and could barely write his name, but did understand animals well.

Narzikul never complained or took part in political discussions. One revolution per lifetime would suffice very well. Besides, he did not have either a revolutionary or reactionary spirit, preferring to quietly blend, refusing to realize that this path sometimes sets the most gruesome snares. He quietly donned his cotton chapan (cha·Pan' - loose robe) and trousers each morning, placed a square embroidered skull cap on the top of his head, and reported to the kolkhoz during the day and to his tanning chemicals in the evening.

At night he buried sacks of grain, the illegal profits of his enterprise, next to the house and in the garden across the road. Ownership of more than two sacks of grain constituted "disruptive hoarding," so Narzikul had to find secret stowages to hide the wheat he had earned.

After each trip to the country, Isakjan led the donkey through the thick wall into the family court, unloaded Eshak, then fed both the donkey and the family cow. Possession of the cow without registration and payment of tax exposed the family to other criminal charges.

When chores were completed, the family sat down to dinner. With the warm weather, they crossed their legs on mats placed on the ground outside, and reached right hands into the common bowl in the Turkistani manner, squeezing a pilaf of bread or rice, butter and carrots between fingers before eating. His half-brother Tura, Isakjan, and young sister sat opposite his father and mother.

His parents swayed in seated position for a moment, face in hands and softly murmuring, "Praised be Allah who has delivered this meal."

The son always waited for an explanation of the soft mealtime chant; he waited at dinner, while driving Eshak, and shepherding the neighborhood cows, but his father never imparted a clarification.

In unpleasant weather, his mother would stir a thin broth over an open fire in the center of the house, smoke curling up to the thatched roof, which sheltered nests of small black birds and snakes. On cold winter nights, she would place a short table (sandal) over the coals, and a blanket over the table. Family members would each find a corner to slide under for warmth, notwithstanding the heavy smoke. A jug of water and open pit in the corner served as sink and shower.

Isakjan's mother dreamed of another life for him, but the realities always pressured them. That summer, his sister died of an ailment that ate a hole in her cheek which widened to the point where the jaw bone was clearly visible despite the salves of the local shaman. Death mercifully followed weeks of degeneration, and the father whispered prayers over her grave.

Just after the funeral, men with long sticks and tablets combed the neighborhood. Isakjan watched as they made their way through the town, stopping in yards and piercing the soil, probing for hidden stores of grain. They also counted the chickens and vegetable plots, comparing records, checking to determine if the tax on these items was properly paid. They noticed the donkey in the Narzikul shed.

"Do you have any cows?" they asked.

The men didn't bother to look and the cow never peered out from the rear of the shed. They didn't need to find the cow, for they had enough evidence.

At night, trucks appeared in the street. The residents only owned donkeys and horses, so the presence of the big vehicles rumbling through the workers' section of old city, kicking grime and noise into the hidden courts, meant the start of a government mission. Isakjan slept while armed men jumped into action, pounding at various doors, and then at his own. He slept as they pulled his father from bed and as they unearthed the evidence, sacks of buried grain, and loaded it on their trucks.

No one was permitted to attend the trial. Isakjan did not see his father again for years. He disappeared into a nether world where Narzikul's fears grew into terror, where mumbled prayers did not suffice as adequate measures of submission. The arrest was part of the many waves of mass imprisonment to shake the Soviet Union that included concentration camps for "destructive" hard labor, costing untold millions of lives. Starting in the 1920's vast numbers of religious leaders were included in the prison population while the property of their mosques was expropriated. Remaining religion practiced underground. [3] Narzikul quietly began to serve his sentence for crimes against the State.

Without the father's support in the fall of 1930, mother, son and stepson tenaciously existed as famine spread, barely surviving on hard bread sometimes dipped into a cup of milk. Isakjan had to assume adult chores. By neglecting to confiscate the family cow, the arresting police spared them from immediate starvation.

Others did not fare so well. In the capital city of Tashkent, the sanitation department worked extra long hours carting bodies, dead from starvation, found in the street.

Isakjan knew only of his own hunger in Jizzakh as he dallied in the yard, thinking about his father's absence. He did not hear a command from his mother. The boy's response took too long, and she set out to quell his insubordination.

"When I call, you get here immediately. What took you so long? No excuses," she yelled with a stiff cuff to the head.

He estimated she stood about seven feet tall, with uncompromising dark eyes.

"Do your chores. Feed the animals."

The boy had already begun to realize, unconsciously, that certain ideas regarding the conduct of life might possibly be incompatible, that rules of behavior are subject to differing shades of meaning, and that the final interpretation of a rule becomes apparent only at your trial.

Isakjan obeyed his mother and delivered hay and straw to the shed. The poor cow, main bulwark against complete destitution, never earned so much as a walk around the court for her contribution to the family. They could never chance getting into the official records as owners of the cow, as they could not afford the taxes for ownership of such capital equipment. As he milked her, a strong stream of white juice squirted from the teats, he estimated the amount available to sell at the bazaar, and then ran to the garden to water and weed, leaving the milk in a pail ready for market.

By his father's example and his mother's tongue, Isakjan acquainted himself with man's most basic privilege and duty: work. He discussed market strategy with his mother over the morning meal, reporting on the fresh green hay procured the previous day as he soaked pieces of hard bread into a bowl of milk. They sat on the dirt floor in the middle of the small central room of the house. After morning bread, Isakjan collected the milk pail and a half dozen glasses, and proceeded to the bazaar in the center of Jizzakh.

While walking, he nodded to the morning's pedestrians, able to identify almost all by name.

"Salaam Alaykum," he called out to each.

"Salaam Alaykum," he waved to his female cousin, promised to him since birth.

The people of Jizzakh lived close together, close enough to know the names of their neighbors and those around the corner; close enough to expect a "salaam" from any person passing on the street; and close enough for each person to take a part in molding the town's character. This enabled them to sustain a unique ability to sift events from the outside. In this secluded atmosphere, small indigent boys did not realize the hopelessness of their plight.

The path he followed to the bazaar passed the building that was formerly a mosque, architectural anchor to Jizzakh. The building traced a history back to glorious days when the Silk Road [3] brought prosperity to the small city. The mosque and town had experienced centuries of scant repair and decline, and yet the building's stone sculpture and commanding minarets still inspired awe even in the youngest of children. Sometimes his mother would impart secrets about the mosque, from the time of the Bolshevik revolution.

"We always stayed alert, keeping ahead of the bullets," she told him. "Then one day the Whites lined up a thousand Reds in front of the mosque, machine guns ready for execution. Something happened, some order or trouble. The Reds were spared and live today as heroes, brigada captains and party bosses who banished the mullahs, converted the mosque to a theater, and then built offices and a school next door."

CHAPTER 2

MILK AND GOLD

The capitalist was able to supply things. He did it inefficiently, charged exorbitant prices, insulted and robbed us...

'But the capitalists were, after all, able to supply things...'

During the past year we showed quite clearly that we cannot run the economy. That is the fundamental lesson. Either we prove the opposite in the coming year or Soviet power will not be able to exist... If all of us Communists, the responsible officials, clearly realize that we lack the ability to run the economy, that we must learn from the very beginning, then we shall win...

--Vladimir Ilyich Lenin to the Central Committee of the Russian Communist Party March 27 1922 [1]

Young Isakjan's thoughts were of commerce as he walked past the mosque-turned-theater. He entered the bazaar area early, observing peasants spreading their mats and vendors displaying their wares. The early arrival rewarded him with a prime spot, at the end of the market next to the melon stalls. He favored this location, because parched shoppers who stopped for melons would also need a drink of milk, which he had to sell that day. Also, customers might leave him their melon skins as a tip, which were loaded into Eshak's baskets and taken home to feed the cow.

The little milk vendor opened his concession while others still trudged in with their produce, spreading out carpets for his customers to sit on while they ate the melons and sipped cool milk. He lined up a row of glasses around a ceramic pitcher on a center mat in the best of bartending tradition. A few of the glasses always brimmed with milk, beckoning a weary shopper to relax for a minute.

The bazaar filled, and he observed a smattering of his best customers, the Russians, who paid with cash instead of bartering and would rather purchase a good glass of milk than share the water of the well with the local residents. The Russians loved the melons of Uzbekistan, and the bazaar overflowed with both Russians and fresh fruit. Every Uzbek market included hundreds of melon varieties in all colors, shapes and sizes up to giant behemoths requiring two men to load.

Preferring their own company, the Russians built an exclusive section of Jizzakh called "New City," to prevent any unnecessary commingling with the locals. These people the Russians disparagingly referred to as "Sarts" from a contraction of Sarmatians, ancient people of the area, which the Russians used in a pejorative manner. Dressed in their Western clothes, the Russians resembled tourists as they walked among the darker-skinned locals who still preferred the flowing dress of the Central Asian plain. The Turkistanis did not lack in resentment towards the Russians, called zhelty (yellow), who had conquered their country, imprisoned their religious leaders, and confiscated their property.

The temperature climbed well past one hundred degrees Fahrenheit in the Jizzakh market, and the little urchin merchant already had sold half his milk, while a number of sweating Russians still roamed the bazaar. He repressed a growling stomach as he watched a plump Russian order a melon. Could he be more clever than his father in claiming a bit of food from the Russians? He filled several more glasses with two-thirds milk and one-third water. Staring at the diluted drinks gave him chills, and he decided to pour them on the ground.

But the Russian approached the row of glasses after finishing his melon. With his light features, fine Western clothes, and confident composure, he contrasted sharply with the mass of Uzbeks flowing past, indistinguishable from a distance in their robes. Isakjan scrutinized his customer, who placed a coin on the carpet and lifted a glass. The small boy watched, uncomfortably aware of his ruse. The man swirled the fluid around inside the mug, to separate the milk and the cream. The boy grew nervous and fearful. His stomach juices curdled; cold sweat broke out on his forehead; adrenaline-charged fear pulsed through his veins. The Russian's eyes grew angry and he glared at the lad.

"What is the matter with this milk? Did you water it down?" the Russian demanded.

Isakjan stuttered while trying to coax his mind into an answer and twisted his hands to stop his body from shaking. In broken Russian he stammered, "It's from a new cow."

"I see," replied the man, relaxing his taut neck muscles.

A glance at the short figure convinced the Russian. He swallowed the milk, gave a refreshed sigh, wiped his brow, and walked away. Isakjan refilled the glass with his mixture.

"Is this the way adults act?" he asked himself, already feeling guilt and self-hate. "What must I do in order to afford meat?" he thought on his way home. When he told his mother, she attacked him, screaming.

"Never, never tell a lie." she yelled. "Always tell the truth." The blows cascaded down as hammer fists descended. "You must become something more than a merchant. You will become a learned one, a teacher or manager. " Even in poverty, the woman felt superior to merchants, as did most of the populace.

Shopkeepers, after all, contrived to barter for petty gains and ventured into demeaning haggling, undertakings fit for small boys, women and effete men. Isakjan's mother gave her son clear instructions to rise above their dismal status through education. When a new schoolhouse opened, she saw to it that he was among the first group to attend classes.

The school and the kolkhoz office next door, both shabby

brick structures, stood unadorned amidst a yard bereft of the slightest consideration for landscape or design. Here, the Soviets trained new citizens with revolutionary ideas. The old generation consisted mostly of those who could read only the Uzbek language using Arabic letters. They had become effectively illiterate when the Soviets decreed that the Uzbek language would henceforth use Roman, and not Arabic letters. This decision limited communication with the Islamic peoples of other countries and between generations. New teachers came from cadres of young enlightened men and women not burdened by the renounced literature of the past.

Isakjan trudged through the door of the Narimanov School, named for an Azerbaijani revolutionary. New buildings acquired names of non-Uzbek heroes since few Uzbeks had earned a name in Soviet history. In school, one room sufficed for five grades, one teacher and the miracle of knowledge.

This miracle raided his senses and body, driving hunger and impotency before it and causing him to forget all else as the numbers and letters hypnotized him. Every subject interested him: Uzbek, arithmetic, history, communist theory, Russian and a smattering of German. Recitations used the Uzbek language with its new Roman letters, while the Russian tongue comprised a minor subject.

"You must study hard," Isakjan's mother exhorted him. "With education your aunt and uncles got positions of distinction."

The child needed little encouragement. After school, while grazing a few animals for the neighbors and collecting hay for the family cow, he sat and took notes on the day's lesson. The concentration on studies lifted his mind and spirit from the facts of his destitution, creating another world where constant challenge fed his yearning for great purpose. He retreated to a special existence: that of the intellect, escaping from the drabness of his endless chores into the make-believe atmosphere of the new Communist future. Here he met with freedom, equality, and success. With this diversion, he could carry the hay home on his back without remorse. He could even accept almost daily maternal beatings for slowness and distraction. He now had his refuge.

An insurmountable wall of imagination protected his refuge except for one difficulty. He chewed and swallowed the books and lessons with enthusiasm in an effort that did not impress his stomach. On too many days the hollowness of an empty belly started him sweating. He had to develop alternatives to scant bread and milk from home.

The hungry boy looked to his classmates, the twins who lived with their grandparents. The twins cared very little for school and spent their time frolicking in the streets or assisting their grandparents in a small home bakery. Their house had a constant supply of bread and fruit on the table and wonderful smells of baking in the air.

Embarrassed by his poverty, Isakjan would roll his pride up in a little ball and casually drop over to see whether his friends needed some assistance with their studies. He knew that the smile on his face must stretch as wide as the ache inside his body, or he would end up as another miserable street cur. After food for his dry palate and instruction for his friends, he could prepare for school the next day.

In class he learned the nature of his deprivation and its cause: the old capitalist and religious systems. The teacher explained, "Hand in hand with the capitalists who took your food were the mullahs. Beware of religion, for it is a tool of the enemy. The mullahs allowed only the rich to attend school, and they helped to enslave women. The old mullahs took the young girls for themselves. Now, Communism has opened schools to all people and to girls. Before, women could not even show their faces, but now they can read. Our country is liberated."

The teacher continued, "The future will change all the inequalities of the past. We Uzbeks have suffered discrimination, but under the red flag, we will walk hand in hand with the modern world, mouths full with food, minds with knowledge, and spirit with class consciousness."

The teachers did not convey the fear of Isakjan's father. They never mumbled incantations or shied from crowds, but confidently explained the mysteries of the world, openly and fully. They spent extra after-school hours with interested students to make them feel part of a tremendous human advancement.

"You are as worthy as anyone in the great Soviet Union," the teachers explained. "Russians are our older brothers, and even though they are building great projects in their own home, they take time to share knowledge with comrades from Turkistani republics. Our Russian brothers have undertaken the task to manage the revolution for the good of all."

Isakjan could see the changes wrought. Communism had reallocated property of the bourgeois class, including his grandfather's grain mill and his step-uncle's bakery. That part of the family made a graceful transition to the new order, pledging loyalty to the Russian leadership and working under Communist

Party direction in their old offices. Isakjan saw this as just, having been told by his mother that those relatives had cut her out of any inheritance because she was only a step-sister. He rarely saw these people, who seemed to avoid the Narzikul side of the family.

The mullahs and small landowners lost the revolution and could lead no more. Korans became contraband, and familiarity with Arabic brought suspicion.

Even though Isakjan lost himself in studies, his impoverished world always waited, a shadow grown over the land. In 1931 his knees, shoulders and ribs cried for some flesh to cover knobby protuberances.

Isakjan's mother woke him before dawn. "We must go for bread today." She put a piece of change under her dress.

The boy knew what that entailed: long lines and nervous people. As mother and son walked from the house, rays of sun pierced the eastern sky, reminding them to hurry. They had slept too long and the line had already formed when they arrived, stretching out a thread of dark veils and thin defeated children. Midday came and went before they approached the distribution point and were told to come back another day.

"No more bread."

At home, his mother acted strangely. She served Isakjan her piece of old bread. "I just don't like stale bread," she complained.

The next morning they awoke early again. "Help me with this," commanded his mother.

She brought out what served as the family heirloom, an old cradle with carved handles and spots of inlaid gold. He watched as she gouged out the metal, collecting a small pile on the table. Then she removed her scarf and tied on the black veil with fringes hanging like hair, carefully retying the scarf again. After drawing her shawl about her shoulders and picking up the shopping basket, she motioned to her son.

"Come with me to the store."

"The store," Isakjan repeated. "That must be different than the market."

The Narzikuls did not go to the bazaar but to one of the government's new Torgsin (commercial syndicate) stores. The government allotted one of these stores each to the old and new cities. They sought the one in old city and soon came to a converted building. Entering the Torgsin removed him from the drab crushing poverty of Jizzakh into the fantasy of consumerism: bicycles, plentiful grains, meat, flour and bright pans lined the shelves and walls.

The boy walked through the store in silence, as though in a museum, without the confidence to touch and too much in wonder to ask. The grain overflowed, enough to fill the caches of many an illegal hoard, and indeed may once have filled secret hiding places before government confiscation. The bicycles held his attention most, all sizes, colors, both new and used.

The Torgsin stores operated differently than other stores. They did not accept the labor credits earned in the kolkhoz cotton field, nor the barter of the bazaar, nor the paper rubles from Moscow. The Torgsin stores demanded hard currency in the form of gold and precious stones. Men with weights, measures and little magnifying glasses assayed the metals and stones.

That day's purchases were quickly exhausted within a few weeks, and without a head of the household, the family entered a free fall into abject poverty and probable starvation. But his older half-brother, born also to his father, saved them.

Tura, a seventeen-year-old born just before the revolution, felt the hunger directly, and his initiative saved the family from the famine. He gained acceptance into a short course for tractor operation and then received admittance into the tractor *brigada*, an independent elite unit that plowed and tilled the fields of several kolkhozy.

"The brigada will give me bread, twice a week," he proudly announced. "Isakjan, you can go and pick it up for me at the distribution station in New City."

Isakjan gratefully added the trip to his chores and announced at the distribution point, "Salaam alaykum. I am Isakjan, brother of Tura from the tractor brigada, come for his bread."

A lady at the counter handed him two fat pieces of black bread, enough to cause a basic improvement in the family's diet. A couple of loaves per week raised their food supply quite noticeably, but Tura brought other surprises, arriving with his tractor to plow their family plot. What Isakjan and his mother would till with sticks and donkey in the hot sun for days, Tura accomplished in minutes.

By the spring of 1933 Isakjan was ten, old enough to find a responsible job for the coming summer once school let out. In the afternoon, he approached the kolkhoz office in the squat brick building next to the former mosque. It shared the structure with the kolkhoz multipurpose man, whose nationalized shop administered haircuts, dental care and circumcisions to the citizens, who still practiced that Moslem ceremony.

"Salaam alaykum," he chanted the traditional greeting once inside the office.

The man there knew him well. Rashid, the kolkhoz boss, sat behind his desk.

Rashid knew very well that the job seeker could calculate and recite better than most adults in the community. Perhaps only one student, Jurabay, outperformed him. Rashid knew this because his own son, Sharaf Rashidov, was among the most educated men in Jizzakh and taught in the school.

Rashid discharged his own job with the authority expected from a man who had risen from the masses to command. He had obtained his position in recognition of deeds in the revolution and service to the Party, but lacked any semblance of managerial skills. The chief of a kolkhoz needed political, not administrative, skills. His assistant, with fewer party credentials but more education, ran the collective while Rashid maintained his Party contacts.

Isakjan came back day after day, badgering Rashid and his assistant for a position. His sincerity and ebullience made the assistant laugh, which in turn encouraged the youngster to intensify his lobbying. One day, the assistant greeted him with news.

"One brigada needs a *tabilci* (ta·bil'·che - bookkeeper). Come tomorrow, and you will take the position as brigada clerk." The brigada constituted one of the six in the collective farm.

"Brigada clerk," he thought, "What fortune!"

The brigada captain handed him a large wooden instrument about five feet high resembling the lower part of a pair of scissors. "You will use this as your measuring compass," the man directed. "Do you know how to calculate area?"

Isakjan nodded his head in the affirmative. The captain tried to explain anyway but trailed off as it became obvious that he could not determine area measurements. No matter, his job was secured by other achievements. He lost interest in the work progress after the first hour each day and, having issued his directions, disappeared till the morrow.

With his bare feet and bone-thin torso, the new tabilci cut anything but a striking figure among the rows of cotton in the hot, baking sun. He thrilled to join real workers, now a part of universal Communism. These were the people who swayed to the chanting on the hill, and their future, like his, held fresh promise.

The eighty men and women laborers of the brigade worked with picks and sticks to trench deep grooves in the soil, connecting branches of the irrigation canal with the long rows of young plants. They lifted water from the canal a pail at a time to the furrows.

All of the workers except young Isakjan were adults. (It was years later that the kolkhoz formed children's brigades that directed youngsters into the fields.) Like a little mouse in the middle of a maze, Isakjan ran down the rows and flipped the compass to count meters, pacing off the outline of the progressing work between the cotton plants. He ran around the scattered brigade, writing down the name of each person, what they worked on, and how much they finished. He dropped off his report at the kolkhoz office every evening.

In the afternoons, the work pace changed, with some continuing their cultivation, others sleeping, and others melting away. Clumps of cotton bolls disappeared into pockets instead of the receiving station, but Isakjan was not able to pass judgment on any adult since his submission to figures of authority was absolute. Furthermore, he liked these people, and his experience observing his father's side business and his own bazaar marketing gave him a sense that the revolution, in its wisdom, gave its workers flexibility. After all, they were now in control of their own destiny.

The tabilci reported no absences, just completed work. As time went on, he became even more lenient with the reports and many of the brigada members earned consistently solid marks for credits.

The skinny lad with the large compass became an odd part of the brigade. With the captain off worrying about party policy, Isakjan fell into a niche created by the power of his own literacy and kolkhoz apathy towards production standards. Favors were traded between groups who trusted each other, just enough to hold off the worst aspects of the poverty they all shared. Trust and discretion dominated this trade.

The work lasted long days, after which he took care of the family cow and chores. Over the course of the summer, he became known to a vast array of common people who recognized him as a person to be trusted, one who could work with the system. Isakjan's confidence increased and he began to think about putting his day off to use. In particular, he noticed the kolkhoz small fish operation.

Two handsome middle-aged men and their donkey trudged each Saturday to a nearby stream well known for plentiful fish. They set up a series of nets, sitting under the shade while the little unsuspecting silver beauties swam into the web. The men emptied the fish into baskets slung over the donkey's back, punctuating their endeavor with sessions of gossip and speculation. Thus did they relax, talking about the next day's work at the bazaar, while the fish lay limp in the sun and the nets filled.

The farm workers' committee, citing the known dangers in allowing this capitalist operation to exist, had nationalized the fishing partnership. The partners no longer needed to worry about their future as the State would see to that, while the population could feel safe that the price of fish from the stream would remain predictable.

The kolkhoz needed a clerk to monitor the machinery of production and Isakjan volunteered for the job. He accompanied the two men to the stream and watched as they drew in the lines and dumped the catch into the baskets. The next day, rather than reporting to the cotton fields, he arrived at the bazaar in time to help set up a charcoal grille and table. The men began to fry the fish in a thick batter and customers stepped up. Some purchased fresh fish, others a fried meal; some paid with rubles, others with the labor marks of the kolkhoz. Ten kopecks bought a tasty meal of three fried fish.

At the end of the first episode with the fishing operation, Isakjan in his position as tabilci counted twenty rubles. He turned them over to the senior partner, who quickly split them, four to himself, four to his partner, ten to a pile for the collective, and two to his tabilci.

"This is your share," the partner winked. "Mark down that we sold fish for ten rubles today."

Isakjan ran home with the two rubles, eager to get them out of his hands and into his mother's.

"My good worker," she praised him.

The praise did not entirely satisfy him, as the contradictions between the responsibilities of a tabilci and the reality of the manner of Communist business haunted him and brought the same feeling of anguish he had felt when selling diluted milk at the bazaar. The revolution seemed to exact a certain tension from those who experienced any success, a problem exacerbated by public inquisitions.

The government reminded the population of the penalties for resistance by initiating open-air trials in front of the town square by the old mosque. The weekend event gave the citizens some entertainment while instructing them on proper legal behavior. During the trials, teashops offered drinks and hot beer to the spectators. Isakjan passed the crowded space in front of the judge's stand, sliding between men already reeling from the effects of the warm alcohol and children scurrying about. The bustle ceased as the judge mounted the podium.

From the buildings to the side, police escorted the defendant, with hands tied and head bowed. The man assumed his position as lead actor in the unfolding drama.

"This is a simple case," explained the prosecutor to the judge and audience. "This man stole from the kolkhoz and the state demands a fair and heavy penalty." The lawyer waved his hand at the defendant. "Did you steal two cows from the kolkhoz?"

The man shook his head and murmured.

"Speak louder," commanded the judge.

"Yes, I did."

"And did you then take these cows and slaughter them for yourself, without giving any meat to the owner, the kolkhoz?"

"Yes I did." With each revealing admission, the man's head sank lower.

The prosecutor threw his hands up in disgust. "Here is a man so depraved that he took animals from the state for his own use. He did this to the state, which supplies him with everything from birth. He deserves no mercy. I recommend ten years."

The lawyer for the defense stood up to "plead" his case. "Your honor," he respectfully addressed the judge, "My client stole from the kolkhoz, which is the state, which is the people. We cannot tolerate disbursement of state property. Give my client ten years."

The judge took the arguments into consideration. He looked fiercely at the defendant. "For stealing from the state, which represents the people, I sentence you to ten years at forced labor."

Isakjan would never steal cows from the kolkhoz. He had already learned that education would provide what hoarding and stealing could not, and therefore in the fall, when his duties at the kolkhoz diminished, he looked to school for his training and camaraderie.

[illegible]

CHAPTER 3

LAST TROLLEY STOP

We must simultaneously develop in the border regions (including Turkistan) a wide network of lecture courses and schools on every branch of administration in order to create cadres of instructors from among local people. For it is clear that without such cadres the organization of native schools, courts, administration, and other institutions in the native tongue will be difficult in the extreme.

Joseph Stalin [1]

Isakjan shrugged off the case of the stolen cow and concentrated on his studies. In fifth grade, the school separated students into different classrooms. Isakjan already associated himself with the literature and grammar Teacher Sharaf Rashidov, a man who dared to differ, to wear Western clothes, to shave his face, and to speak his mind boldly. Isakjan, recognizing his own disadvantages, knew that his path sided with change, with unexplored ideas. Many an afternoon he spent at the home of the Rashidov's, enjoying snacks of meat with heavy bread and listening to reports of progress in the revolution brought about by the efforts of father and son. These men understood the revolution and the place of the Uzbeks in Soviet history. They walked as equals to the Russian managers of destiny. They told Isakjan how the revolution worked, and gave him an inkling of how a family, how a father and son, could relate with congeniality rather than silence.

Isakjan learned that the Soviet constitution guaranteed a future to all people, living in equality and fraternity. He memorized large parts of that document, as a sign of the better world to come. He particularly enjoyed the opening:

"Since the formation of the Soviet republics, the states of the world have become divided into two camps - the camp of capitalism and the camp of socialism.

"There, in the camp of capitalism, national hatred and inequality, colonial slavery and chauvinism, national oppression and massacres, imperialist brutalities and wars prevail.

"Here, in the camp of socialism, mutual trust and peace, national freedom and equality, peaceful coexistence and fraternal cooperation of peoples are to be found.

"....Only in the camp of the Soviets, only in the conditions of the proletarian dictatorship rallying the majority of the population, has it become possible to destroy national oppression root and branch, to create an atmosphere of mutual trust and to lay the foundations for the fraternal cooperation of peoples......" [2]

Rashidov also pointed out that, "in America, individual states can not secede, and, indeed are held by force of arms which caused the U.S. Civil war, but in the Soviet Union, every Republic shall retain the right of free secession from the Union." [3]

Isakjan found more in the communist ideology; he found faith. Before, his poverty was comprised not only of economic scarcity, but also of faithless existence. The Communist Party brought him from that misery and gave him belief in the community of man.

Sharaf especially enjoyed a reputation as a leader, for as much as Uzbeks disdained the petty shopkeeper, they revered a man of learning. With mullahs in disfavor under the ruling Communist regime, secular teachers filled a place of status in the community.

Sharaf rose to the stature that possession of knowledge could bring. His poems taught the people of the advances brought by the revolution. His presence at a dinner table brought more honor to the host than that of ten shopkeepers and five kolkhoz officials. He befriended Isakjan, encouraging him with schoolwork, challenging him to excel, and instructing him in the ideals of Lenin, Stalin, and socialism. He constantly reminded the boy and the class:

"Marxism is the best thing to happen to the Uzbek people. Our brothers in Russia realize our state of poverty and send their own talented managers to help us modernize and advance to take our place with the workers of the world.

Perhaps some of you saw the play in the theater over the weekend. It showed how the workers have overcome the tyranny of the upper class and taken their lives into their own hands. You, as the new generation of freed people, will enjoy a better life because of the revolution."

Isakjan had seen the play, as his aunt and uncle often appeared as actors in productions at the mosque-turned-theater, and he watched rehearsals. The teacher continued.

"Here in the Soviet Union, the working man is improving his position, while in the rest of the world the capitalist managers force people to work long hours or suffer arrest and starvation."

After the lecture as Isakjan walked from the classroom, he paused at the trashcan and, as was his usual habit, picked up a used copy of the newspaper "Road to Socialism." Usually he could expect to read a poem or article written by Sharaf.

"Isakjan, wait a minute," called out his teacher.

"Yes sir?"

"I would like you to compose a story for our newspaper. Go over to the kolkhoz office and interview my father."

Isakjan became a writer, recruited by Teacher Sharaf, keeping readers informed of new irrigation jobs, the harvest plans, and the progress of the Tenth Anniversary of the Revolution

Kolkhoz.

His work pleased Sharaf to the extent that one day, when Isakjan submitted another article at his teacher's house, Sharaf offered him a present, a book of poetry he had written.

Sharaf won the loyalty and firm pledge of Isakjan for the Soviet government. The boy accepted without question the inevitability and superiority of a Communist world. He made his first political judgment and commitment.

While he grazed the donkey Eshak and various cows, Isakjan read Sharaf's poems. His celebrations of the progress of Uzbekistan arising from its association with Russia, praised the uniqueness of the USSR. Sharaf worried that other nations did not have the same future, the paradise where workers were free, where the bread lines were short, where the largest nation on earth was leading the world to a new era of contentment.

In the summer of 1936 the government found it necessary to measure the private plots of the community, since some citizens exceeded the law which bequeathed a small plot of land to anyone desiring to raise his own produce. With the recommendation of the Tenth Anniversary of the October Revolution Kolkhoz, tabilci Isakjan Narzikul helped in this task. Now quite practiced in the art of surveying, he set out to measure the plots, marking down in his little book those exceeding the allotted amount of land.

A wrong mark in his book could instigate a review by the authorities, and confiscation of the excess land by the government. He felt this practice too severe, and was once again thrown into a confusing blend of duty, anxiety and expediency. In most cases he determined that leniency was in order and simply overlooked violations. He lacked the resolve required to place his neighbors in trouble.

The surveying brought him to the yards of many citizens of Jizzakh, including that of the town's best student, Jurabay, who sat reading a book under a tree. The two befriended one another, talking for the rest of the afternoon. The borders of that yard were never subjected to the scrutiny of the surveyor's compass. Instead, the two students talked of education. Jurabay already had enrolled in a high school far from Jizzakh and spoke of the adventure that still awaited his young friend. Jurabay planned for a career serving the socialist government, expanding his considerable expertise into municipal management. Both lads wanted something better from life, which meant something Russian.

That summer Isakjan's clerking activities also extended to the mill in New City, the one that his mother's family once owned.

He knew about the mill from previous occasional visits with his father. When they arrived early, he would witness men opening the wooden gates in back of the dam to direct water over the huge wooden wheel, sparking the round grinding stones into plodding circular motion.

People came to the mill with grain they obtained, either from their own sweat or the black market, and stood in line for a turn. For each hundred kilograms ground, the kolkhoz wanted six as payment for the service. The workers ignored this, and Isakjan, as clerk, followed their instructions, marking the records to hide whatever private deals the operator and the customer set.

Isakjan discovered how the clerk could gain popularity by respecting the will of the people. He filled in time sheets for field hands, sometimes adding hours to those in need or those nice to him. He learned what his father didn't: the way to cooperate within the system. He felt so lucky, so privileged to live in the Marxist socialist society where a boy could work hard and get ahead, but he also felt plagued with depression at the contradictions and felt that only time was needed to perfect communist society.

Isakjan came back home from the bazaar one winter night to find his mother's half-brother, an editor of the Tashkent newspaper "Red Uzbekistan," in the living room. Such an important man rarely came to Jizzakh and only saw his sister once a year.

"I hear your studies are going well, young man," the editor addressed his nephew.

"Yes, sir."

"Your mother tells me you would like to attend technical school."

"Yes, sir."

"Well, I would like you to take a little trip to Samarkand and apply to a boarding school there."

Few towns provided education beyond the seventh grade and those larger cities that did often offered boarding.

In spring, 1938, he boarded a train for the first time in his life and went to the big city of Samarkand. He sat on the wooden benches which backed up to the windows of the passenger car, and twisted his head to view the terrain all the way to Samarkand, the last stop, nervously excited about the chance to continue his education and join the ranks of men like Teacher Sharaf.

He returned to Jizzakh and waited. The letter which finally arrived expressed appreciation for his application -- and rejection.

A second letter from Tashkent, home of his uncle, proved more rewarding. The Lenin Teacher's School in Tashkent agreed to admit him.

On the train to Tashkent, he read a newspaper retrieved from the trash. Great changes were happening in the Soviet Union, enough to concern Isakjan. Stalin discovered numerous foreign agents undermining the Soviet system and was forced to initiate a number of extreme actions to deal with the problems. The Soviet State and his future were threatened. He was amazed and shamed to find that some of the conspirators were Uzbeks, and he followed the details of the trials and the treachery uncovered by the confessions.

Every day, the trials in Moscow brought out more discoveries. He read the printed transcripts from the courtroom interrogation of two Uzbek officials:

Prosecutor: You worked for a foreign power?

Defendant: I did.

Prosecutor: Did you have secret meetings, and why?

Defendant: Yes, I met in secret with foreign representatives to plot the overthrow of the government.

Prosecutor: Did you defame the Soviet State at these meetings?

Defendant: Yes, we gave false information about the Soviet Union.

Isakjan marveled at the evil in these men and felt relief at the diligence of the authorities in preserving the revolution.

He entered Tashkent, flower of the Soviet Orient, a few days before the start of classes, meeting the secretary of the school and asking her where he should sleep. His assignment to a room followed, where he found himself the youngest, at 15, by a couple of years. Others in the room came mainly from Ferghana, the historic center of the Uzbek language. He was the only student from a small town.

Isakjan placed his extra shirt at the foot of his bed, contrasting starkly with the lockers and possessions of the other residents. The families from Ferghana must have been quite prosperous as the other boys displayed many articles of clothes and jackets while they boisterously arranged their living quarters. The disparity did not bother Isakjan since he lived for things more important than clothes. He smiled at his fellow countrymen, comrades and future partners.

"Where are you from?" asked one of the others.

"Jizzakh," replied Isakjan.

"I thought just mountain people lived there." The others laughed.

"Don't you dress there. We don't want to have to look at you. Are those all the clothes you have?" Again, laughter.

Isakjan reminded them, "All people are equal under the Soviet constitution. You have no right to discriminate."

"Well, what did you do for the revolution, mountain boy? My father runs a collective farm."

"And mine works for the Party paper," chimed in another.

"Come, let's go to a restaurant and leave this mountain goat behind." They left.

Isakjan, thinking that class distinctions were gone, was surprised that these boys could get enough money to go to a restaurant. In Tashkent the revolution seemed not to take hold. He wished his uncle, who helped him enter the school, would explain the ways of the city to him. When the uncle called, he did get a dinner, but no advice.

Back at school, more derision followed as the other students bragged about their fathers and made fun of him. Then they wanted to know, "How come you only have one pair of pants?"

"Hey, Gypsy, when do you take a bath?"

"I guess he is just an Uzway, mountain Mongol."

It just didn't make sense. "How come these students have so much money and I have nothing? In a socialist republic, everyone is equal," he brooded.

In the morning he went to the dining room for breakfast of tea and bread. After soup at noon, his stomach still growled, and the meager suppers turned the growl into a constant ache. He had no mentors or patrons in Tashkent to offer snacks of bread or pilaf, but a kitchen job finally soothed his stomach.

The teasing grew worse and incessant, but he never fought back. The smallest boy could never win anyway. He internalized all disputes, blamed himself, and took everything personally. The elegant clean rules of Communist behavior fell apart in the Tashkent school. When his frustrations became unbearable, he walked away rather than get enticed into a fight, admonishing his fellow students, "This teasing is against the Constitution."

The teachers of the school, his hoped-for friends and patrons, did not help. They conducted formal classes and offered no personal contact, not even when his grades rose to the highest in the class.

One Saturday Isakjan set off for the bazaar by himself and observed strange sights including men and women dancing together in the center of a square while a band played. They even held hands and waists. He stared for an hour at this sight of flagrant loose morals before continuing through the market. And such a large bazaar! As a merchant himself he had seen many displays of wares and produce, but never any to rival the luscious fruits of Tashkent. However, the fruits were not for him, not for those without money.

Somehow his goals became blurred, as did the philosophy that a poor boy can work hard and make good. He retreated into his books, constantly studying in classrooms after sessions and in his room, learning about the great social strides made in the Soviet Union while strikes and worker beatings occurred in the United States. He just wanted to finish the last few weeks of the first year and then leave the school. Even the thought of returning uneducated to Jizzakh for a few years started to tempt him, but an ad in the "Red Uzbekistan" newspaper gave him another alternative.

TASHKENT MILITARY SCHOOL

SOLICITATION

CANDIDATES WANTED

OFFICER SCHOOL

He read on. Candidates for officer school must be a citizen of the Soviet Union, understand Russian, possess a degree from a technical school, and be age 18.

Isakjan considered his position, a boy whose father had been jailed trying to provide for his family, scorned by his peers, and with diminishing hope of a trade. A military background might unite him with those who believed in the socialist cause and who lived by its rules. It might open the doors that now were closed before him.

The most important qualification, that of a Soviet citizen, he knew would stand him in good stead. Never mind that he had not quite turned 16, that he spoke crude classroom Russian and that he lacked a year for a technical school degree. The tabilci experience led him to understand these details. His faith in the overwhelming charity of the Soviet system lifted his expectations and hope.

He sauntered into the secretary's office and bid her, "Salaam alaykum." She remained his only friend.

"And how is Isakjan today?" she inquired.

"Oh, just fine," he responded, and after a time, added. "You know that I am leaving, that this is my last year?"

"Yes, and we will miss you."

"I thank you for all you have done for me," he said with conviction. After another pause, he continued, "Would you mind giving me a transcript of my grades? I might be needing it when I apply to another school."

"Certainly, I'll prepare one for you today."

"You are so busy," he worried. "If I prepare it for you, all you will have to do is sign it."

She hesitated. In 1939, documents in Uzbekistan were hand-drafted in a style suitable to the author.

"Yes, that would be fine. Write the transcript and I will check it."

He spread oversized paper out on a desk in the next room. On the very top, he carefully inscribed the statement "First Year Transcript." Leaving a wide space, he wrote "Tashkent Technical School," and thereafter listed his marks, noting that due to achievement in grades, the holder received honors.

The secretary scrutinized the paper, compared the grades with her records, stamped a certification, signed the document, and handed it back to Isakjan.

"Good luck."

"Thank you."

Back in his room, he cut the top of the transcript above the space he had carefully left. In that space, which now stood at the top of the cut paper, he inscribed the words "Graduation degree and last year transcript."

He took the trolley to the end of the line and got off at the Tashkent Military School, asking directions at the main gate. He lied about his age and produced his false certificate of graduation. They gave him a test, in which he scored well in math, poor in Russian.

Staying temporarily at the technical school, he took the trolley every day to the last stop and read the posting of successful applicants. After days, a message appeared for Isakjan Narzikul to see the colonel in charge of admissions.

The colonel sat at a large desk, looking more like royalty than an officer, with distinguished white hair, immaculate uniform, handsome fine face, and radiant blue eyes. The colonel had served in the army of the czar long ago, and one of his most famous maneuvers was a successful jump from the White army to the Red. If this was an example of how officers turned out, Isakjan could make the military a career.

The Red Army placed the colonel, after appropriate service and loyalty, in an easy position for his last years, at the Tashkent Military School. No frozen wasteland for this officer, but warm climate in the sun belt of the Soviet Union, there to supervise the sons of the well connected. These well-connected sons did not come from the republics of Turkistan, but from Moscow, the Ukraine, Byelorussia and Moldavia.

"Why did you apply for admittance to the Tashkent Military School?"

The question came as a command from one who dispensed the privilege of admittance to the School, and the small boy shriveled.

"I want to serve my country," he stammered in what he realized was very inadequate Russian.

"Well, your math grades are passing, even good, but we frown on admitting those who can not speak Russian fluently," he spoke in a commanding voice.

At this juncture the youth's ability to respond almost departed from his shaking body. The report on his grades in math and his own desperation gave him added strength. Also, the grand dignified admissions officer was a Russian, and his kind were known to buy watered-down milk from small urchin boys, thanking them for the drink.

Isakjan burst out in a unsteady stammer, "Sir, please give me a chance. I learn very quickly and will study every day and learn Russian very well. I will work very hard. You will see. You will be proud of me, and I will serve my country well."

The colonel smiled. "I will think about that."

The next day, his name appeared on the bulletin to get a medical exam. A week later his name appeared again, a successful candidate for Tashkent Military School.

CHAPTER 4

THE RED ARMY ALWAYS WINS

Every citizen in Soviet Uzbekistan enjoys full opportunities for education and the development of talents. The sons and daughters of factory and office workers and farmers become prominent scholars and cultural workers. This is one of the vivid illustrations of the Soviet way of life.... reference to Article 27 of the Constitution of the Uzbek republic which says: `The state concerns itself with protecting, augmenting and making extensive use of society's cultural wealth for the moral and aesthetic education of the Soviet people, for raising their cultural level.'... Things were very different in the past. At the time of the Russian empire and all the preceding centuries, Central Asia had an extremely low level of cultural development, although the peoples of the region gave the world many great scholars, philosophers and enlighteners. All the cultural wealth created in Central Asia in the past remained the property of a handful of rich. The October Revolution of 1917 changed the state of affairs radically. In order to build a socialist society it was necessary to accomplish a cultural revolution.... Within the first two decades of Soviet power, this task was resolved in the main.

---Uzbek Society for Friendship and Cultural Relations with Foreign Countries, Tashkent, Uzbekistan, USSR, 1983.

The School stood at the end of Tashkent, on the central thoroughfare, with large iron gates at the entrance and a tall fence along the property. Pedestrians entered a smaller gate next to the main one. Inside, an enormous yard spread out on either side of the drive; the layout afforded visitors a view of the houses of the officers in front of the school buildings. The commanding general occupied the first house, a graceful structure that set the tone for the architecture of the campus with its imposing early Russian motif. Playing fields for soccer and volleyball skirted the officers' homes in a plan that rivaled the best of municipal parks. The entrance road veered to the left, separating the school on one side and a six-story dormitory and administration building on the other, all with minarets and spires.

The guard at the gate admitted Isakjan, giving him instructions which guided him through the campus to a building where clerks waited to process him. He thrilled at his acceptance into the stately school and prepared himself for assimilation into communist brotherhood.

Gangly lines formed by the recruits accented the fact that Isakjan stood a full head beneath the other students. He stretched to see a few isolated tan faces and black hairlines, which readily distinguished his fellow Turkistanis from the mass of light Russians and Ukrainians. The barber pushed his shears over light and dark heads with a determination to reduce each one, regardless of ethnic origin, to a tiny fuzzy patch. The tailor and bootsmith shared a similar detached desire to produce regulation grade models from a disheveled mass of bodies. Isakjan melted into the program, happily losing consciousness of his unique past.

Before the cadets could don their new garments, the officer in charge supervised a shower and inspection. Isakjan then dressed in his first set of new attire. The uniform included a white collar attached to the jacket with matching sewed-in sleeves, making the suit very hot in the Asian sun, no doubt designed by a procurement department located in cool Moscow. He lost no time in acquiring modern Russian tools, beginning with a toothbrush, and readily became proficient in its use.

Other utensils presented a more difficult problem, especially forks and spoons, since he was accustomed to eating with his fingers in the Uzbek manner. In social behavior class, when most officer candidates laughingly practiced military posture, he worked on the proper manipulation of flatware. While others found the class a silly diversion, he discovered that it unlocked the secret of his inferiority and that serious application of its lessons could make him equal to the Russian culture. He assiduously repeated the trivialities of manners: how to shake a hand, proper posture, correct gait, and graceful greetings. He lacked only a razor for his toilet kit, something not needed for the clean face of the smallest and youngest cadet.

An officer assigned him to a company of a hundred boys, consisting of a few platoons. Each platoon and company had a commander. He lined up with his company for another of the frequent inspections.

"Issacaan," read out the instructor.

The Russians could not pronounce Isakjan, no matter how hard they tried.

In the dormitory, the entire company shared a hall, with bunks lined up along the walls. Isakjan looked around for Turkistanis to associate with, but saw precious few. He was the smallest, youngest, skinniest, darkest and most foreign; an alien in his own land, unable to communicate in the language used in the school.

"Ssakacan. What kind of a name is that?" they taunted. "We don't need any *natsmen* (nats·'men - dirty foreigners when used negatively, but literally means `national minority') in our army."

Isakjan looked away. He didn't want torment in his new home. Inwardly, he brooded and resolved to change. His energy took a nervous turn in attempts to improve himself to the point where he could deserve positive rather than negative attention. While he fretted, the remarks became more degrading.

"Hey, country bumpkin, why are you so dark? Cherny, that's what you are. Cherny. Blacky."

As the only Turkistani in the entire company, he had no countryman to turn to. Others, however, also received a hail of derision, and he made his friends among a group of outcasts.

Among the little band of cadets was the Jewish Krasinski, especially subject to intimidation even though he was Russian. A slight fellow, very passive, he yielded to their pranks. He could pronounce Isakjan no better than the rest, and because of a speech impediment, could not even pronounce many Russian words, particularly those with heavy "r's." The anomalies of the two outsiders challenged the cadets who possessed the accouterments of status to greater heights of ridicule.

"Why don't you work harder in the field?" they asked Krasinski. "You Jews think you can just do paper work. You'll learn here."

Krasinski ignored the taunts as best he could. Worrying about his friend, Krasinski gave advice to Isakjan. "Why don't we call you Ilja? It's a Russian counterpart to your name."

Isakjan agreed. After all, he knew that good things came from Russia, and he should be willing to compromise. Entering the circle of Russians, people from the land of his dreams, might entail overcoming a few obstacles, but he could make a first step to demonstrate good will.

"Ilja, I like that," he thought. "Teacher Sharaf guided me correctly. The Russians will take care of their friends."

He could prove himself again as he had in Jizzakh. His misfortune resulted from his birth, and the Russians would ultimately not bear a grudge against a victim of misfortune. He believed that good will of the Soviet leadership would disperse prejudice, even the kind that he endured from his classmates.

During the first class, the instructor began to explain the principles of topography in Russian. Ilja understood hardly a word, and realized how much he must learn to carry on the simplest conversation with his fellow cadets. Every day he sat by himself after class and after dinner, reviewing Russian vocabulary or experimenting with various methods of memorization.

He forced himself to read newspapers printed in Russian rather than Uzbek. The political teacher encouraged this, especially in the realm of international events. Ilja read with fascination the articles, which decried actions of the fascist Germans. They outlined the weakness of the Western powers in not resisting Nazi aggression, bemoaning the loss of Austrian and Czechoslovak independence to the boot of the Nazis. The British Prime Minister Chamberlain, a traitor to the rights of free people, could never deserve the admiration of a Soviet citizen. Only the Soviet Union protested bold aggression, while the spineless Britain, France and the United States ignored treaties and allowed former friends to succumb to evil forces.

"The Soviet Union, with its extraordinary power, alone resists the blatant ambition of the Nazi regime," explained the press.

The political introduction class underlined the need for a

strong army and outlined the duties of officers.

"Officers will ensure the freedom of the proletariat. As such they receive an honorable profession and respect from grateful citizens. However, the enemies of socialism will not be kind to captured officers. The hideous Germans, for example, will commit unspeakable acts of barbarity on any Soviet officer they might capture. They will cut off ears, nose and body parts, just to delight in the screams. That is why no Soviet officer will ever surrender, but will fight to the death. It is in our statutes that surrender is a crime, so if he can not continue his battle, then a soldier will have mercy on himself and point his gun to his own head rather than submit himself to torture and interrogation. The worst disgrace and traitorous activity of an officer is capture."

The political officer spurred them to great xenophobia, but did not explain that the Soviet soldier was the only one in the world who could not surrender. In any other country, a man who loses a limb in battle and is held in a POW camp but eventually makes it home receives a hero's welcome. In the Soviet Union he was jailed. [1]

Ilja's roster included much more than reading and academics. Rising at 7:00 a.m., he reported for lineup, then gymnastics. His young age and small stature widened his susceptibility to pranks and mischief. Attempts to launch his body over the exercise horse convinced the other cadets of his helplessness.

"What are you doing here, cherny? Make way for men. You can't expect to really serve in the army."

Many of the older athletic youths attended school to avoid draft and Mongolian service. Compared to Ilja, they all had money, important fathers and influence, continuing the Russian tradition of nobility in the military.

Again he was thrown in with a group of privileged youngsters while he remained the runt and the poor boy. This especially hurt because these youths were not native Uzbeks, but visitors displaying the most rude manners to their hosts. Only the fabric of military rule held his grief in check. The food, instruction and uniforms issued were equally available to all. He would show them by excelling in school. Uzbeks could learn as well as Russians.

"Hey blacky," someone called. "At least other natsman are white. Why do we have to put up with you?"

"Don't call me that; it's not nice and it is against our law, since we are all equal," he admonished. "Our constitution abolished chauvinism." Isakjan believed the principles of the Soviet constitution would one day prevail.

"Well, that part of the law doesn't apply to you, cherny," they concluded.

The students hastened back to the dormitory, shouting, pushing, and laughing. Isakjan welled up with the same curling of the stomach, rush of adrenaline, and heavy dose of self-deprecation he always seemed to develop in his efforts to equal the Russians. Next morning they prepared for inspection again, making beds and dressing for roll call. Following inspection, they marched to breakfast.

At the mess hall, Isakjan savored the enticing aromas from a heady mixture of scents given off by rich black bread and eggs. He looked at the huge slabs of butter and pitchers of milk, all accessible in unlimited quantities. He sat down at the table with his smart uniform and his first machine-made shoes. In ever more understandable Russian he asked for second helpings, slowly and carefully lifting them to his mouth using the novel fork and spoon, while holding his head erect.

Even though the tormenting became a way of life, the busy schedule, a few friends, and the military leveling gave him areas of shelter. The study and workload gave him challenges, with little time for despondency.

Four hours of morning math and military science usually went well, with his crude Russian hindering him in the military course. The early afternoon classes, accenting the history of the Communist Party and the theory of Marxism, returned him low grades, not for lack of attention or effort, but from confusion with the Russian language.

Later in the day each cadet got a turn to march his company, practicing military discipline, saluting, and formation. Krasinski, without ability to pronounce the Russian "r" in commanding a right turn, commanded the company to make three left turns in order to accomplish a right.

After six weeks in school, eligibility for the privilege of city leave came up. Every third week, upon passing inspection, he could take the streetcar to the center of Tashkent. Isakjan thought that his allowance of several rubles might make a difference from the previous disappointment experienced at the technical school, especially since he now wore the uniform of a prestigious establishment rather than the rags of a lowly urchin. But a few rubles were not adequate to shop at the stores or even to buy dinner.

Occasionally, a fellow Uzbek in another platoon whose

family lived in Tashkent took Ilja to his house. The boy's father held an important position in the party, and the food in the house exceeded any standards known to Ilja. At this table he heard epithets hurled at the Russians. "Those Urus (despicable Russkies when used in the negative) always try to run the show. They give no credit to anyone else." Isakjan did not disagree, and had accumulated a number of resentments toward the "big brothers" of the revolution. However Ilja saw personal progress as well as suppression, and could not bring himself to criticize.

Entertainment in the city still eluded him. The fruits in the bazaar still grew fatter and larger than his allowance, and without a circle of friends, adventure managed to turn every corner before his approach. Perhaps a little excitement outside the school would have pulled him away from his paramount goal, learning Russian, or perhaps that concern prevented him from enjoying what every lad of sixteen should naturally do. However, he spent his weekends under the trees just outside the gates of the School, pouring over Cyrillic letters and phrases of the Russian language, fitting them into his mind.

He worked hard, remaining true to the pledge given to the academy admissions officer, learned quickly and studied hard. By the fall, he could participate in all of his classes, and even felt some muscle development from the gymnastics exercises. His body could vault the horse and use the parallel bars. As the grades were posted on the bulletin board, the name of Ilja Narzikul began to appear in the honor group.

He had switched completely from reading "Red Uzbekistan," the paper his uncle edited, to the Russian language paper, "Pravda Vostoka (Truth of the East)." Both papers printed essentially the same stories in their respective languages. In August 1939, Ilja read in the newspaper about a new non-aggression treaty signed by Hitler and Stalin. At the end of the week, his company gathered for their regular political discussion under the guidance of the academy political division chief, who lectured the group. He had more power and authority than the head of the school.

"We are very pleased at the efforts of our great leaders in convincing the Germans and the Japanese to accept the USSR's formula for maintaining peace in the world. Due to this change, our leaders have been able to sign a peace accord with Germany, which will benefit the Soviet people. Germany will now be our ally, and has signed a twenty-year agreement. We will start exchange programs in the arts and in agriculture. This is a day to remember.

"Naturally, it is to the advantage of the Germans to

associate themselves with the Soviet people. Since we defeated Germany in the World War, she has become a weak nation compared to the Soviet Union, which is many times the size of Germany."

In one week, the lecturers and newspaper had totally reversed their rhetoric. Only days before, articles and speeches had vilified the Germans and Japanese.

Ilja marveled at the capacity for rapid change and the powers of persuasion demonstrated by the Politburo.

September 17, 1939: the USSR joined the already initiated German invasion of Poland, and on the 29th, in Bialystock, partitioned that country. The last Polish troops surrendered October 1, at Hela.

The newspaper discussed the partition of Poland, explaining that, as in Turkistan, the Russians, even though busy building up their own republic, extended aid to brethren. Ever alert, the Soviet leadership routed anti-socialist elements in Poland and responded to a plea from the workers to allow them to join the Soviet Union. The country of Poland, formed by an unholy capitalist plot, had illegally seized lands properly belonging to the Ukraine and Byelorussia from a weak Russia after the last war. The Soviet Union complied with the wishes of brothers in Poland and accepted the invitation to help them in their cause. Sometimes, in order to save world order, Moscow had to exhibit its awesome force.

In Tashkent, the press reported victory after victory for the Soviet cause. Ilja read:

Comrades in the Baltic States of Estonia, Latvia, and Lithuania asked the Soviet Union to send detachments of troops in order for the population to control oppressive elements and to join the revolution.

The audacity of the capitalist nations and their agents outraged Ilja. He saw that his own complaints of teasing paled in light of the exploitation of brothers and sisters in other parts of the world. He longed for a chance to aid the communist cause, not realizing that far from Turkistan, other reports circulated in the West asserted that over a million intellectuals, aristocrats, officers, religious leaders, and landowners were forced to board transports for Siberia to join Moslems and other people from Turkistan in forced labor prison camps. Half of Poland was ceded to the USSR and the other half to Germany.

The rapid movement of peoples and countries to the Soviet orbit exhilarated the cadets, and the political discussions drew active participation. The instructor could see Ilja's raised hand with greater frequency.

Ilja appreciated that his hand had grown longer in the eyes of his instructors; in gymnastics, he began to do more than just jump over the exercise horse. The sensation of accomplishment lightened his mood and made him want to dance with joy, but he didn't know how to dance. However, with new-found self-confidence, he realized that even learning to waltz was possible. He entered a class to learn dancing. The cadets waltzed around the floor, usually with brooms as partners, for girls were in short supply.

"Cherny thinks he can dance," taunted a more talented waltzer.

Ilja clutched his broom and twirled around the room. His broom was one of the prettiest - smartest too - and probably better at math than the woodenhead that teased him, he silently told himself.

At the next political session, one officer expressed concern over the problem of teaching the native Uzbek population the Russian language.

"The Soviet government wishes for all its people to have equal access to knowledge. In order for Uzbeks to share prosperity and advance themselves, I see a necessity for them to change their alphabet. A special commission of Russians and Uzbeks has determined that an alphabet change for the Uzbek language from Roman letters to Cyrillic would help minorities learn the Russian language better. Stalin has issued a proclamation which will change the Uzbek use of Roman letters to Cyrillic. "

The Russian concern for improving Uzbekistan impressed Ilja. By then he approached a mastery of the Cyrillic letters used in the Russian alphabet. He anticipated ease in reading Uzbek when expressed in Cyrillic letters rather than Roman, and acknowledged that if he had learned his native Uzbek using Cyrillic, subsequent studies of Russian would have been easier.

It never occurred to Ilja that many Uzbeks considered the change in alphabets a debasement of their culture. Just a few years after the time Ilja was born, another change had replaced Arabic letters with Roman. Parents afraid to speak, pro-Russian schoolteachers, and Russian military instructors, exposed Ilja to only one view.

CHAPTER 5

THE PROFESSOR IS DRAFTED

We have internal enemies. We have external enemies. This, Comrades, must not be forgotten for a single moment.

...the private manufacturers and their servitors, the private traders and their henchmen, the former nobles and priests, the kulaks (small landowners) and kulak agents, the former whiteguard officers and police officials, policemen and gendarmes, all sorts of bourgeois intellectuals of a chauvinist type, and all other anti-Soviet elements...

They set fire to warehouses and wreck machinery. They organize sabotage. They organize wrecking activities in the collective farms and state farms... (They) include certain professors...

And so, the 'have beens' from the ranks of the exploiting classes play on the private-property habits of the collective farmers in order to organize the plundering of public wealth and thus shake the foundation of the Soviet system...

The Central Committee of the All-Union Communist Party considers that physical pressure (beatings) should still be used obligatorily, as an exception applicable to known and obstinate enemies of the people, as a method both justifiable and appropriate.

– Joseph Stalin [1]

Ilja had heard dissatisfaction with the Russians from Uzbek friends, but nothing serious enough to sway his faith in the Soviet Union's promise to the world. Other Uzbeks considered the Russians and their communism or czarism to be the main cause of misery in Turkistan, and the change of alphabet added to the dissension coming from this adversary group, which included professors several blocks away from the Military School, at Tashkent University.

The University provided a special opportunity for the native population to excel, for while Russians tightly controlled the military, the government, and the legal system, many Uzbeks gained positions of responsibility by teaching. Among them was Dr. Ergash Shermat, chairman of the law department in Tashkent University. While Ilja conversed with his political advisor, Shermat walked to a poetry discussion group seething with rage.

Shermat slipped down the stairs to the small room where the club held its sessions. Since Turkistanis admire poetry, many of the clubs sprouted up throughout Tashkent. They professed a love of Russian poets and devoted their charters to the study of them. Shermat opened a book of verses by the Russian Lermantov (1814-1841) while his friend called the meeting to order. With a nod from the convener of the meeting, one of the participants sauntered to the doorway to stretch his legs. Immediately, the books of Russian verses slammed shut.

"Dr. Shermat will deliver our talk today."

The men sat close to one another, so the speaker did not need to stand, and in fact spoke in quiet tones. However, the hushed voice did not hide the fervent strength of the message. "The actions of the imperialist Russians in their attempt to change our language makes my talk all the more important," Shermat began. "I want to relate the story of our national hero Chokay, a man who stood up to the Russians and is now publishing the truth with magazines in Paris and Warsaw."

Shermat, like Ilja, had attended the new Soviet schools. His brothers and father supported a series of meetings held throughout Turkistan before 1920 meant to set up an autonomous government. The Russians could not muster up any popular support for a rival Soviet government, but they did control the rails and an organized army. The Red Army ravaged the countryside to destroy talk of autonomy, after which his brothers each took a horse and rode with the rebels into defeat.[2] Shermat's kin returned to their fifty-acre farm, which the Soviets shortly confiscated and folded into a kolkhoz.

Shermat was isolated from the battles since he attended school, but the boy listened to the tales. Young Shermat contributed small articles to the newspaper in his city. The editor harbored resentments against the Soviets for their assumption of power, unlike Ilja's teacher and editor back in Jizzakh.

His involvement with the local newspaper editor led Shermat further information about the history of his country and its national heroes. One of those heroes was the poet Chokay. Shermat shared with the assembled members of the poetry club the events surrounding his newspaper experience:

One day as Shermat barged into the editor's office with an assignment, the chief stuffed papers into his desk and changed the topic of the conversation he was having with a distinguished poet. Hoping to see some poetry, Shermat begged the editor, "What was that paper you put in the desk?"

The editor reflected a moment. Then, with a deft sweep of his hand, a small booklet appeared on the desk. "Before I show you this, you must promise to never, never divulge the source."

Shermat agreed.

"This is a copy of a magazine called `Young Turkistan' published by the Chokay. You should read it and learn the true history of your country, but," the editor cautioned once more, "you must not mention where you obtained this. Open your mouth and lose your head."

Shermat devoured the magazine, reading of the elimination of the Turkistani leadership by the Soviet powers and planned suppression of regional culture. Within a couple of weeks, twenty other students had read the magazine and also pledged not to disclose the source of their information.

After Shermat spoke of his personal history, the poetry club discussed the changes in Turkistani culture and the coming alteration of the alphabet. After the club ended its meeting, some of them dined with a visiting Kazakh singer at the same teahouse which other leaders of the city including Isakjan's editor uncle frequented. The singer cried through the meal.

"In the capital of Kazakhstan (a Turkistani Republic), our intellectuals decided to test the new constitution, particularly the clause which allows any republic to secede. They proposed a referendum to determine what the people wished. In one night, 300 of them were arrested by the secret police and we have no idea what happened to them. I much prefer our old Muslim law to this Russian implant."

Shermat, as a professor of law, especially deplored the

practice of interference in the operation of the constitution by politicians who overruled judges. Shermat saw that, in practice, the old Moslem Shariat law gave a reasonably fair trial and the Soviet law resulted in a manipulated one.

Ergash Shermat had hoped to change the attitude of his government by working with it, and wished to battle for the rights of his countrymen. He had taken to heart promises from the Soviets, which proliferated after the revolution. The sign in the park, "No Sarts or dogs," which the Czar's agents erected came tumbling down and new laws came flooding into the court system, changing rules of labor, property, family, and estates. The rapid codification of so large a body of law produced constant revisions, but those revisions came mandated from Moscow without input from Turkistan.

Shermat's advancement in the University's law department came from his acquaintance with Marxist law, since the older lawyers had only studied antiquated Shariat law. He, on the other hand, possessed a degree from Moscow and knew the details of communist legal theory.

He rapidly became head of the law department, presiding over the training of people who would apply the Soviet code, which affected every aspect of life imaginable. He saw to it that young law students studied German rather than Arabic, so they could read Marx, Engels, Hegel and Nietzche.

Shermat's position at the University brought him to the attention of the court system, and he became a head of Tashkent provincial justice with supervision of 54 district courts. Although he admired many of the Russian teachers who came to educate the Uzbeks in Soviet law, those in the justice system generally came only to promote their careers.

Thus, when Shermat fired a justice department official from a part-time University teaching job due to incompetence, complaints about Shermat's performance at the justice department began to surface. His proclivity for causing trouble and favoring Turkistani rights was deemed anti-Soviet.

Nevertheless an offer came to him from a deputy in Moscow working closely with Stalin's chief aides, to become Minister of Justice of the Uzbek Republic. Appointments of any importance came from the Communist Party in Moscow and not from the Uzbek government, and so Shermat traveled to Moscow to discuss the new position. He hesitated to accept, as enemies in the justice system were mounting a lively campaign against him and could cause him a short term ending in banishment to Siberia. As he recollected the ever-longer list of public servants who had recently disappeared or were publicly liquidated, he realized that the promotion implied a shortened life expectancy. Then came the kolkhoz case and the Kazakh judge.

The Soviets had ordered the arrest of one of the most popular kolkhoz chairmen in the Tashkent area, who wasted away under torture and imprisonment for almost two years without charges while an investigation progressed. Finally he faced a trial for anti-Soviet activity, and a Kazakh judge, a friend of Shermat, sat on the bench.

The Kazakh received a call from the Second Secretary of the Tashkent Provincial Party Committee. Whether in county or republic government, the first secretary position normally went to an Uzbek, who usually remained in office until he displeased the second secretary. The second secretary, virtually always Russian, kept his post for many years and held the reins of power and the connections with Moscow. So when the Kazakh judge talked with the Second Secretary, he listened carefully.

The secretary wasted no time. "That kolkhoz chairman you have on trial: give him life at hard labor or death."

On the following day, the Kazakh judge presided over a courtroom overflowing with friends of the defendant. As the trial wore on, the judge grew impatient with the prosecution's trumped-up accusations and complained to Shermat, who attended the proceedings. After the closing statements the judge stood up to deliver the verdict. The crowd grew silent.

"I have listened carefully to the arguments," announced the judge. "No proof of guilt has been presented. This man is not guilty and may go home."

Excited arms lifted the defendant from his seat, and the courtroom filled with cheers. "Long live Soviet justice! Long live our chairman!"

Later, Shermat called the judge's office on the phone to congratulate him on his courageous decision, but his assistant claimed that the judge was away from his desk. Shermat grew alarmed and suspicious, but tried to repress his anxiety. A later call produced the same result, and Shermat knew something ominous had developed. He rushed to the judge's house where his wife answered the door. Her contorted face, red and swollen with crying told him what he didn't want to hear.

"The NKVD took him this afternoon," she wailed. (Cheka, GPU, OGPU, NKVD, and KGB are successive names for essentially the same organization.)

Shermat, badly shaken, stumbled home in disbelief at the action of the feared secret police. He could not contend with a system so corrupt and cynical, and reeled from the sickening truth, so blunt and brutal. Then he did the unforgivable, declining the offer and promotion to chief justice, an offer which would inevitably lead to his own arrest. He had to find a way to make himself vanish for a few years, to take some time to think, to try to make sense out of chaos and to find a way to remain true to higher moral law.

A friend who worked with foreign service positions promised him a consulate job in East Turkistan, China (Sinkiang), and he attended a processing school in preparation. The friend, unfortunately and unwisely, circulated opinions of the problems in Soviet government. This earned him a night visit from the NKVD secret police, after which he was liquidated. All appointments that the bureaucrat had contemplated were canceled. Shermat reached a state of panic as he sensed walls closing in on his life. Moscow insisted that he accept the justice position, and his refusal to immediately take the job already constituted insubordination. He presented himself to a friend in the Tashkent Red Army headquarters.

"Please," he begged. "I know I am exempt from service, but you must do a favor for me and issue an immediate draft into the army."

The professor put on an army uniform and was stationed in the Ukraine when the USSR presented Finland with demands which were refused. On November 30, 1939, Soviets invaded that country and bombed the capital city of Helsinki. The drafted Shermat, as a political instructor with the Red Army, heard of the effective fight mounted by the Finns. Typically, a handful of Finnish skiers suddenly appeared dressed in winter white to ambush and eliminate entire companies of Red Army soldiers.

Back at Tashkent Military School, the students heard no dissension from the Soviet view of the world, and they shortly became concerned about news from Finland, which the press reported as, "Finland invades USSR, bombs and attacks our country at 6:00 a.m." The cadets were outraged.

Seemingly, the mouse attacked the elephant, but the cadets didn't see it that way. At the military school, Ilja was dumbfounded at the atrocity committed by Finland's attack on his own peace-loving country. Finland pushed the Red Army back of the Mannerheim line, and the Soviet defense minister was replaced. The School political officer assured the angry cadets that the Soviet army would punish the invaders, never mentioning the defeats encountered. The students clamored for more than mere punishment, taking special offense to transgressions on Soviet soil. The future officers of the Red Army knew that their strength, well founded on the good tidings of the peoples of the world, stood invincible.

In the Western press, predictions of war grew rampant, but none of those predictions made its way to Tashkent. In fact, Ilja saw the military as an easy career, and permanently set aside ideas of textile engineering. He began to see the outline of his life work: to serve his country faithfully and competently as a model officer bringing respect to himself, his family and his people. Towards the end of that career, he would live in one of the houses at the Tashkent Military School, inviting Turkistanis and Russians to share bread and ideas together.

In March 1940, Finland acceded to Russia. The students of the Tashkent Military School cheered. The first year of studies came to an end, and his grades rose dramatically. Warmer weather found Ilja resuming a position in front of the school on weekends, books and notes spread out on the lawn. He moved his papers ever so slightly, inside a fence next to the volleyball courts where the children of the officers spent many afternoons. These children attended schools in Tashkent.

Over the edges of books, he looked admiringly at the line of officers' houses, watching their families as they entered and left on the errands of the day. He could see, in the yards, faces of Russians, Byelorussians and Ukrainians, with a few Georgians and Tatars.

Above him, a great tree soaked up the ever-warmer sun while he occupied himself writing notes, always writing notes, allowing himself quick glances as a volleyball game commenced. The group formed a discussion knot, choosing sides. One shortly emerged from the group and walked up to Ilja.

"We need another player. Would you care to join us?" he asked.

What a question. Would a lonely lad far from home and without companionship like to join a merry group of youths in a game of volleyball? But he prepared them for his shortcomings.

"I have never played volleyball."

"Come. We will teach you."

Next weekend, the same school cadet joined again. Afterwards the group went to the house of Nora Melkakze and her brother, where Major Melkakze, second in command of the school, and his gracious wife treated everyone to food and refreshments. The Melkakze family pronounced their Russian speech with an accent and their faces revealed features a little too dark for natives of the Northern Republics. Georgians. That's what they were: representatives of a minority who preceded Turkistan in alliance with the Russians. The Major had succeeded in accomplishing what Isakjan envisioned for himself and his people.

After sampling a few snacks, Isakjan balanced his cup of tea with the greatest of care and gently eased the fork into a piece of cake, anxious to hide any sign of his coarse upbringing, and pronounced each Russian word with a little too much premeditation, displaying a lack of spontaneity. The hosts and guests didn't mention his lack of polish, and in fact ignored his obvious deficiencies while pursuing a spirited review of the volleyball game.

Isakjan's participation in the weekly game and social hour afterwards became a regular affair, and his interest in volleyball was soon eclipsed by a friendship with the delicate Nora Melkakze. She invited him to her birthday party, giving him a triumph that bypassed the harassment of his tormentors. The Melkakze family offered him their home. Even during weekdays, in free study period after dinner, Isakjan wandered over to the Melkakze house, chatting with the mother over snacks if the children were out. She elicited admissions of his battles with discrimination and assured him of his own worth and the possibilities available to minorities, using her own family as an example. She insisted on sewing the dress sleeves of his uniform and involved Nora in discussions of the stinging barbs of the Russians. The major wanted names of the perpetrators, but Isakjan declined, wanting to make his own place. After visits to the Melkakze house he floated back to the platoon dormitory, where his immunity from outside intrusions ended.

"Ilja Narzikul. Telegram."

He opened his hands for the message from his brother Tura. Their father had entered the medical facility in Jizzakh in very poor condition.

With five days leave of absence, he traveled by train to Jizzakh, and visited his father in an old building converted into a clinic where men lay in shabby metal cots. Jizzakh did not yet have a hospital. His father gained some strength and the undiagnosed attacks no longer seemed life threatening, but he still refrained from delivering a wise message to his son, one that might teach the boy something of the old man's faith or creed. His mother's eyes sparkled when she saw her son in the uniform of a cadet and future officer.

"I never believed that the Russians would allow one of us into the officer corps," she beamed. "You will be famous. I never guessed what was written on your forehead." (Turkistani saying)

She put on her scarf and walked with him to the kolkhoz office in order to claim respect for the family. He strode beside her in an easy military cadence with his crisp clean uniform, the soldier and the mother. Neighbors who used to throw bread scraps into Isakjan's burlap bag as he gathered cows came out to view the parade. The former trades people and small farmers, now cotton pickers, touched his jacket and imagined it on their own sons. At dinner, Party workers preferred his company to that of a teacher.

He tended to other Jizzakh business. The cousin promised him in marriage needed to know his intentions, as she was then of age and had other offers. He advised her that he had chosen a military career rather than a wedding and she should accept another proposal. He was still a boy seeking a stable home and pursuing studies. The concept of marriage remained remote and not an immediate prospect.

Back at the school a few days later, another telegram arrived. "Father was moved to Samarkand hospital, where he died yesterday," the message read. Isakjan attended the burial.

Upon his return to the school, spring rituals started. Grades were posted, Ilja Narzikul posting honors 4.1 average out of a possible 5.0. Almost half of the students had to repeat. After a few days of relaxation, the officer candidates packed up and moved to the country, setting up camp in tents for summer exercises, practicing military maneuvers and chemical warfare.

Without a recess, regular classes resumed after camp in the early fall for the second and final year of studies. News of tension in the world increased, raising the patriotic fervor in the school, but such news affected him just a little less since he had Nora's friendship.

Nora Melkakze agreed to attend dancing classes with him. Proudly wearing a newly won medal for marksmanship, which hung on the breast of his uniform, he stopped by her house and escorted her to the school building. In the activity room, cadets jostled with broomsticks before the instruction began, challenging each other to duels with slaps on the butt. The few candidates with female partners stood aside, quietly conversing to show good taste and manners. Ilja and Nora entered the room, and the swish of rotating necks replaced the clang from crossed wooden sticks.

Nora took his hand, and tossed her head. The cadets had

seen her walking the grounds before and every student desired a place next to her. A heavy silence permeated the floor as covetous eyes and gaping mouths followed the couple.

Someone whispered, "So, Cherny can go dancing with the Major's daughter, but that doesn't help to make him a better man."

The music started, and Ilja whirled her around. As he danced, he pitied the Russians and Ukrainians with long thin brooms and long thin mouths. He felt sorry for them, with all their advantages, ending up with brooms as partners. And he felt like waltzing all night, enmeshed in the sweet embrace of Nora and the sparkling uniform of equality.

When the couple walked on the grounds, the stares and whispers filtered over to him. "How can Cherny, a lousy natsman, deserve that girl? She must be crazy."

Major Melkakze often called the duty officer to allow Ilja to stay out late, going to plays and sights of town. He generously supplied cash for these undertakings. Tashkent took on a new vitality for Ilja, as visits to the movies introduced him to Charlie Chaplin, Douglas Fairbanks, and Mary Pickford. Besides movie stars, other American influences entered the streets of Tashkent, most obvious in the numerous "Amerikanka" which supplied quick-service beer and refreshments across a standing-room-only counter on most busy commercial blocks in the city.

Mrs. Melkakze's special liking for the boy led her to mend his garments and bake him treats. This turned into a timely benefit when the School altered its mess hall policy, downgrading lunch to a light snack, and instituting a ration day once a week to "support the people of the world." Ilja supplemented his meals very nicely at the Melkakze household while others did so at the bazaars. For the still shy Ilja, the relationship with Nora stayed platonic.

He attended plays at the Tashkent theater, often without his friends and at no cost. The School obtained ten tickets to every performance and handed them out to officers and cadets. In deference to the Russians in the city, half of the presentations used their language, and the other half were delivered in Uzbek. Only high-ranking officers and privileged cadets acquired tickets to the performances in Russian, but those in Uzbek went begging. Isakjan, with fond memories of his trips to Jizzakh rehearsals, became a regular at the theater, familiarizing himself with plays and operas from Gilbert and Sullivan to La Traviata.

Hamlet tied his emotions in knots. The boy from Jizzakh who grew up with a father poisoned by some mystery, choked when he saw the prince of Denmark discover the poisoning of his parent, the king; the son of a leather worker sniffled when the gravedigger recited that it took ten years for a tanner's body to rot; the youth longed for his father who had died alone without sharing his faith or creed. He cried upon seeing the skull of the trusted court jester, the drowning of Hamlet's love, and the foul death of his mother. He walked away from the play despondent and lonely, thinking of his father and the substitute Melkakze family.

During January 1941, he was invited to a birthday party for the son of the School's commanding officer. The general gave a wonderful party. Ilja was the only one with military attire, his special badge of stature that took the place of proper upbringing.

During the height of the festivities, Ilja noticed the time approached 9:30. He walked over to the General and requested permission to leave the party.

"Permission to leave, but why so early?" he inquired.

"I must make roll call, sir." Ilja answered.

"And what unit do you belong with?" the General pursued a line of questions.

"Sixth Company, sir."

"You may stay. I will call your unit." The General rang up the school.

"This is the commanding general speaking," he told the party at the other end of the line. "Candidate Narzikul is a guest at my house and will return late tonight with my permission."

At morning roll call, the officer in charge called the cadets to attention.

"Gentlemen," he announced. "Our company was honored yesterday to have a member in attendance at the house of the Commander of the School."

Ilja enjoyed the compliment. He had demonstrated that a poor starving cherny Turkistani could match the accomplishments of Russians, and that he and his countrymen were equal to the highest ranks of world brotherhood. He had overcome the unfortunate accident of his birth and finally inherited a meaning and a goal for his life. Thus Ilja energetically assisted in the May 1941 preparations for summer exercises. He anticipated entry into the army later in the year as a man with a trade and mission and knew he could master the final exams in order to qualify for the graduation scheduled for September. What a grand ceremony that would be; but as the company departed for the field, rumors spread.

CHAPTER 6

HOW LONG DOES IT TAKE TO DIE?

The Fighter of the Red Army Does Not Become a Prisoner

--- Soviet Army pamphlet

Nothing, including even the threat of death, can compel a fighter of the Red Army to become a prisoner.

--- Infantry Combat Regulations [1]

"Did you hear that the next class will have a different course load, and that the entire school will change its orientation?" asked Krasinski. There was no answer and no confirmation. Field practice began several miles from campus. They practiced marching, artillery and firing range.

But the Red Army desperately needed officers, since Stalin had arrested some 30,000 of them during his purges, and in the process executed three of the five Soviet field marshals, thirteen of the nineteen army commanders, and over half of the generals. Then he signed the non-aggression pact with Germany as a substitute for a strong army to resist the Nazis. [2] The Red Army had designed the T34 and KV tanks, superior to the German machines and models for future armored vehicles, but the designer also met the fate of a bullet in the skull. Superior numbers of Soviet airplanes and an impressive production capability meant little in the face of political interference with the military.[3]

In early June, Ilja reported to his company morning roll call and assembly.

"Attention!" sang out the platoon commander. "We will march to assemble with the company. Line up. Forward, march."

The entire class was called for a meeting. The heads of each company, who had remained at the main campus, made an unusual trip to the field.

"Cadets, you have brought honor to our school by making tremendous progress, and learning your studies well. The government has decided to reward you with an early graduation. I now proclaim that you all will become officers of the great Soviet army in three days."

In early June 1941, the school had orders from the Ministry of Defense in Moscow to graduate the students immediately and dispatch them to military units.

After the announcement, cadets dispersed for artillery practice. Ilja stationed himself apart from the huge gun, giving the crew an estimate of how to aim by sighting the target. After firing, a scout from the top of a knoll signaled the distance between the target and the shell explosion. Ilja adjusted his orders.

That night, they discussed the unusual turn of events.

"Ilja, did you notice anything special about our class that we should graduate so quickly?" the inquisitive Krasinski wondered.

But Ilja had not developed such a sense of open questioning. "I guess they are rewarding us for something. Things sometimes happen quickly in a new socialist state."

In the last sessions, the use of gas masks, tanks, communications and field maneuvers were quickly reviewed, receiving little attention from students granted graduation without exams and regardless of grades.

The School held graduation the next week in June, canceling the remaining summer exercises and final examinations. This stimulated a great feeling of relief among the students. Undergoing no further preparation, the officers arranged to conduct a ceremony right in the field, without notice to friends and relatives. Helpers distributed army uniforms to replace the student dress, and they prepared to receive orders. As new officers they speculated on the possibilities for initial assignments in the various Soviet military districts.

The class assembled, five months early, for review by the general and commander of the school, who read the order of graduation.

"By order of The National Army of the Union of Soviet Socialist Republics, the class of 1941, Tashkent Military School, is hereby granted degrees in military science and a commission in the Soviet Army, together with the appropriate rank and salary. Listen carefully, gentlemen, for your assignments."

The General proceeded to read out the names of the cadets and the location of their first duty, with many of the Russian names inevitably ending up in the Turkistani areas, while the Turkistani, Georgian and other minorities drew orders to report to far away places. Ilja did not give up hope for a post in his native land, as he reasoned that his exceptional grades and patriotism should make him a candidate for local duty, a sort of symbol and example of the uplifting spirit of the revolution and recognition by the military to a minority boy. He had shown his trustworthiness to the highest officers in the School, and now believed they would nominate him as a pioneer of the Turkistani military establishment. The general's voice boomed over the silent faces.

"Isakjan Narzikul, Baltic military region."

He hardly believed it. Latvia, Estonia and Lithuania would take him a long way from home, while the vast majority of White Russians were assigned to the Turkistan district. But, if the Soviet government needed him in the Baltic region, he resolved to serve with honor there. A commissioned officer knew his duty.

The graduates reported to the tailor's tent, set up for the occasion, to turn in the student outfits and receive a regular army uniform with closed, raised collar, jacket, headpiece, white belt crossing in the front, holster, shoes and new underwear. A merry confusion of exchanging clothes to procure the right size followed. He engaged in the same sort of procession that, in his first day of military school, had introduced him to a different world, but now he moved between locations with the skill of an accomplished veteran and the physical strength resulting from two years of diligent exercise.

The very next day, with four other Turkistanis and a few Russian cadets also assigned to the Baltic district, Ilja transferred directly to the train station, with no last opportunity to talk to his mother or to visit the School and tell Nora what had transpired. New officers reporting to the Baltic region clasped their one-way tickets to Moscow, where they looked forward to three days leave.

The group looked excitedly out of the train windows. And why not? They had received an early graduation and could smugly congratulate themselves, careers assured with little risk. After all, they reminded themselves, the Soviet leadership made friends with all their neighbors, assisting the aspirations of the people in Latvia, Estonia and Lithuania while blunting the aggressive tendencies of Finland. The Soviet Union was the largest and mightiest nation on earth, with the clearest direction, that of the future, entrusted to it. The Baltic peoples would welcome them as leaders, affirmation that a tremendous power protected them.

Ilja sat next to a handsome ethnic Russian lad for a portion of the train ride.

"I guess you are from the Ukraine or Russia." suggested Ilja.

"No, actually, I live right in Tashkent." he offered. "My family moved there years ago. Where are you going?"

"Riga, capital of Latvia," answered Ilja.

"My name is Alexei. We can be partners, as I also must report there. Riga is a nice city. We should like it," smiled Ilja's new friend.

The train that ferried the youths to their assignments stopped to pick up more passengers and freight along the route. In Kazakhstan, Ilja and his Russian friend stepped off the train to get some refreshment. He tried some kumiss, the thick fermented mare's milk of the plains. As the train continued on its journey, the alcohol spread through his body, adding a carefree gaiety to the ride.

After a five day trip, the boys exited at their destination, found a small hotel to spend the few days leave in Moscow and set out to tour the capital. Each carried an issuance of 200 rubles, enough to buy a watch in Moscow, in the unlikely event they could find one for sale. Ilja wandered the streets of the big city, the largest he had seen, gawking like a peasant boy at the buildings and people who passed by him.

On the second day, he visited an agricultural fair where all the Republics were represented with displays and restaurants. At 11:30 he entered an Uzbek restaurant, feeling accomplished with his graduation, and ordered pilaf and tea, the perfect picture of the officer at leisure. His uniform and military bearing brought respectful stares.

The public radio blared. Always, in gathering places, town squares, teahouses or restaurants, the manager kept a radio constantly transmitting. With the broadcasts came announcements and proclamations, reminding the workers and farmers how they now owned the country, which was the best country in the world, whereas in capitalist countries, workers were beaten and forced to strike. In a socialist country, people received the right to work, and therefore did not want the right to strike.

The waiter brought his bowl of pilaf, and he sat back to watch the festivities and listen to the radio. After two spoonfuls of the rice and vegetable mixture, the program was interrupted for a message from Molotov, who rarely spoke except on significant occasions. The date was June 22, 1941.

"Germany, at 5:00 a.m., attacked our homeland, entered our territory, bombed our cities, and heinously abrogated our non-aggression pact. We have declared war and will move to rapidly repel and punish the invaders."

He dropped his spoon of pilaf back into the plate, and could not take another bite. War. Insanity. Who could believe it? How could Germany, destroyed in one war and still weak, attack the megalithic USSR? It was too much to comprehend, almost like a bad dream. The Red Army would crush them in days.

Now he understood the early graduation. The Soviet leadership knew of the intentions of the Germans and had to prepare in secret for defense of the nation. He, as an officer, needed to rush to his assignment to protect his country.

Other thoughts ran through the crowd. Men and women started to panic, run and cry. Lines wound around blocks in front of grocery stores while citizens tried to buy sugar and staples.

Next morning, he and his Russian comrade took the train

to the city of Riga, reporting to the 9th parachute brigade. The troop owned no parachutes and had no access to a plane.

"This will be a quick war," suggested the Russian cadet.

Ilja laughed nervously and agreed.

At the barracks of the 9th brigade, the few guards who were stationed informed the recent graduates that the troops were in the field. The new officers were assigned beds and awaited further orders for the next two days, time they used to explore the area, including the city of Riga.

Riga proved more surprising than Moscow. The merchandise in the store windows completely amazed him. Shoes, watches, shirts, cameras, anything and everything imaginable crowded the shops, and for very little money. Watches that were unavailable for two hundred rubles in Moscow were in plentiful supply for twenty. One ruble equaled one lat, and the lats went far in the shops. The city still operated as part of an independent country and not one that was occupied by the Soviet army.

After two days, a soldier arrived with instructions and drove them fifteen miles into the woods, where they marched farther with a guide to find their new quarters and troops.

"Did you ever hear of anything so asinine?" asked one of the guides next to Ilja. "Imagine a small country like Germany with the insolence to challenge a great nation like the Soviet Union. We have many times the population of their little nation, and will dispense with their false sense of superiority."

Ilja felt the same and repeated the viewpoint of his political instructor. "We defeated Germany in the last war and they have had no time to re-equip. In no time our forces will punish them." [4]

"This unexpected bit of action might prove a timely lift to our careers," suggested his companion.

At the front, Ilja met his first command, a full company of one hundred soldiers, very green. He surveyed the men and saw a group of untried new conscripts and volunteers. The youngest must have been five years older than Lieutenant Narzikul, who had yet to apply a razor to his face.

But he determined to make a fighting force out of them before marching out to demolish the Germans. He placed a newly issued pistol into his holster. In a day, he distributed the standard Soviet rifle with its five- shell clip to each soldier, and began the task of teaching them how to march and how to fight.

The unit resembled a crowd at the fair more than a fighting force. Its composition included a mixture of many Republics. Not all of them spoke Russian, and those who did, spoke it as a broken second language to their own ethnic tongue. He called them to attention and could see instantly that they were not prime army material.

"Attention!" he shouted.

"Eyes left."

Half turned in the proper direction, and the other half equally divided between those who looked the wrong way and those too confused to do anything at all. The young and inexperienced officer felt like an old pro next to these troops. It would not take long to mold a group strong enough to tame the Germans.

The battalion commander held a briefing for all officers. He explained that the Soviet command was surveying the German action and was creating a master blueprint. At the briefing, the political officer addressed those assembled.

"The Soviet Union is preparing for its victory against the German barbarians. You officers should train your troops for action in the near future. As you know, only recently the Baltic states invited their Soviet brothers to aid them in their path to socialism.

"Unfortunately, we have not had enough time to fully accomplish this goal, and a number of fascist reactionaries still inhabit the towns of Latvia. Hence, if any officer finds it necessary to reorganize his troops in a temporary position to the rear, he should never go through a Latvian town. Bandits, counterrevolutionaries and fascists sometimes fire on Soviet troops from windows."

The political officer could not bring himself to talk about possible retreat, and thus described a backward movement as a reorganization, in order to emphasize the brief nature of any yielding shift of troops.

The political officer continued, "You should also never subject yourself to capture by a Nazi. The German army lives in a primitive state unchanged since ancient days. They will slice off your private parts, cut off your ears, and dismember your arms before finally allowing you to die."

Ilja knew of the terrible behavior of the Germans from discussions back at the School. He asked one of his sergeants about the fascists in Latvian towns.

The sergeant verified this, saying a retreat through a town would produce two enemies, townspeople and Germans.

And Ilja thought Riga was such a lovely city.

The next day, the entire regiment of close to 2000 men marched along the Dvina River, where they expected some sort of attack, and proceeded to dig foxholes and entrenchments on the East side. Hand-crank telephones connected each company to the battalion commander's post. The summer weather in Latvia, although not as hot as Uzbekistan, still kept the men sweating as they dug their ground works and trained. Equipment consisted of pistols, rifles, machine guns, and hand-held anti-vehicle guns. They had no idea what armament the German infantry possessed.

Then, in the blue summer sky, a small German plane buzzed and circled the area, unchallenged. It paced the river and descended to only a few hundred feet above the defenders. A bold swastika flashed before their uplifted heads. The plane repeated its forays a number of times without giving or receiving fire. No Soviet antiaircraft artillery and no Red planes greeted the intruding aircraft.

The men took this as an insult and began firing into the air. The shots from their rifles could not reach and the little plane swung merrily along, teasing the angry lines below.

"What the hell is that? Call the Air Force and get rid of him," someone yelled, fruitlessly firing a rifle towards the craft. The assembled troops had no anti-aircraft capability and only assumed that some higher command prepared a plan to counteract the surveillance.

The plane circled lower, drawing more fire from the lines of the Soviets, exposing its swastika to the aim of the soldiers, and laughing at the efforts to down it.

Next morning about 7:00, the same plane circled even lower, ejecting flares and whistling smoke, signaling the position to German artillery, which then began a bombardment on the entire east side of the river. Still no orders or plan. For Ilja, graduated just over a week before, no hair on his eighteen-year-old face, the war began.

Just as the Military School textbook recommended, German heavy artillery adjusted its positioning, lofting shells ever closer to the recently dug entrenchments. But the artillery came from the enemy side. No matter, the textbook recommended ways to alleviate this situation, by moving troops, counterattacking, bringing in air strikes, and firing defense rounds of heavy shells. However, no orders came to his company, and he noticed no countermeasures. Sometimes the subtlety of the Soviet initiatives was frustrating, but the leadership always came through with solutions.

The line of fire from unseen cannons mesmerized Ilja, as he watched the effect of the artillery finding its range, raining imminent death down upon his troops. He sat like a child at a carnival watching a dancing snake, swirling and luring, until he realized that his position was the object of the venomous fangs, which spat fire and destruction. With the artillery range established, a tremendous outpouring of carnage followed.

"I'm hit. I'm hit."

This frantic chant chilled the ground, backed by a chorus of screams and moans. Dying men sank to the earth, soaked it with their blood as they tried, too late, to reestablish their line as the political officer advised. Ilja knew that the enemy would achieve its first objective, to soften the ground in advance of a thrust forward.

"We must be prepared for our reinforcements!" Ilja screamed to a figure next to him. "Or maybe, our troops are counterattacking on the other side of the river."

His mind reviewed all the theory taught in school. Usually artillery that bombarded the front stayed a couple of miles behind the line of interaction, with tanks and planes accomplishing surveillance and gaining ground from the adversary troops. The Germans had read the textbook also.

The artillery attack decimated the ranks of the defending Soviets, with sporadic disorganized sections of the line flying into the air among explosions of dust and dirt, while other, luckier troops ran to the rear unaware of the dangers coming from housetops if they ventured into the towns. Ilja's troops came under heavy deafening explosions.

He called for a tactical retreat of sixty feet in order to avoid the murderous penetration of the heavy guns. Then the enemy showed itself.

German troops appeared across the river. His anger grew at the brazen barbarians, and he fired his pistol with very shaky hands, trembling, thinking about death. After a few more rounds of artillery missiles rained on his position, his senses concentrated more on avoiding incoming shells and repositioning his men.

"Fire at will!" he commanded.

Only a few heard his order, but those who weren't dispersing commenced firing.

The defensive fusillade, without coordinating orders or plan, brought no damage to the enemy due to its randomness. He grabbed a rifle from a body lying still, its calm face denying the frenzy in the air. He forced a clip into the magazine and fired two rounds at the Germans across the river, but discovered that the shells could not reach the other side of the river. Furthermore, the clip jammed and refused to yield another round to the barrel.

"Where are our orders, our reinforcements?" he yelled to no one in particular.

On the other side of the river more foreign troops appeared, delivering hard unexplainable blows to the Soviet prestige.

Tanks roared out of the woods on the German side, violating USSR soil with their boisterous grinding and destructive turrets. Alongside the tanks, two or three German companies, about three hundred men, challenged the Soviet regiment of 2000.

Finally, a call from battalion headquarters summoned Ilja to the commanding officer. He traveled military style. First he crawled through the dirt, then ran in a crouched position for a few feet behind a small dirt mound; then reached the captain's foxhole, where he kneeled with another company commander to get instructions.

He looked at the other lieutenant. There sat one of the cadets just graduated from Tashkent Military School, Alexei, his fellow train passenger, in the same battle. They hardly had time to acknowledge each other.

"My friend," he said as much to himself as to his classmate.

"Isakjan," the graduate responded in a bewildered tone.

"Orders, finally orders, finally the plan will be revealed," Isakjan muttered.

The captain looked harried, panicky, and not at all the striking figure of a couple of days before. He started to explain.

"We expect German tanks to try to cross the river any minute now," he motioned in the direction of the bridge. "Arrangements have been made to blow up the overpass when the tanks begin to cross."

Ilja and Alexei nodded their agreement with the plan. Each of the other company officers of their battalion had already received instructions, and now the youngest officers sighed with relief.

As the captain began instructions, large artillery barrages increased in intensity, and German troops with tanks began to cross the bridge. The three in the foxhole waited for the bridge to explode.

The tanks and troops kept advancing, never letting up their pressure. Twenty tanks crossed the bridge, firing into the foxhole area, causing panic among the troops, none of whom had received instructions.

The German tanks never paused, but pushed rapidly forward and fanned out at the base of the bridge to perform a simple pincer movement, with tanks leading two coordinated thrusts and troops crouching and firing behind them. In between the two columns, they flushed out the Red Army soldiers, overwhelming them with superior firepower, coolly reducing the population of the regiment. Many on the Soviet side died, many retreated, and many were wounded in an atmosphere of complete hell. Ilja's company languished a couple of hundred yards away from his meeting place with the captain, with no weapons to match tanks.

Every soldier made his own decision on what to do. No authority existed. The result amounted to retreat and confusion, their light five-shot rifles having no effect on the German heavy tanks. All contact with regiment headquarters was lost.

The captain's alarm grew to fear as he realized the hopelessness of the situation, now deteriorated to the point of complete encirclement. The Germans, with tanks, airplanes, artillery and troops marched across the bridge without serious impediment. They overran and decimated the more numerous Red defenders, who sat without orders, even to start retreating, a maneuver they had not yet practiced.

"We Soviet officers know the ruthless behavior of the barbaric Germans," the captain lectured as he prepared to die. "We must do something to avoid capture."

It was the middle of the day, about noon, with tanks overriding them everywhere. Most of their troops lay dead or wounded, and very little visibility existed through the belch of battle.

"We must fight to the end or take our own lives." the captain repeated himself, struggling with the probable conclusion of his life.

Ilja did not flinch from this conclusion. He possessed no individual identity, his own completely merged with the Soviet cause, a cause that needed soldiers to fight and die. He only needed an order to do whatever was necessary for the good of the country, whatever the Captain desired. The two junior officers nodded their agreement. Ilja, almost in a trance, remembered the instructions back at the School never to allow himself to be captured. He shuddered to think that his contribution to the war would come so soon and without glory.

"What should we do, Captain?"

"Take our own lives. Each man will shoot himself. Yes. Fine. We all have pistols."

The captain waved his gun as if to show the item in question. His eyes grew wide with delirium.

The two new lieutenants took guns in hand and pronounced their willingness to die for country, Stalin and family. They said goodbye and embraced, thankful for an order that would help the Soviet Union, and grateful to be spared the horrible torture awaiting an officer captured by the heathen Germans. Ilja could hardly breathe between the heat of the raging battle and his frustrations at such an abrupt ending to his life.

The Captain then turned to the young Russian officer, who, due to his ethnicity, received more authority than Ilja.

"You know, I have a wife and two children, and can not kill myself." He stopped short of sobbing.

The two new officers leaned close to the captain in order to hear the details of their suicide and to hear the captain's last words.

"I assign you to shoot me, then shoot lieutenant Narzikul, and then shoot yourself."

The lieutenant stared at his Captain, dumbfounded, and immediately grew hysterical. "I can't. I just can't."

Ilja Narzikul got the order. He didn't understand the reluctance of his compatriot to execute perfectly logical orders, as he attributed no value to his own life or that of his fellow soldiers.

The German tanks growled, ever closer.

"Yes, Captain." he answered, at last feeling relieved at receiving an executable order, concluding that his own life and those of his fellow officers stood in the way of the inevitable Soviet victory. He could obey his commander and spare all of them from torture: his pride as a Turkistani soldier and officer demanded it.

That was the order he willingly obeyed for his country, without further thought. His personality lined up to obey, so melded into the military and Communist movement that he could not think to question the order. So they again said goodbye, this time with less emotion. Time grew short.

Ilja could not point his gun at the captain's face. The emotional state of his fellow officer passed to him, now in charge of the executions, but he fought to repress any tendencies to value his self over the needs of his country.

"Please, sir," he requested, "at least turn to the side." The horror that had gripped his captain and fellow lieutenant began to strike him and overcome his fervor.

But the captain rapidly complied, by turning around to expose the rear of his head and removing his helmet. Ilja put his gun to the captain's head and pulled the trigger several times, producing instant death, blood, exposed brains.

Ilja lurched backward, aghast at the sight, but before he could gain his bearings, the Russian cadet turned his head in imitation of the captain and demanded the same ending. Ilja repeated his action on behalf of his fellow graduate cadet. Poor boy. Death in a foxhole to start a career. Ilja gagged as he fought waves of stomach churns attempting to induce vomiting and tried to think of his hometown and family. This was not why he joined the military.

He turned the gun to his own head, delirious with grief from the deaths, confused from the slaughter and panic from the imminence of the tanks. He moved it to his chest, wavering back and forth, thinking maybe he should fire at the heart instead. The sight of his dead comrades distracted him, prostrate in the foxhole, covered in their blood and with heads blown open. Did faith in the Soviet Union demand an end like this? All the time tanks approached the top of the foxhole. In the midst of the wavering, he fired, with the bullet entering his shoulder just below the clavicle bone and above the rib cage, through muscle, causing bleeding, but not unconsciousness.

He put a hand under his shirt and pulled out a fistful of blood.

He wondered, "How long does it take to die?"

He had not paid attention to the battle above for a few moments, and now the rumble of the tanks and the firing of turret guns overshadowed all the other sounds of hell. The Germans pulled to within yards. He heard the metallic sounds of the furious tracked wheels braking at the lip of his universe, the little foxhole so quickly dug a few days ago by the mighty Soviet Army.

A tank stopped at the top of the foxhole, and he dropped his gun to lie between the bloodied bodies of the other two, listening as German voices approached the top, looked over, and then left. He recognized only a few German words, but his fear of the situation prevented any concentration on the voices. He lay frozen for what seemed a century, shivering with terror and apprehension, hearing the tanks trail off as they resumed their rapid pace across the territory. His uniform soaked up the blood and brains of his comrades. The voices receded and the tank rolled out.

The sounds of battle diminished as the Germans raced across the Latvian plain. In the middle of the afternoon, he put his head up and saw no moving person or thing, only bodies, smoke, devastation. The once pulsating veins of his company spread out across the riverbank with red blood emptied, attracting flies.

He found himself behind enemy lines, having improperly followed orders. He thought about taking his pistol and shooting himself again, but the flowing waters of the river distracted him. He determined to try to cross the river with a small boat lying several feet from the bank, but he did not have enough strength to push it to the water. If only he could get some help, and rejoin his troops and the revolution. After almost fainting with his efforts, a civilian appeared and approached him, responding to his request for help to cross the river.

As the civilian rowed, his pain increased. The man took him to a Latvian household in a little village. The man's wife washed him and replaced his uniform with street clothes. They had no medicine, but took some black bread soaked with water and bandaged it with cotton cloth against the wound.

Ilja continually asked how he could reunite with the Red Army, crossing the enemy line through the forests. Somehow, he hoped that the deaths of his fellow officers in the foxhole had been a bad dream and that he cold reunite with them. His hosts told him his condition must improve first, but they would investigate the possibility of meeting up with Soviet troops.

He listened to this advice for a few days, growing more despondent and concerned over a separation from his army. During the nights, vicious dreams haunted him as he relived the foxhole scene a thousand different ways until he could stand the tension no longer. Waiting until his hosts went on errands, he ventured outside to seek directions from the villagers.

A man sauntered at the end of the block, and Ilja approached him to inquire about the likelihood of obtaining a guide to the Soviet side of the front, and to ask where the respective armies were located. The man spoke hesitatingly, surprising Ilja with his knowledge of Russian, nervously wringing his hands before abruptly walking away. Ilja continued through the village, but before he progressed more than a half block, a motorcycle with sidecar carrying two German soldiers raced from the end of town to his side.

"Halt, halt!" they shouted, with machine guns aimed.

It happened too quickly for him to think or escape. Ilja raised his hands and submitted to a search.

He now remembered that his political officer warned him that fascist elements lived in some of the Latvian villages. Now he was caught behind enemy lines in civilian clothes, liable for a firing squad as a spy.

Soldiers escorted him to an assembly point for prisoners,

and deposited him with a group of about fifteen Soviet soldiers and a flyer, with a burned face. A guard detail patrolled outside the compound. He stayed with the group that day without food or instruction, waiting for a firing squad to line them up and shoot.

The prisoners passively waited for death, silently parting ranks as more defeated soldiers were added to the compound until evening came and darkness surrounded all. No questions or comments so far from the Germans, but the Reds huddled and talked among each other, exchanging stories of the battles and the brigades and divisions they fought with. They convinced themselves that the setback was temporary, that the Soviet Army was extremely strong and would recover to become ultimately victorious.

The pilot with a burned face was the first evidence of a Red Air Force he had seen. And the last.

CHAPTER 7

MEDICS WITH CLUBS

Our people see all hope has dwindled,
While foulest falsehoods flourish rank.
Throughout our life we're cheated, swindled.
We fight, but all our shots are blank!

-------Abai Kunanbayev, Kazakh poet

The Soviet POW's were escorted under guard late at night to a large building surrounded by towering stone walls and huge steel gates. They congregated in a hall while German soldiers removed them one or two at a time. None returned. No sounds were heard, but the remaining prisoners believed that the Germans surely executed their comrades, perhaps after interrogation and torture. They expected no less from primitive barbarians and steeled themselves for flesh-stripping agony. Ilja sat silent, a child compared to the others. His civilian clothes made him seem even younger than he was.

His turn came, and a soldier guided him through a dungeon maze of very dark unlit halls. He followed closely, nursing his hurt shoulder from which emanated a bloody pus, while the guard poked a flashlight into the stone recesses of the granite walls until he found a doorway that interested him. He called his captive forward and suddenly pushed him through the opening and closed the door behind.

Ilja tried to look about, but the room was extremely dark. Sounds of movement and whispers came from the black space before him.

"Who are you?" someone called out in Russian.

"Ilja Narzikul," he replied.

"And where do you come from?" the same male voice struck out from the depths.

"I am from Uzbekistan, and was captured. How many people are in here?" He took a turn questioning.

"About twenty, all from around Riga."

"What are you doing here? Are you soldiers?"

"No, we are Jews."

"Jews? Why are Jews in this place?" The whole episode twisted his sense of equilibrium. He couldn't conceive of a reason to imprison civilians, but the Germans had mistaken him for a local lad, and assumed that he must be Jewish.

"When the Germans occupied the city, they told all Jews to assemble in the square and then transported us to this building, which was, before the invasion, a high security prison. We do not know why we have been brought here or what will happen to us." The spokesman from the dark continued. "Are you Jewish also?"

"No, I am Moslem, if anything."

In the morning light, the Jewish leader questioned him further and realized that it was his civilian clothes and youth that caused the Germans to mistake him for a noncombatant and that he certainly did not belong with the Jewish detainees, but rather with the POW's. All the people in the room were herded outside and forced to exercise by running around a fifty meter circular path, including men and women ranging from adolescents to elderly. Ilja stretched his memory back to German courses from grade school and came up with a few words, which he used with reference to his shoulder, saying "Ich bin krank, (I am sick.)" and showing the guard that he was wounded. The sentry showed no interest in the laceration, and pushed him back in the line.

"You must explain to the Germans that you are not Jewish," the leader concluded, supplying him with the necessary German words.

He approached the guard again, "Ich bin nein Jude. (I am not Jewish.)"

The German guard said, "You are not Jewish?"

The guard asked Ilja a few more questions, and, with a crude exchange in German, convinced himself that Ilja was Uzbek.

The next day they did not take him to march in the morning, but left him in the room, while the Jews were forced to march until they were exhausted. After another day, a trooper called his name and led him out of the dark cell to a compound with a half dozen wounded Red Army soldiers by a railroad station.

A German who spoke Russian came to interview him. "Why do you wear civilian clothes?"

"Sir, I was shot in a battle by the bridge on the Dvina River, and taken to a small village, where the people dressed my wound and gave me clean clothes."

The interviewing officer asked a few additional questions involving serial number and division. He suddenly stood up and moved to the front of his desk.

"Pull down your pants," commanded the German.

He looked at Ilja's penis, obviously circumcised. "Why are you circumcised? Jews are circumcised."

"I am Moslem, as most Uzbeks are. Moslems are circumcised. It is done in my town in the building next to the mosque."

"Well, you certainly don't look Jewish." he concluded, looking over the dark eyes, hair, and round nose.

"Return to the compound."

Ilja shuddered as he arrived back in the army compound, thinking himself in a more secure place than the dank prison. None of the original Red Army men remained. He knew nothing of Hitler's attitude or policies towards Jews or other peoples, and certainly nothing of the Fuhrer's racial orders to his legions, commanding them to gather all political commissars or Asiatic "criminal types" for immediate liquidation and Jews for separation into ghettos or firing squads. Not trusting the army to carry out these orders, Hitler arranged for Himmler's SS Einsatzkommandos to follow the army and carry out executions. The SS combed the prisoner of war camps, shooting anyone looking Asiatic or Jewish. In one Polish camp alone, 28,000 Oriental-looking Turkistanis were liquidated. [1]

Ilja and the other POW's were loaded in cattle cars, packed tightly like animals, and transported for several hours to Kaunas, a big city and the capital of Lithuania. Other prisoners recognized the city upon being herded out of the boxcars. The wounded entered a large hospital.

A doctor inspected Ilja and applied dressings. After a couple of weeks, the wound started healing in the front, where the bullet had entered, but he still experienced a weeping of blood and pus at the exit hole where the bullet had torn a large amount of flesh. The stay at the hospital came to an end well before the gash closed.

Again he was transferred by bus and cattle car to a small town, which he later found out was called Ebenrod, Prussia. He watched for hordes of bandits and other savages among the enemy, but saw well-dressed people riding bicycles and driving cars on paved streets with sidewalks and impressive buildings. The barbarians all enjoyed a life better than that known in Turkistan. Somehow, the capitalists had not destroyed Germany and they hadn't sacked Latvia or Lithuania before those two countries sought refuge with the Soviet Union. Citizens of the archenemy Germany enjoyed a standard of life higher than in his people's paradise.

Guards escorted them past the town to a big open field sprouting sharp barbed wire and lookout towers at regular intervals. Back-to-back square wire compounds about four hundred feet on each side, separated by long dirt streets, defined the compounds. Captives could talk to inmates in adjacent compounds.

At a POW clearing station he waited for his turn with the German clerk.

"Name," the soldier asked brusquely in Russian.

"Isakjan Narzikul," he answered, ignoring his Russian

nickname.

"Nationality."

"Soviet Union."

The answer did not suffice. "I mean what republic."

"Uzbekistan."

"Home."

"Jizzakh, Uzbekistan."

"Where is that?"

"Uzbekistan. Turkistan."

The clerk motioned to a guard and he was led to a new residence. He looked out on an open dirt expanse surrounded by the ever-present wire, with a small shed near the entrance. Bleak clods of dirt and threatening rolls of sharp wire surrounded over five hundred men. They came from the Turkistani Republics, places like Uzbekistan, Kazakhstan, and Tajikistan. Another compound held a contingent from the Trans-Caucasus area - Georgians, Azerbaijans, and Armenians. Other nationalities also were grouped together, so that Ukrainians, Latvians, Estonians, Great Russians, and Lithuanians each had separate wired areas.

The prisoner-of-war-camps for Soviet soldiers amounted to transfer stations to mass graves. The Soviet Union never ratified the Geneva Convention of 1929 regarding wartime prisoners, a pretext that the Nazis used to withdraw the most minimal human support from the Soviet POW's. [2] The men herded into the wire prison came with the wounds of war; a few missing hands and legs, but most suffering lacerations, exhaustion, and deprivation, which rapidly deteriorated further from malnutrition, starvation, exposure and beatings. Those with more serious wounds died in the battlefield.

One compound harbored a different arrangement. Within the square outline of wire, a second, smaller circular fence further isolated the occupants. In this special circle extra guards watched over 100 people, whose plight the others could watch through the wires in the open field. The people in the center circle were always marching, driven by clubs and kicks of the guards, who forced their charges to hustle around in small orbits until they dropped. This was the Jewish compound.

Unknown to the Germans, a good number of the Turkistanis were Jewish and therefore potential candidates for the foul treatment meted out to their brethren. This situation shocked the entire compound. Rumors abounded that the Nazis did not like Jews, but many of the other minorities also suffered discrimination. Many speculated that the circle prisoners would be shot, but then they themselves might be also. The various degrees of the prison abyss mattered little for those who expected to die, and so the Turkistanis followed their orders and the Jews in the circle followed theirs.

A large metal gate for trucks and a smaller one for pedestrians stood at the front of the Turkistani enclosure. Immediately inside sat a small wood shack, about ten feet square with a flat roof on top and a single desk inside. Max, the German Sergeant in charge of the compound, maintained his office there. He relied on his assistant, a twenty-five-year-old Latvian POW who served as translator and took charge when Max was away. Max never spent more than three to five hours of any day in the compound.

The Latvian took roll call, supervised the digging of a big hole on the edge on the compound to be used as a squatting latrine, and slept in the wood shack.

Prisoners huddled at night on the dirt with whatever scant garb they wore and without facilities to wash or drink because the Germans did not even supply water. Poorly clothed and fed, they suffered without relief. Isakjan witnessed no escape attempts; at night the streets were patrolled with dogs, blazing lights, and the wire fences were tightly woven.

He slept on the hard cold ground among a knot of men from central Uzbekistan, the area of Jizzakh. The tight pack of bodies held a lingering bit of warmth, but very often someone turned cold, blue and motionless before sunrise. Once again, he was the youngest, but this time he was not ostracized. Small consolation. But his youth served to advantage, because the cold and the hunger ripped through the bodies of the older men faster, tearing remaining flickers of life from their eyes as they prepared to fade into the care of Allah. Resignation to this inevitable demise never occurred to the youth.

"What is your name, boy?" they asked him.

"Isakjan," he answered.

His Russian nickname of Ilja suddenly seemed distant: a fanciful dream from days when he danced with Nora Melkakze in his crisp uniform back at the Military School. Her name signified acceptance, knowledge and achievement, qualities for which he had fought so hard and which now served no purpose. Even a little bowl of bread and milk on a mat in Jizzakh seemed extremely desirable and so far away.

The cart for the dead arrived in the morning after roll call. The men could see blue bodies slung in a heap on the wagon, to be buried without the slightest pretense of Moslem burial, without a word from loved ones, without a last pleasure. Death dealt an undeniable punishment, but the horrible blue color shocked Isakjan most. Usually a few, and sometimes twenty bodies lay on the hard dirt, swollen and discolored from exposure, wounds, hunger, sickness and then the ultimate stiffness that attracted flies. Summer still lingered, but the evenings were cold, and the men had no blankets or heavy clothes. More prisoners always came in the afternoon to fill the spaces vacated by the morning death cart. The constant influx indicated the Germans had no shortage of prisoners or victories over the Soviet homeland.

At roll call, the Germans asked for a sick count. Often a group of three uniformed men arrived at the compound to witness the roll call and inspect those claiming to be sick. They carried no stethoscopes or cotton, but long clubs the length of a baseball bat and slightly more narrow.

Isakjan tried to show his not-yet healed wound to the inspector, who began shouting in rapid German, bombarding him with a fusillade of blows from his club. The unexpected force of the club threw him to the ground, where he curled into a ball to protect himself from a continuing rain of kicks, hits from the wooden weapons, and curses. The attack suddenly ceased, but the boy lay in shock for a long time after the inspectors departed.

"If you want treatment," advised one of the older inmates, "tell them you have diarrhea. That will get you out of here and maybe at the treatment center you could show an attendant the bullet hole."

Isakjan observed the medical process first. Those complaining of wounds, pneumonia, exhaustion or most other ailments were beaten with bats, unless the sickness was diarrhea, for the Nazis feared typhus. In that case they would remove the diseased person, but what exactly happened next did not seem obvious because the sick rarely returned. Most men preferred to take their chances in the dirt on the field, hoping their aching bodies would not weigh down the death cart with another swollen mass of twisted flesh. He decided to let his shoulder worry about itself.

In these conditions, the winter would finish any man hardy enough to last through the autumn, provided the SS squads looking for Asiatics did not find him first.

He realized the mistake he had made by not committing suicide. An ugly dark hole of human misery in prison showed its face to him as it had to his father. To advance beyond chauvinism and destitution, then be caught and returned to a base existence as though his personal determination to advance meant nothing, constituted the very worst torture. This damaged him more than the hunger and cold, deprivations that had made his acquaintance from early childhood. But the hunger stimulated a natural reflex in him from times in Jizzakh when he found a way to survive and where his driving energy had always led him to someone willing to champion the underprivileged. So he searched for some strong leader in the camp needing help. He looked toward the camp boss.

The Latvian spoke none of the Turkistani languages, and only jagged Russian. As manager of the temporarily alive, he wielded a great deal of power over the inmates. The Latvian signaled to the prisoners, mostly with gestures. Very few Soviet Central Asians knew Russian, and especially not those subject to military draft. Yet he needed to nominate POW's to work on German farms. Those returning from such assignments told of lush farms where the families owned their own fields and marketed their produce as they saw fit.

Isakjan was drawn to the Latvian.

"Ich gerna arbeit. [sic] (I like to work.)" he claimed.

"So you do." answered the boss. "And you speak a little German too. What is your name?"

"Isakjan."

"Well, Isakjan, you will go with the farm detachment today."

They passed bountiful fields on the way. In his crude German, Isakjan talked with the farmer.

"Is this your land?"

"Oh yes, I own all these fields, the house, barn and livestock."

The entire Tenth Anniversary of the Revolution kolkhoz did not possess a building or field comparable to that of one German farmer.

The war brought much confusion to Isakjan. The German farmer did not look the least bit oppressed, as the Soviet press claimed. With a guard overlooking, he worked the fields, digging potatoes, keeping a few in his pocket and feeling thankful for the assignment. The farmer prepared a large meal and fed them well with bread and even a little meat, a better meal as a prisoner than the kolkhoz ever provided for his family.

"How can the Germans give this land and house to a mere farmer?" asked a fellow Uzbek on the way back to the camp. The Uzbeks gathered around Isakjan, the speaker of German.

"What did the farmer say? Is that his farm, his beautiful

house?"

But they already knew the answers. Even though only Isakjan could converse in German, the others did not need to confirm what they could see. The farm was so attractive, the house so exquisite, unlike the dull flat buildings on the collective in Jizzakh.

They talked among themselves, observing the discrepancies. On the many days with no activities they initiated great conversations about the smallest details of their captors. Isakjan thought about his father, jailed for saving a few sacks of grain and pursuing a trade on his own. His father knew enough about animals and agriculture to have owned a farm like the German. And yet Isakjan had joined a mighty Soviet army to combat this farmer's country, to prevent the spread of his methods into the Soviet Union. Isakjan had worked himself into a fever in preparation for killing Germans, but observing the enemy from within his house changed his mind. The life of the Germans did not look barbaric at all.

The activities in camp produced the most dour boredom and misery. After roll call: nothing. At noon, the entire compound marched to an outside kitchen at the edge of the camp where a crew dispensed thin watery soup. Toward the end of the day, a select group, hand-picked by the Latvian, marched to the kitchen, obtained bricks of lard and black bread, brought it back to the compound, and distributed a piece of the bread and a tablespoon of lard to each man.

Always looking for a place where something was happening, Isakjan usually found himself loitering near the boss's hut, and he made himself available to the Latvian, translating his orders and establishing a communication between the overseer and his slaves. He noticed that at the end of the distribution there always was bread left over, and that those who went to gather the bread ended up with an extra portion. He guessed that the kitchen never really knew how many prisoners occupied the compound, because so many died each day. The conditions and inadequate food combined to shorten life expectancies to months rather than years.

The Latvian started picking Isakjan to help get bread as the boy stayed by the shed and watched for any moment to extend his interaction with his boss. With his wound closed and healing, Isakjan could become more active. When Max the guard departed, he wandered over to the Latvian and struck up a conversation, slipping back into the throng of miserable prisoners when Max returned swinging his menacing club. One day, the Latvian motioned Isakjan to stay as Max approached.

"Herr Sergeant, this is Isakjan. He speaks German well and can work hard."

"Good," grunted Max, without acknowledging the boy.

Isakjan soon regularly accompanied the evening bread detail to the kitchen, learning that the number of prisoners recognized by the kitchen was somewhat arbitrary as expected. The Latvian doled out extra bread to his kitchen squad, who then melted back into the mass of prisoners. Isakjan stayed to keep the boss company. He ate some of the second portion given him as they talked, gaining strength with each day, and saving food for his coterie of friends.

"What do you think about the war?" the Latvian wanted to know.

"I'm hungry and want to go home."

"Well, you are just a boy."

He practiced German and conversed for long hours with the Latvian. The compound overseer could speak to no other man informally and grew fond of Isakjan. He had no kind word for the Russians, however.

"You're not Russian. Your country, whatever it is called, was overrun by them and they are just exploiting you."

Isakjan nodded. "I see."

It was a new theory. The Latvian had a grudge against the Russians, and maybe he was a capitalist reactionary trying to justify himself. The lad decided not to disagree with his patron.

"We were once a free country," the Latvian continued. "Russians stole our freedom and reduced us to vassals. We will fight to be free once again, and, with the help of Germany, we will succeed."

Isakjan nodded again. He was a good listener, but the Latvian suggested that the news he read and heard in Uzbekistan amounted to complete fabrications and lies. The Latvian convinced him that maybe the Germans deserved more consideration than the Soviets credited them for. The German nation did not consist of oppressed peasants or a weak military.

He listened and nodded. After all, the Latvian controlled the amount of bread available to Isakjan and the other prisoners.

"You say you could not retreat into the Latvian towns when you were in the Red army? Let me tell you that the whole population, not just a few Fascists, would love to shoot Russian soldiers, and they would not distinguish between Russian and

Turkistani when they both wear the same uniform. Did you ever think why the Germans found you? Anyone asking about joining the Soviet army should be considered an enemy. You were waiting for the bridge to blow up? Maybe the Latvians wanted that bridge to stay so the Germans could chase the Russian bully out forever. And how many Germans did it take to defeat your regiment? Very few."

Maybe the Latvian had a couple of points, Isakjan was forced to concede.

"Anyway, why did you come to fight in Latvia? You should have stayed at home and let the Russians do their own dirty work. How does it feel to be duped by the Russians?"

Isakjan brought the message back to his little group, but he learned that they already harbored anti-Soviet inclinations, and that many had suffered imprisonment for the crimes of owning land or practicing religion.

From morning to evening, the boredom beat down upon the men as menacingly as the cold and hunger, giving them nothing to do except wait for a frigid end to life. The coveted farming work came only irregularly. One older person with a long beard, Nuriddin (Namangani) Qari, turned out to be a mullah, but one who commanded only a little appreciation from the men since his religious fanaticism was so extreme. Isakjan held a great deal of respect for his elders, and the mullah reminded him of his father. He saw to it that the man got a little extra portion of bread.

Nuriddin felt that Allah was watching over them and therefore everything would turn out satisfactorily. He preached to the men incessantly, invoking the Almighty for help. The Russians had locked him up in jail far from his Uzbek home for practicing and preaching Islam, and therefore he hated the Russians most, but also the Germans, who had released him during their Baltic campaign and taken him to the POW camp.

While Isakjan's new position helped him distribute a bit of extra lard and bread to his immediate circle of friends, the Latvian controlled a greater quantity of food, and Isakjan looked for ways to transfer it to the men in the compound. He interested the Latvian in the trade of the camp, which involved shirts, pants, cigarettes, coats, rings, items from the dead and from the newly imprisoned. New arrivals brought cigarettes, the currency of the camp. Since the overseer could not talk to the Turkistanis, who did not like him anyway, Isakjan obtained several garments for him in exchange for bread. This barter continued and increased the amount of food to the prisoners.

The days and hours passed slowly, with the Latvian going into further detail about how residents of the Baltic states hated Russians because they took over and robbed the people. He elaborated on the backward state of the Soviet Union compared with his country, and vowed he would never submit to Soviet domination.

Further news of the war drifted into the camp as more of the prisoners died and others took their place. Reports circulated that the Germans were making tremendous progress in the war, approaching all of the great cities of European USSR, with a penetration of over 700 miles. The new prisoners confirmed this simply by detailing the place of their capture, with each group coming from deeper into Soviet territory. One of the prisoners remarked, "The Soviet Union was very vulnerable, and they tried to hide that from us with their speeches, but the fact of their weakness is as big as the sun and, as our Turkistani proverb says, "you can not hide the sun with a handkerchief."

CHAPTER 8

PROMOTIONS FOR POW'S

A handkerchief cannot cover the sun.

-- Turkistani proverb

The German Wehrmacht advanced so fast across Soviet territory that they did not have time to pick up all the defeated Red Army troops. Just as Isakjan had found shelter in the house of civilians after tanks crushed his Soviet battalion, so did thousands of other scattered soldiers.

One of those soldiers was Ergash Shermat, former professor and chairman of the law department at Tashkent University and justice department official, who had fled into the army to escape harassment from party leaders who labeled him for anti-Soviet activities. As a Turkistani regionalist, he had vowed to oppose the revision and control of Turkistani history and interests by Moscow ever since he had realized the hostility of the Soviets to both.

June 1941 found Shermat on the line between the Ukraine and German-occupied Poland as a political instructor following orders to deny rampant rumors that the Germans were preparing to invade the Soviet Union. The denials of the obvious did not enhance his standing with the officer corps, who hated the interference of the political advisor anyway. His commissar commander, however, told him to ignore the German intelligence plane that circled the Soviet positions during mid-June and the buildup of German equipment and soldiers because Stalin had assured the army that the Nazi alliance held firm.

At 5:00 a.m. on June 22, exploding shells abruptly awoke Shermat to the chaos of an advancing German army. The Red Army put up no discernible defense, but instead evaporated into a mob of scattering panic-stricken men and piles of burning and mutilated corpses. Shermat belonged to the group of panic-stricken men who overran the lone commanding officer trying to rally the troops, and thus he lived as witness to the humiliating defeat of the Soviets.

After hiding in the woods during the day and traveling at night, he asked and received shelter in homes of Ukrainian families. One family invited him to stay for a longer period, even though they detested the Soviet regime and its army. The Ukrainian village residents had not transferred their loathing of the Moscow leadership to individuals also suffering under the same duress.

"We are anti-Soviet, not anti-humanist," they explained, and gave him civilian clothes. As the German troops marched by, family members gathered bread and salt, the welcoming symbol of the land, and presented them to the liberators. They flew flags and signs proclaiming "long live Bandera," the Ukrainian nationalist revolutionary leader, and "long live Hitler." Shermat remained in the attic during the day, but joined the family often at night, sharing conversation and meals with village leaders who came by to appraise him. Thereafter the villagers agreed to cooperate with the family's offer of asylum and to help Shermat. During these conversations, he grew close to the family and the village members. They shared their food with him and displayed an open Ukrainian warmth that made him feel a member of the family. Months passed.

In the aftermath of the regular troops, German auxiliaries and bureaucrats arrived, bringing the SS, the Gestapo and the SD, a security agency harsher than even the SS. They began to arrest leaders of Ukrainian nationalism, often the very ones who, months earlier, had brought salt and bread to the conquering soldiers. Searches of individual houses brought arrests of many Soviet soldiers who sought refuge.

Very early one morning, about 5:00, a knock on the door awoke the family downstairs and Shermat in the attic. Shermat heard voices and the woman cry, "Why does this evil exist in the world? Why is the world such a place?" Shermat came down after hearing a summons, but the family was speechless. The husband and wife tried to bring words to their mouths, but could only choke and cry. A village leader explained that the Germans had ordered all Soviet soldiers to accumulate at a central camp, and anyone not cooperating would be subject to severe punishment. The family promised to petition for his release. Shermat ended up in a prisoner-of-war camp over the protests and tears of his host family. As an educated professor speaking German, Russian, and various Turkistani languages, he was immediately separated and set to work with other educated prisoners recording the incoming masses of defeated Soviet soldiers, writing down names, ranks, and units.

As the new prisoners filed into the clearing room, either the camp doctor, the commandant, or the SD representative supervised. German SS men instructed each POW to pull down his trousers as they filtered in, and then separated the men into two lines. One line completed processing, and the other headed out the back.

Shermat asked the German at the entry table, "Why do they want the men to pull down their pants?"

"To see who is circumcised so we can sort out the Jews," answered the soldier in a matter-of-fact voice.

"What happens to them?" Shermat wanted to know.

"We take them in the rear and shoot them," was the SS reply.

"But Moslems are circumcised also," pointed out Shermat, realizing that he himself would not pass the circumcision test.

The German was surprised. They were killing Moslems, thinking they were Jewish. "Maybe you should tell the commandant," he suggested.

Shermat immediately went to the man in charge and explained his point.

"But we can't spare the Jews," the commandant explained, willing to liquidate hundreds of Moslems in order to get one Jewish person. "How can we tell Jews from Moslems anyway?"

Shermat persisted, "All Moslems will know this prayer: God is one. Muhammad is his prophet."

"We will try that," promised the commandant.

Soon the great majority of circumcised men traveled into the camp along with the rest of the defeated army, and only a small line filed out to the back. Shermat saved thousands, but despaired at the destruction of the Jews, and decided to get himself into another risky situation by overriding authorities as he had in Turkistan. He sauntered over to the group of arriving prisoners and started a conversation out of hearing distance from the guards.

"Who here is Jewish?" he asked. He quietly began talking to those pointed out. "Listen quickly," he ordered. "When the guards see that you are circumcised and ask your religion, tell them you are Moslem. Then, if they ask you to recite a prayer, say that God is one and Muhammad is his prophet."

"Why should we do that?" questioned one of the men suspiciously.

"Because they take anyone Jewish out back and shoot him," said Shermat. "So spread the word and don't mention how you heard."

Many of the men listened. A few claimed that they must be separated for special consideration since many Jews had advanced education. Those died that very day.

Some of those saved that day met a slower death by sickness, typhus and exposure in the camps. As they jammed into the wire compounds and told the events of their capture to other inmates in dozens of prison compounds, the men questioned the power of the Red Army.

Every additional prisoner brought into the camp where Isakjan was housed told of tales similar to Shermat's, depicting the immensity of the Soviet defeat. For Isakjan, this war news, trips to

German potato farmers, and talks with the Latvian forced him to reconsider the might of the Soviet Union and the inevitability of Marxist success.

At the end of September 1941, all POW's from Latvia, Estonia and Lithuania were released to go home since the Germans considered them friendly allies. The Latvian recommended Isakjan to succeed him, and Max gave him a promotion. He now had the responsibility for picking the kitchen and farm crews. The comrades who lived around Jizzakh all benefited from his promotion and he increased his circle of associates to other Turkistanis.

The summer faded, making room for colder weather and each frosty morning prepared the field for another harvest of blue dead flesh. Those not dead or dying lined up, with shirts off in the frigid air, picking off the lice. The compound still had to manage with no water. Very few of the early groups avoided the death cart.

The pain permeating the wire enclosure from wounds, sickness, and yearning for home was overwhelming, with most prisoners falling into deep depression and then death. Isakjan shared the pain, but his outlet was work rather than languor, and he busied himself.

In the mornings, he organized the roll call, reporting to Max the German the number of prisoners and number of dead and sick. Despite the tremendously squalid conditions, he busied himself with structure and routine, insisting on straight lines and orderly announcements. The absurdity of his precision did not occur to him because his need to work dictated a course of constructive activity. The little extra food from the kitchen brought back his energy and he released it with attempts to instill military discipline into his ranks. He knew the difference between animal resignation and self-respect. They could die with dignity and organization.

Elsewhere, SS squads continued to work their way through prisoner camps, meting out cruel and instant death to racially unacceptable stock. At the same time the German East Ministry developed an interest in the Turkistani population of the camps and conducted its own search for Asiatics. This Ministry began to plan uses for the captured soldiers other than death, but lacked the political power of the racially biased SS liquidation squads.

As winter approached, Max instructed Isakjan that a number of extremely important visitors were arriving at the camp and the lineup should be very formal, according to size, in straight lines, with military attention. About 10:00 on the designated morning, Max gave the signal that the visitors were coming, and Isakjan put everybody in line.

The boy instructed the men, all of them from a few years to twenty-five years older than he, lining them up with military precision. The only vestige of his former life amounted to his training in military formation, and he scurried about to stake a claim of some kind on control and competence. The group arrived, headed by a German major, a tall man with dark hair, well groomed with a neat mustache, followed by a small staff, one of whom dressed in a beautiful civilian suit.

Isakjan marched forward and reported the number of detainees.

The major addressed the prisoners in German. "My name is Major Meyer-Mader. I have come here to see you in person. I know the people of Turkistan suffer under the dictatorship of Russia, and I am working to make your life better, with improved facilities."

Then, to the surprise of the prisoners, the major repeated his message in Uzbek.

The man in civilian clothes started speaking in Uzbek, which could be understood by all peoples of Turkistan. "I am Uzbek. My name is Veli Kayum-Khan. I was born in Tashkent and came to Germany in 1922 when the Soviet government wanted helpers that could control Turkistan and were sending people to Germany to school. I decided to stay in Germany where we have a political organization formed to liberate Turkistan from Russia.

"You will hear very soon from me some good news."

The men murmured among themselves. Good news sounded like a trick.

He continued, "Do any of you have a university degree or a rank of officer? If so, step forward."

No one moved, afraid. He spoke again in Uzbek, saying with passionate pleading and earnest motions of his hands, "Don't be afraid. I am telling the truth, and if this is not the truth, may Allah punish me and strike me dead. This I swear on the honor of my mother."

This oath struck home. The Turkistani people regard that pledge as holy.

About a dozen stepped forward, including Isakjan and Nuriddin Quari, and their names were taken. Veli Kayum-Khan thanked them very much, promising to return shortly. The dozen scolded each other afterwards, wondering what they had wrought upon themselves.

Two weeks later, a troop of Germans came in and read the names of the officers and degree holders, telling them to follow. They were taken to a compound at the other end of the camp, given their first shower in four months and new clothes.

The clothes fit well. Isakjan looked at himself, standing in a clean Red Army uniform, recycled without insignia. Hair cuts and shoes followed, causing him to feel that he might not be shot, at least not soon.

A soldier took them to the train station, guiding them to the rear of a passenger compartment with civilian riders. The guard traveled with a rifle, as the train passed German towns and neat little villages with careful masonry houses and paved roads far superior to those in the Soviet Union. The prisoners stifled their apprehension concerning what would happen.

The trip took many hours. Isakjan was the only officer; the others possessed university degrees. Finally the train stopped and they got out where the sign said Lukenwald. They disembarked and sat by the station and waited for a bus like a group of tourists. When an army truck came, they got in the back and drove through a forest to an empty compound with freshly painted barracks. Closer inspection revealed the camp was brand new and they were the first inhabitants.

A German soldier speaking in Russian greeted them.

"I am a Volksdeutsche, a German ethnic born in Russia."

He took their names and assigned the group to barracks with individual beds, sheets, blankets, table, and chair. Any furniture represented a big change, but this furniture even exceeded the amount most were accustomed to back in their native land. They joked morbidly, saying that maybe the Germans would fatten them up before shooting them. At noon, the guide took them to the mess hall, with tables and chairs, bread, good food. This small group of Turkistanis were the only occupants in the camp. Ten days passed, days with three big meals, bread, butter, meat, ever so good. For those few who had accomplished the art of eating with a knife and fork, those utensils were placed at the tables.

More arrived, educated minorities, and at the end of the month about forty people came together. Ethnic Germans from the USSR arrived speaking Russian, and also native Germans who had learned Russian. Then the German mind again surprised them.

"Welcome to school, students."

Class started in the morning, teaching everyone the German language. Isakjan excelled, having studied German before. He remembered how much he loved school. After a week, more surprises.

Gunnery school. Isakjan was handed a German rifle, taken to a range and taught to fire; how to operate German machine guns; how to shoot, take apart, clean, repair them. The guns were far superior to the Red Army ones, but the group had no idea what they would be expected to do with their new skills.

They made it a practice to ask no questions and enjoy the good food and surroundings. Teaching included marching, German language, and political orientation. In the political class, the Turkistanis learned about their own country, with emphasis on the failure of the Soviets to properly care for the Turkistani republics, taking the former countries by force, and then exploiting them.

For the first time, Isakjan attended a class on the history of Turkistan. He discovered, much to his surprise, that Central Asia once thrived as one of the richest areas on earth, as a major trade center on the Silk Road, as a significant producer of cotton, and as a center for mining many minerals. These fortunes were exported to the Russian republic from the Turkistani Republics.

When the Germans successfully defeated Russia, Central Asians would be brothers with Germans as free men in a free country.

One day, Veli Kayum-khan appeared before them again.

"Very soon your lives will undergo an immense change for the better. Our country is now under Soviet dictatorship, but soon we will have a new homeland for ourselves."

The rapid change in political thought took some time to seep into the minds of the students, some of whom came from apolitical or Communist backgrounds, while many others had felt the heel of Russian rule and expressed strident anti-Soviet views. The strident ones related their stories of woe to the others. The students passed the courses; they were being fed, were under guard and remembered harder times in prison. The claims of the Germans contained much sense and could not be refuted.

The group knew that the Germans had some grand scheme for them, but the exact nature of their plan was not disclosed. The camp did fit into a larger effort. Two other camps joined to teach courses along the same lines, giving views and histories of Germany, Russia, Bolshevism and the repression of the Soviet peoples. Nazi propaganda regarding Jews was muted. [1] Moslem and Jewish (unknown by the Germans) Turkistanis set aside memories of suffering at the hands of the Nazi prison guards while they heard teachers detail the plight of their homeland due to Russian domination

The prisoners listened intently to the German instruction. At 18 years of age, Isakjan felt happy to be alive, to study, to eat three meals a day. He wished his fellow cadet and his former captain, both dead from his bullets could have lived and been exposed to this strange turn of events.

His standards of expectation had been considerably compromised. Any speculation regarding the future amounted to an uncertain and precarious proposition. He suspended his unquestioned adulation of the Soviet Union, and started to resent the life forced upon his parents. He decided to open his mind and listen to the German claims.

After six or seven weeks in classes and training, the Soviet minorities were put into a train accompanied by a few Germans, and traveled for a couple of days. They arrived in a small town called Zelonka, 50 miles from Warsaw, Poland. Turkistanis emptied a number of trains until they assembled 1200 to 1300 strong in a large barrack camp with beds and a mess hall. A wild wind of jubilation and homecoming prevailed, seeing so many together, so many friends thought to be dead.

Even in Zelonka, Poland, where the population had supposedly petitioned the Soviets for permission to join the socialist revolution, Isakjan observed that the locals lived better lives than available in the Soviet Union. Although not as grand as in Germany, Polish farmers owned their farms, livestock, and homes. They were their own masters in a more direct sense than the dictatorship of the masses through the party bosses back home.

The Germans assembled the group from Isakjan's camp, and, knowing their individual backgrounds and specialties, assigned positions.

Major Meyer-Mader, the man who had addressed them in the POW camp, commanded. He told them, "We have over 1200 people here, all from Turkistan. We will divide you into seven companies, which make our group, called the Tiger battalion. One will serve as staff for artillery and communications. The others will serve as fighting companies."

Fighting companies. Whom would they fight? Would they enter their homeland to establish a new government?

The instruction continued. "One of the fighting companies will be a company with Isakjan Narzikul as commanding officer. He will report to a German liaison."

There were 240 in Isakjan's company, all of them in recycled Soviet uniforms. The German advisor's name was Schneider, a career soldier in the German army with the rank of sergeant, and, although called just a liaison man for the company, he was in actual charge. His word was final, but Isakjan was the mouthpiece and titular officer in command, taking orders from Schneider.

In the morning, Schneider outlined the activities planned: one hour exercise, shooting range, tactics. The program provided more instruction and detail than the one given Isakjan's troops in the USSR, when he attended military school, and certainly when he trained troops in Latvia.

But in the field Isakjan suffered a sudden attack of deja vu. He noticed that his troops consisted of men far his senior, 30 to 45 years of age. Furthermore, when he called attention and commanded a right face, only half the men turned in the right direction, with some of the others turning left and others too confused to do anything. These were sad excuses for soldiers, the same stock he had dealt with in Latvia, awkwardly marching, undisciplined, nonmilitary people, and Isakjan wondered how he managed to get stuck with this group. He determined to make good soldiers out of them, to practice his trade as an officer. With these recruits he had time and equipment.

"Soldier, stop," he ordered a recruit. "Where do you come from, and how did you get here?"

"Officer, if you please, I am a student of Islam, placed in jail by the Soviet authorities for practicing my religion and released by the German army."

Others were charged with various crimes against the Soviet regime. He asked them how many years in the service they had, and many answered that they were never in the service, but had been released from Ukrainian penitentiaries by the Germans only months before, political prisoners under the Soviets. The most common charge was the open practice of the Islamic religion. Most of the soldiers were mullahs, students and people who didn't comply with collective farming orders or who spoke out against the policies of the Soviet government.

They had no experience as soldiers, but with anti-Russian attitudes, they made promising material. The troops treated Isakjan like royalty, the boy officer who would lead them back to their homeland. They offered him presents of cooked oranges and other delicacies to show him respect.

Baymirza Hayit [2], an Uzbek school teacher captured in the German advance, worked his way up in the ranks to the command of the Turkistani forces in the war of liberation He traveled often from his home and office in Berlin to address the men.

"You are the foundation of the Eastern Legions, and one day, when the eastern countries are free, you will be the backbone of the homeland."

Isakjan performed his duties, alongside other Turkistani officers, with whom he became acquainted. Among them was one of the platoon commanders who reported to him, Kamal Alimov. Alimov worked hard and exhibited a knack for military procedure, making friends and promoting himself. He won advancements through popularity rather than military precision. Although he was only a sergeant in the Red Army, the Germans quickly marked Alimov for higher tasks, and sent him back to training camp to initiate the formation of another Turkistani battalion.

Two weeks before Christmas, 1941, the Turkistani Battalion was issued new uniforms, Wehrmacht uniforms. The men were in the German Army, with the door back to the Soviet Union closed. Isakjan received the rank of master sergeant. The only difference between their uniform and the regular German army one was a patch on the side arm, which read "Allah Biz Bilan (Allah is with us)."

Hayit proclaimed their trust in Allah: "Let the First Turkistani Battalion be strong."

PART II

GERMAN PROMISES

The aim of our policy, to me, therefore, appears to lie in this direction: to resume, in an intelligent manner and sure of our aim, the aspirations to liberation of all these peoples and to give them shape in certain forms of states, i.e. to cut state formations out of the giant territory of the Soviet Union and to build them up against Moscow, so as to free the German Reich of the Eastern nightmare for centuries to come.

...the most important premise is a corresponding treatment of the country and the population.... The conquered territory as a whole must not be treated as an object of exploitation, even if German food and war economy will require large areas....

----Alfred Rosenberg, German Minister for
Eastern Territories under Hitler. [1]

CHAPTER 9

ALLAH BIZ BILEN

In the mist of the sky I was a bird,
I flew like a blade of straw,
I weighed nothing more than fine hair,
I obeyed each order in patience and calm.
But my heart was aflame for liberty.

The crows are cawing in the garden
I know not whose fate they announce.
Their claws reach for the ripe nuts
I know not whose hopes they renounce.
You who come, ugly, from the cold North,
Your grating voice will be silent in the desert.
You who plunder the fruits of my garden,
Your black heads I will bury in the earth.

The last stone which lies on my land,
I shall hurl against the Goliath,
The last wish lies still in my heart
That I reach at last my goal.

----- Cholpan (Abdul Hamid Suleiman), Uzbek poet, liquidated with friends by N.K.V.D., 1937.

Sergeant Narzikul called his company to attention. They snapped smartly, prepared for his review. He marveled what a little time could do for training civilians in combat procedures. Their German rifles and machine guns caught the crisp December sun and reflected back a well-ordered force.

Just over a half year ago, he had held Nora Melkakze's hand and walked through the fruit stands in the Tashkent bazaar. Since then he had stood witness to the destruction of the Soviet Baltic Defense Army, executed his classmate with a pistol shot to the head under orders, and earned a promotion to POW straw boss. Although his eighteen-year-old mind attempted to bury these events, vestiges emerged in daytime hallucinations and in nightmares.

However, this new start made more sense. He understood better now that the Russian attempts at socialism amounted to unsophisticated, exploitive imperialism. He realized that the Russian help extended to Uzbekistan was more an anchor than a sail. The relentless tormenting by his classmates could now be explained since the Russians simply held Turkistanis in contempt and he had been duped. His isolation from world news in the face of Soviet propaganda led to the most erroneous conclusions and convictions, and he felt ashamed and embarrassed. The Soviet system was the kind that could be viewed in its entirety only with a magnifying glass held from outside. No person inside could begin to appreciate the disease.

No longer the innocent teenager from Jizzakh, he had traveled through parts of Europe and Asia to gain experience of war on both sides of the conflict, which gave him perspective and a new attitude. Isakjan saw that his path to the future lay with a powerful nation that stood for liberation of the backward countries. Ushering in revolutionary changes in order to protect the rights of individuals was Germany, the country that enabled his troops to train and arm themselves for the liberation of all Turkistan. When they arrived home, they would not need to beg the Russians for a little courtesy, but instead would boot them out, so if a bullet felled him in the process, his death would be purposeful. He wanted to contribute his life to the purpose of liberation.

Isakjan faced his men and introduced the official mullah of the First Turkistani battalion, his friend from POW camp Nuriddin Qari. Nuriddin raised his hands to Allah and thanked the Almighty for honoring the soldiers with the privilege of emancipating their homeland. "Praised be Allah who has blessed us. We who were slaves to the Russians and imprisoned upon sight by their police will return victorious."

Isakjan listened. He knew all too well that he could return to the Soviet Union only as part of a liberation army and that any other visit would mean instant death or torture. There could be no excuse the Soviets would accept for his behavior, as the duty of a Red Army soldier was to kill all the Germans he could until he himself died.

He did not congratulate himself on his good fortune at having discovered the truth about the Soviet system. The mere fact that he lived signified traitorous activity in that he had disobeyed an order to shoot himself. Even though he realized that the order was unreasonable, his instinct did not favor disobedience. He wished there had been a solution that did not entail his insubordination and the horrible order to kill his companions, but now, willingly or unwillingly, he and his troops wore German uniforms and carried German weapons. This quandary placed him in a moral dilemma, for back in Latvia he had behaved unprofessionally as an officer and had lost a battle, notwithstanding his later discovery that the Red Army abused his professional devotion. The problem caused his nerves to twitch until he resolved to revive his military honor and the subjugation of his homeland with a military and moral victory against the Moscow tricksters.

Isakjan's reflections were interrupted by Nuriddin's address. "Allah in his wisdom has given us the ability to commit fully to his cause."

The soldiers nodded their agreement. "Praised be Allah."

"You will one day be free men and heroes in our own land."

The men cheered.

Isakjan prepared to dismiss the company, but first added his own comments.

"We have committed ourselves," he reminded them. "There will be no mercy if any of us are captured. We are trained soldiers ready to fire our weapons and fight until death. Thank Allah that we have the honor to die from the slice of the enemy's sword rather than the crack of the master's whip."

In their evening talks, the Turkistanis realized that the Germans would use the minority troops against the Red Army, but still harbored reservations about actually entering combat against their old employer. The mullahs, however, had not the slightest qualms, and they proclaimed the wisdom of fighting Russians, whether they be czarist or Soviet, because it was they "who took our homeland and spit upon us." Isakjan kept his opinions to himself.

The training proceeded in almost eerie isolation from the war, which raged somewhere far to the East, no doubt even more ugly than before. Isakjan enjoyed the respite, taking the chance to practice his trade and mold his troops. The exercises suited his need to work on something constantly, to try to perfect it.

Schneider summoned Isakjan to his office, where a line of men covered with brass stood spread out next to the desk. Isakjan saluted in the Wehrmacht fashion, on the side of the head with open palm rather than the Soviet salute, from the front with flat hand.

"At ease, Sergeant, and shake hands with a few of your friends."

The German Major Meyer-Mader, whom Isakjan recognized from his speech at the POW camp, greeted him. Meyer-Mader took charge of forming the Turkistani battalion, and Hayit, the Turkistani military commander, provided a liaison between the Turkistani political group in Berlin and the Wehrmacht. Both majors smiled and congratulated Isakjan on the fine work he was doing in organizing his men. Major Hayit, a handsome man who preferred a business suit to military green, glanced at Isakjan's shoulder stripes.

"Why," he asked, "as commanding officer of a company, do you only have the rank of master sergeant?"

"I don't know, Sir," Isakjan responded.

"I will look into that."

A few days later, Isakjan was again summoned to Schneider's office. Several other officers stood by.

"By order of the Germany Army, Isakjan Narzikul is hereby promoted to the rank of lieutenant."

His sergeant's stripes were replaced with those of the higher rank.

Thus Isakjan Narzikul became one of the first lieutenants of the Eastern Army of the Wehrmacht. The term "Eastern Army" applied to troops from the predominantly Moslem part of the Eastern Soviet Union who were coordinated by an exile liberation government in Berlin. Some German officers saw these men as key to a Nazi victory. Many in the Wehrmacht were anti-Nazi and predisposed to counteract many of Hitler's directives, particularly the one that planned to turn the attack on the Soviet Union into a mass enslavement of its inhabitants, something they felt was sheer lunacy.

They realized that the Soviet government could be overthrown if the energies of the various nationalities in the USSR

- the Baltic states, Ukraine, Caucasian States, and Turkistani states - were organized. Peoples in these areas hated the Russians for their forced collectivization, repression of religion, and Stalinist dictatorship (even though Stalin was Georgian). German army officers encountered villages offering the "liberators" traditional welcomes of bread and salt and received aid from former Red Army personnel; captured soldiers volunteered to fight the Soviets and provided specific information on Red Army positions. [2] These men regarded the Soviet Union as a front for Russian imperialism. The way to mobilize these anti-Russian sentiments could follow only one path, and that path required dividing up the Soviet Union into many separate countries, thus utilizing the enormous potential for revolt among the Soviet peoples.

If Hitler's racial policies could be circumvented and then changed, victory against the USSR was possible. Otherwise, this German coalition of certain professional army officers and men from the East Ministry knew that defeat and death awaited them. To this end, without the official approval of the Nazi high command, the group had already added over 200,000 Soviet citizens to the ranks of the Wehrmacht.

The Germans uncovered the hard proof of Stalin's great fear: revolt in the Soviet Union. Soviet secret police had exported over a million Poles to death and labor camps. In the Soviet retreat from Eastern Europe, communist police murdered thousands of prisoners and other citizens who were suspected of anti-Soviet sympathies, and in so doing, continued to lay the groundwork for dissension and revolt. [3]

The German Army sought to add more Turkistanis to this growing mass of volunteers. To that end, the East Ministry sent Veli Kayum-Khan into prisoner-of-war camps in a macabre race with the SS hit squads and mortal diseases for recruitment into his Turkistani army of liberation. [4]

Veli Kayum-Khan and Major Meyer-Mader reached Isakjan before the SS. Meyer-Mader spoke Uzbek extremely well and he served as a forgiving father to his men, not even reprimanding Isakjan for a time that he had broken open a barrel of brandy and distributed it to the troops while the Major tended to duties away from his battalion. Instead of disciplinary action, the Major scoffed at the incident and complimented Isakjan on his command of German. This fluency with German served to cement a friendship between the Major and the Lieutenant.

The Turkistani officers bivouacked together, six minority officers sharing the same room. Their German liaisons, however friendly, always kept separate quarters. In a sense the two quarters housed entirely different peoples, with the Turkistanis stooped over open fires, eating their meals with their hands and speaking very little German. The Turkistani soldiers, compared to the German brigades, carried on in a wild manner, sitting on their haunches and dipping fingers into the same bowl. But some of the minority officers drew invitations regularly into the dining rooms of the Wehrmacht. These were the ones with command of the German language and ability to carry on conversations about the plays of Shakespeare or the geography of Europe. Isakjan dined often with Meyer-Mader and his staff.

As Christmas approached, Schneider cheerfully called out to his lieutenant, "Isakjan, I will be going to Germany for the holiday. Would you like to be my guest and visit Berlin?"

Schneider and a couple of other German liaison officers rode the train to Berlin with their Turkistani assistants. In Berlin, with ice cream in hand and the thriving city in the background, the men lost any doubts the new Eastern Legion had about the superiority of the German nation. Isakjan and another Uzbek walked the city. They roamed and marveled at the German citizens traveling in cars and modern trains instead of cows and donkeys. Signs of military preparedness were everywhere, from uniformed men to great caravans of army supplies.

The Turkistanis concluded that the Germans, with tremendous organization and intelligence, not the Russians, could save Turkistan from its decline and restore its former respect. He suddenly realized how his capture had been inevitable. He understood how the Wehrmacht, with a couple hundred troops, completely surprised, surrounded, and eliminated his entire Soviet regiment in a matter of a few hours.

Isakjan bought a razor, one with good German steel, for he now shaved once every few weeks. They passed a distinguished gentleman dressed in a beautiful suit, with stylish cane, someone with a familiar Eastern face, and turned around to take another look. The gentleman did the same. Isakjan sort of recognized him, and the man walked back toward them.

"Hello my countrymen, do you remember me? Veli Kayum-Khan. I spoke to you when you were still in prisoner-of-war camp."

"Yes, yes, we do."

Veli asked them what they were doing in Berlin.

"Just a visit."

Veli was so pleased. "I cannot tell you how happy you

make me, as the first time I have seen Turkistanis in German uniforms. All of our work and prayers are rewarded."

He continued, "If you are wondering what I do, I work in the German Eastern Ministry. Now, you must honor my family and our country by coming to my home."

He called his wife and asked her to leave her work and come home to greet his friends properly. They met her, a lovely German/Spanish woman who worked in the Ministry of Information in broadcasting. She expressed her delight in meeting the young officers.

She prepared food, wine, meat, potatoes and Isakjan lunged at the food, holding fork in left hand, knife in right as taught in military school. Veli laughed.

"We are not in the Soviet Union any more. You can set an example for the other Turkistanis on the civilized way to eat."

He corrected Isakjan, showing him not to cut the potatoes into little pieces, but to slice them with a knife and press them open with a fork.

After the meal, Veli took them to the arranged place of meeting with Schneider. Isakjan's German, as he referred to Schneider, took him to Stuttgart, and put him up in a boarding room near his small house. Isakjan attended a circus, took full leave around town, and dined in Schneider's house, met his German friends and relaxed for five days.

Isakjan bought a Siemens radio, which became his traveling companion, and he thrilled at its excellence and its power, at being able to listen to so many stations. He formed a bond with the radio that only a teenager could consider.

Schneider and Isakjan returned to Poland and resumed training. Isakjan immersed himself in this activity, resolving never again to find himself on the side of the least-trained troops. He drilled using every exercise recommended by the German advisors and added a few from his Tashkent training. In private, the Turkistani lieutenants complained about reporting to German liaisons who were sergeants.

"We need to do something about this," Isakjan claimed. "We don't need to be as cooperative as our fellow Turkistani officer Alimov, with his ready `yes sir, yes sir."

Having seen the glittering city of Berlin and having witnessed the training given his troops by the Germans, Isakjan believed that his new allies were committed to the goals of his childhood, namely brotherhood and equal opportunity. Pride in his Turkistani heritage drove him to test the German ability to grant their new allies fair status.

In the mornings, one of Isakjan's sergeants placed the company in line and took roll call. After each of the other companies performed the same exercise, the Turkistani lieutenants reported to their German master sergeants to give the results of the attendance and receive instructions for the day. Isakjan refused, sending his sergeant instead. Schneider came huffing to the Uzbek company. Isakjan waited, making the man walk right up to where he stood.

"Lieutenant Narzikul, I was waiting for you, and you sent a sergeant in your place. I demand an explanation."

"Sergeant," Isakjan explained patiently, "it is customary for someone of your rank to report to a lieutenant and not the other way around. I can not command the respect of my men and lead them into battle if they think that I can not even hold myself up to a sergeant."

Schneider fumed, "But I am a German."

Isakjan agreed, "Yes, and I am a lieutenant. Why did you put me into a German uniform, if you don't want me to follow the proper military procedure? How do you think it looks to our people if a Turkistani lieutenant reports to a German sergeant?"

"I will take this up with my superiors," promised Schneider.

The superior officer was Meyer-Mader, who brought the matter up with Lieutenant Narzikul without waiting for the coming dinner the two expected to attend together. The Lieutenant had formed a closer social contact with the Major than had the Sergeant. The Major reached a decision that German sergeants would report to Turkistani lieutenants each morning.

But Isakjan did not advance his career by his actions. He urged his fellow Turkistani officers to stand up for their rights while the cooperative Alimov got the next promotion along with an order to return to the indoctrination school to aid in forming another Turkistani battalion.

With its hierarchy established and training complete, the first battalion was prepared when an order came to pack up guns and gear, to report to the railroad station. The men rode the wide track Russian gauge rails to 300 kilometers northeast of Kiev in the Ukraine, to the town of Glukhov, a town just behind the edge of the German advance.

Most of European USSR then came under Nazi command. The blitz attack crossed all of the Soviet Western Republics, including the Ukraine. With the exception of the Leningrad area, the line between Moscow and Stalingrad now defined the Western limits of the Soviet Union. Millions of Ukrainians sided with the Germans, many to the point of donning Wehrmacht uniforms.

Before flinging their recruits against experienced Soviet troops, German advisors planned to break in the newly formed companies with a clash against anti-German partisans. The mettle of the Turkistani troops could be tested against these small numbers of partisans who, like pesky gnats, crept behind German lines and blew up supplies and factories.

The battalion was divided, each company taking control of a separate town, looking after railroads and important buildings with heavy armored vehicles and weapons. Each company got one mullah to serve as religious leader.

They swept the forests looking for partisans, but after five months of frequent combing, the men only engaged in isolated skirmishes, as the partisans were small in number and ineffectual except in their ability to outmaneuver the larger foreign forces.

Not war; not yet. But a trial, and the men were up to the challenge. Isakjan remarked on the cohesiveness of the battalion to other officers. The German liaison Schneider was delighted.

"Our sources brought us some information," Schneider announced in an excited manner. "Now we will get some action."

He pointed to the map.

"We suspect that partisans slip into this porcelain factory to pick up cows and other supplies. They will come tonight."

During the day the company moved close to the factory. Well after nightfall, with only a few hours to dawn, they encircled the building and part of the town, setting up nests of machine guns and posts of rifles along the road.

As the partisans emerged from the factory, the Turkistanis pressed their triggers, cutting down the exiting men like so many sheaves of grain. Some of the wounded moaned in the morning mist, but the deadly crossfire killed most of them outright. On the victorious side, the battle assumed far different proportions, with light casualties and a feel of power and purpose. The screams of the wounded did not come so close either. The captured partisans were turned over to the Germans, who removed them from the area. More troops came to aid the battle and scan the countryside, but after a few days the effort diminished from lack of contact with any more partisans.

The company mullahs were ecstatic and held a special prayer meeting. He told the troops they were fighting for their country and the Russian yoke must be overturned so they could be free. After a service, the mullah asked for comments from their commander. Isakjan congratulated them for their heroic efforts and reminded them to continue the fight so as not to disgrace their nation.

The Turkistanis performed very well, for they were urged by the mullahs and by the horrible thought of being caught as traitors by the Red Army. Aside from their cause and mission, the terror of any possible capture sealed off any thought of surrender, and so the Turkistanis never backed off. The German commanders must have been pleased to see that the use of ethnic troops could help their cause. However, the forays with the sparse partisans were only games compared to the action of the Eastern front.

Schneider received new directions and showed them to Isakjan. The battalion troops boarded a train and headed South, on a bearing that would take them to the Southern part of the USSR, just across the Caspian Sea from their homeland of Turkistan. They detrained near the city of Astrakhan, administrative center of the Kalmyk autonomous republic, on the Volga River just before it greets the Caspian. Large groups of Kalmyks bore arms on the German side. An historical epoch arrived, with entire peoples sensing the possibility of freedom from the Russians within a few short years. The mullahs were ecstatic.

Isakjan rode with the officers. He discovered that his medical officer, Sattarov, came from Samarkand, the famous ancient trade city of the Silk Road situated close to his home in Jizzakh. Sattarov was Jewish, one of the many in that city and in the new Wehrmacht Eastern Legion. Jew and Moslem blended well in Uzbekistan and had common names, so Sattarov's features were indistinguishable from the typical Uzbek's.

After leaving the train, they marched for four days West to Yashkul with their nostrils filled with the air from the Caspian, and memories of their home charged their adrenaline. It seemed so clear now why the Russians assigned the Turkistani officers to far-flung provinces and jailed their mullahs in places like the Ukraine. The Germans, however, prepared a possibility for a homecoming that they all anticipated with excitement.

Someplace across the Caspian, his mother breathed the same air as she wrung her hands and suffered for her son. She didn't know about the course of the war, for the press and official news outlets were less than frank with the population, but the rumors told her the worst. The lack of a specific report on her son caused her to worry all the more.

The First Turkistani battalion marched to the front line of the war and was given a section to hold, separated from the Red Army by about ten miles of no man's land. The daily orders were "halt and see." After creating a stable line of trenches on the home side, commanders sent patrols forward every few days to engage the enemy and ascertain the strength of his lines. Sometimes the Soviets would send an excursion to probe the German lines.

As a German company, Isakjan's men carried much better equipment than the Red Army: more operating tanks, artillery support, better hand weapons. He envisioned the men on the other side, expecting victory as he had a year ago.

In the "halt" phase of the routine, life assumed a dull trench existence with the troops exceedingly bored. In this phase, duty consisted of protecting the front line against infrequent Soviet incursions. Men played cards, got a portion of liquor - some vodka or other spirits. The mullahs did not object even though they did not drink, realizing that everyone compromises in time of war. The task of war was reduced to day and night shifts covering the foxholes and trenches, with troops exchanging positions for eating and sleeping.

Hunched by their fires at night eating pilaf with fingers, the Turkistanis prepared to seek the Russian enemy as their distant ancestors had just over 700 years before when, coming from the East, those forebears sat in front of similar fires in preparation for their first of several burnings of Moscow, then a minor town. That ancient battle was swift and certain, resulting in complete submission of Russian principalities, whose princes for generations traveled to the encampment of the Khan of the Golden Horde on the lower Volga to "strike their foreheads" to the ground before him, asking for permission to assume the title of prince. [5] Many Eastern Legion troops hoped to participate in a new sacking of Moscow.

Orders came from Schneider, at battalion headquarters in Yashkul. "Narzikul, take twenty men, and meet a transport at 1000 hours. Proceed to this point for assembly." Isakjan looked at the detailed maps.

He and his men met a few troop carriers and other assembled soldiers, driving off to rendezvous with a handful of tiger tanks. The Germans deployed the tiger series along the Southern parts of the Volga to succeed the lighter panzers. With its roaring 650 horsepower engine, four-inch armor, 62.8 tons of steel, and three cannons, this vehicle presented a considerable problem to its adversaries. It flew across the plain with its five-man crew while swiveling its Krupp-manufactured turret high above the gnarled treads [6] and kicked up clods of earth, wood and bodies. The tanks aged according to the amount of action, and the troops resembled dusty fragments of the bulky metal monsters.

The commander of the operation directed the iron dragons to go and "see." Three tanks fanned out, with armored troop carriers behind them, storming the Soviet lines. They raced across the no-man's land and quickly came into range. Then they got angry and spit out streaks of explosive death at the Red Army foxholes just ahead. Isakjan signaled his men to leave the transports and fill the gaps between the tanks, drawing fire from the enemy side. Then he jumped into the column, directing some men to slipstream behind the tanks and carriers and others, the vanguards, to press an open attack, running infantry style for a dozen yards and diving into the dirt.

He and the other vanguards attracted the fire of the Reds. Triggering his machine gun and sprinting in a crouched angle, he flung his infantry toward the Red Army line.

The terrain was very rough, with holes, mounds and thin weeds. This line of exposed men rushing the enemy foxholes insured casualties for his men, delivering death to some. Inevitably the Soviet units had some machine guns, but no artillery and no armor-piercing capability. Many of them fired with the familiar clip rifles while claiming their gruesome quarry. The Red Army soldiers concentrated their aim on the middle line, dropping a few Turkistanis and claiming a head start in numbers killed.

That claim sealed their fate. This was the moment waited for by the tanks, as they now could identify the dimensions of the defending line. The tanks veered to each side of the Soviet position, while the transports behind began dropping off more soldiers. The Soviet quarry continued to fire, unaware that defeat had found them.

Quickly, tank cannons zeroed in on the entrenched gunners and moments later, exploding shells dispersed great balls of dirt and dust. Bodies flew into the air as tank shells pounded their lairs. The Soviets hardly ever damaged a tread of a tank, as their rifle shells bounced off the steel dragons.

The tanks, having prepared the ground for the foot soldiers, raced to either side of the Soviet front to expand the boundaries of the German territories another couple of miles, as the Turkistani-Wehrmacht soldiers picked off the exposed defenders and raced in for the final kill of the cornered quarry. The tanks sealed any escape route. They blistered the ground, turrets revolving, shells exploding, debris thickening the air, and finally overwhelming the inflexible, inadequately armed defenders.

In short order, a pincer developed, the favorite German maneuver, and the Soviets were surrounded. Unlike the time when the Germans attacked inexperienced defenders along the Latvian river, no escape route lay open with tanks to their rear and attacking men to the front, no option to retreat into a town or countryside presented itself. Red soldiers begged to surrender. Some, screaming with pain from wounds, pleaded to die.

Isakjan held one of the dying, a Russian, who cried in his arms and in his last breath, blasphemed the creed of his atheist army by imploring, "God help me."

And then the count, the numerical evaluation: over twenty dead, all Russians and another twenty captured. On the German side, a Turkistani lay dead and two wounded. Isakjan's troops led the haggard, spent prisoners behind the lines. When the quarry consisted of Ukrainians or any of the Soviet minorities, Isakjan wondered if they might shortly don a Wehrmacht uniform.

"Today's prey was ethnic Russians from a special unit. I wonder if the Germans will allow them to join their army?" he thought.

With the additional captives turned over to the German command and the advance mapped out, he returned his strike force to the company position on the trench line. The unit's mullah prepared a ceremony for the killed Turkistani hero.

The only limits to the Nazi advance came from their own organization: the number of tanks and supplies they could garner. The USSR army provided no impediment, standing like heated metal waiting for the German tank wheel to stamp them under treads into final handiwork.

Back at regimental headquarters, five miles outside Yashkul, Isakjan settled back into a few days of routine, checking supplies, receiving replacements, coordinating with the Germans. He gave reports on the status of the lines, and troop numbers, oversaw the cleaning of weapons, and conducted exercises for the men on the rear shift. He ate at the officers' mess, usually sharing meals with other Turkistanis, but sometimes with the Germans, who became more respectful as the war progressed.

Narzikul came to realize that some of the officers he had considered “German” were actually Austrian. Many Austrians did not necessarily agree with the Germans, particularly one chef and a lieutenant from the vicinity of Vienna.

"You know," the chef complained to the Austrian

lieutenant, "I once served in the best hotels of the country and not like here, in the lowest dumps. Come see me after the war and I will treat you to a real meal."

The Austrian lieutenant gave him full sympathy. "I don't see why we had to unite with those pushy Germans. We were at peace. We don't need land to the East. Why should I give up my job as forester to risk my life to free their country?" He pointed to an assembly of Turkistanis.

Isakjan wanted to assure them that his country would repay their kindness after liberation, but somehow that seemed short of the question. He would just press to fight harder and end the conflict sooner. Every day or two, he requisitioned a jeep to inspect his men in the forward shift and review the field situation with his sergeants, often bringing with him the company mullah for exhortations and guidance.

The main headquarters for communications up and down the front, and for the high command, occupied buildings in Yashkul itself. Tatars comprised most of the local population, inhabiting a large part of the North Caucasian and Crimean parts of the USSR, and although they intermarried frequently with Russians, received the occupying Germans very well.

As future leaders of free Turkistani provinces, the company commanders shared residences and socialized together. Besides the communication and staff company, each republic, Uzbek, Turkmen, Kazakh, Kirgiz and Tajik had a commanding officer. The similarity of the Turkic languages enabled them to communicate freely, except with the Tajik Persian dialect.

The company mullah guided the troops in their prayers to Allah, and, in his understanding mood, did not chastise them for praying to Mecca only a few times per day instead of the required number. Besides, he realized that a number of the troops had not benefited from the teachings of the Prophet Mohammed during their childhood, and could not be expected to follow the Koran without more training since religion had been suppressed in the Soviet Union. Those who did practice had different interpretations of the prophet but it never led to disruption; a few of the Turkistanis were Shiite, but the vast majority were usually Sunni. Differences were set aside so that all possible energy could be used to gain the coming liberation.

Isakjan treated his men to leave every two or three months. By allowing a rotation of ten to fifteen of the company's soldiers for a week, they could go to a larger city like Stavropol or Rostov for some recreation. The Germans supervised houses of pleasure for enlisted men only; these establishments kept a supply of willing girls, drinks and hot meals.

No such pleasure arrangements existed for the officers, and the front was no place to start an officers' club, so each was obliged to find entertainment on his own. Isakjan and his friends took this as an open invitation to tour the Caucasus and the Ukraine after tiring of the provincial village of Yashkul and the slightly larger Elista.

They drove by military jeep two hundred miles over the small hills that meld into the Caucasus Mountains South to Stavropol. Along the route, people on the road waved to them, cheering the liberation army. The soldiers drove in jeeps with open tops and no need for security. In Stavropol, the German command post assigned each officer on leave quarters in the homes of residents, who could not thank the liberating soldiers enough for ridding them of the communist rein.

Churches closed by the Soviets reopened and newspapers proclaimed, "Christ has risen." Many of the area's Cossack population rushed to join the Wehrmacht. [7]

Isakjan drew a room near the center of Stavropol city in the home of a dentist. He knocked on the door and spoke Russian to the man who answered.

A smiling man faced him. "Another Wehrmacht officer, and one who speaks Russian. What a pleasure. You don't look like a German. But come in. Come in."

Isakjan entered the comfortable home and accepted tea in the parlor. The dentist introduced his daughter, only two years younger than Isakjan, and the whole family listened to their guest as he told his story.

The dentist was tremendously pleased to host an officer of the German army, and even more, one who spoke Russian, which was understood by the professional class of Ukrainians. "You can visit us any time you like," the man assured Isakjan. "I hope to see men from our country fighting with you to free us."

They moved to the dining room where his wife served dinner. The dentist viewed the boy from Turkistan as an example of achievement, a model of proper manly behavior. Isakjan saw that he need not consider his ancestry as an impediment, and that the fact of his oppression under the Russians gave him inherent companionship with a co-dissenter. Hence the acceptance for which he devoted his life in Turkistan under the Russians became an automatic right in the German army.

The dentist's daughter escorted him on a tour of the city, to the movies and to supper. Pedestrians, storekeepers and restaurant patrons wanted to talk with the Wehrmacht officer who spoke Russian and fought to liberate the Soviet republics. He, in turn, liked these people and came back to visit Stavropol and the dentist's daughter.

The feeling of recognition gave him confidence to try all his social skills, and they were well received. His Turkistani troops had not entered social behavior class as he had during military School days, so they did not always understand the customs and non-verbal cues of the civilians. To many soldiers and officers alike, a woman who exposed ankles, arms and face in public invited all to her bed. Isakjan interceded at a number of restaurants to prevent misunderstandings from becoming incidents.

He called his off-duty troops to order. "Today I will review with you how to conduct yourselves while on leave. Welcome to social behavior class." The men did not give him looks of encouragement, but he pressed forward regardless.

"We are stationed among people with different customs, and if you learn to conduct yourselves according to their manners, we will be better accepted and you will avoid trouble. If you are not in the house of fun, but go to dances or meet girls in towns, you don't grab them or force a kiss. I will now tell you what you do.

"First, you ask the girl to dance, but don't pull her. If she agrees, you dance, but if she says `no,' then go to someone else. In European culture, you do not take offense if the girl does not want to dance. It does not mean that you are no good, but just that she does not want to dance. If she dances with you a couple of times, that does not mean she is ready to go to bed with you. You never force anyone to do anything. Remember that we want these people to like us and not think that we are a wild company in the Wehrmacht. I don't care what other units do; this unit will get respect from the people of the area. We will show them that we are not backward or without training."

He dismissed the men, but determined to continue his instructions to shake them out of a mold of thinking that did not allow for divergence from tradition. Isakjan himself jumped back and forth, from the company of Turkistanis to that of German officers, eating one night with utensils and conversations of the theater in Berlin, and the next with fingers and singing to the music of a Turkistani dutar, an instrument similar to a guitar. He became a man of two cultures.

A mannered liberation soldier speaking Russian always ended up with friends. He was ready to visit larger cities and drove to Rostov on the Don, where the Don River meets the Sea of Azov.

Rostov, a pearl of a city. Never did the men see such broad straight streets, with numbered avenues perpendicular to named streets and buildings with lovely minarets. Here, they discovered again that they did not have to wait until they entered their homeland to be treated as heroes. The residents conferred that status upon them instantly, greeting them as liberators. The town's streets, restaurants, dances and daughters swirled about them. Isakjan, handsome in his uniform, was besieged by the hospitality of the town. He found in himself a personality that attracted girls at each town's dances, and a manner that led to long discussions with the tradesmen, who came to regard him as a friend.

This success inspired longer ventures. Why not a week's vacation, crossing the Volga and heading into the Ukraine to Petrovosk? The countryside was beautiful, and the security precautions nil. They drove in open jeeps, blowing kisses to the girls, waving to the newly liberated nation. At the age of 19, Isakjan was an eligible, handsome hero.

The weeklong trip to Petrovosk pleased him so thoroughly, that he and a few fellow officers configured a requisition for two and a half weeks to Kiev. They had never seen such a metropolis, replete with the kind of beauty that could be built only with inspiration and faith rather than the calculations of a bureaucrat or an investor. Although not so bustling as Berlin, they felt that Kiev was clearly the most beautiful city in the world.

Turkistani officers enjoyed popularity even greater than that of many Germans, since many of them spoke Russian and could converse with the people. From once-oppressed minorities in the Soviet Union, they achieved an important status since they marched with the liberators; they were treated to the best of restaurants and accommodations. People feared the Russians, and no one was afraid of the Germans. They had not yet gotten to know the dark underside of their liberators, although the insidious plans of the Nazis had begun to affect areas to the north.

The Ukrainians invited them into their homes, introducing them to their families and glowing about the possibility of a new life. Kiev was free.

The number of Turkistani soldiers and officers increased with their value to the army proven, but their commanders still were considered junior officers to German "liaisons". Nevertheless, they achieved much more authority and stature than in their homeland under the Russians.

In November the weather severed its alliance with the

Germans and clasped the Russian cause. Headquarters had trouble supplying troops, a problem exacerbated by the required change at the German-Russian border to rails with different gauges.

In its pact with the other side, winter served up an unexpected fury, delivering horribly cold weather and deep snow. The dirt roads, coupled with the inclement weather, bogged down the troop carriers and trucks. In addition to the inclement weather, the Soviets gained another ally: the interference of Hitler with the Wehrmacht.

When the German Army commanders recommended a concentrated assault on Moscow, Hitler diverted strength to the Ukraine; when they wanted to avoid stagnation in Kiev and Stalingrad, he ordered them not to yield an inch, all while the Soviet industrial capacity beyond the Urals was gearing up with promised support from the West and the Red Army put forth unexpectedly strong resistance on several fronts. Forbidden by the Nazi government to make the best use of Blitzkrieg, the Germans no longer were the mobile force.[8] Their front, stretched out beyond German ability to maintain regular supplies, became subjected to organized Red Army and sporadic partisan attack. The Uzbek company came under heavier fire than usual. The Red Army took the initiative and the Germans, in an orderly manner, retreated.

In Yashkul, headquarters explained that the weather and other extraordinary circumstances would necessitate a temporary change in the German line. The orders directed to battalion headquarters explained that a strategic retreat was needed, and instructed them to take a few companies back and dig more new trenches. Somewhere down the line, the Soviets broke through, and, because the purpose of the retreat was to avoid encirclement, and to maintain a straight line, the retrenchment accelerated. The orders and senior German officers never disclosed exactly where or if a line severance had occurred, and no breakthrough by the Soviets happened at the Turkistani point of defense.

Major Hayit visited his troops, praising them and encouraging their spirits. He introduced a publication from the Liberation Front, the active Berlin-based exile committee for Turkistan. The two-page paper informed readers of German advances in any war theater, Turkistani soldiers' accomplishments, facts about Central Asia, and the events in Berlin. It was a small newspaper, easy to hold, to the point, and was often accompanied with copies of the latest issue of "National Turkistan" magazine, founded by the Turkistani nationalistic hero Chokay, which probed the issues and policies of the war in more depth.

CHAPTER 10

THE HAY WAGON WITH MACHINE GUNS

The Soviet initiative was never to ease, as, on the footsteps of spring, came American supplies. These eventually included 427,284 army trucks, 13,303 tanks, 35,170 motor cycles, 2,500,000 tons of high octane aviation fuel, countless tons of vehicle fuel, 20,000 aircraft, 1966 locomotives, 20,000 railroad cars, 4,500,000 tons of tinned foods, machine tools, industrial plants, small arms, ammunition, and textiles. The land Isakjan fought to liberate, Soviet Turkistan, received aircraft manufacturing facilities, coal mining machinery, copper mining mechanical shovels, drills, and steel mills. In addition to the authorized supplies, Soviet espionage managed to pilfer huge quantities of United States secret documents, plans, and uranium while the massive relief effort pushed forward. [1]

The unprecedented flow of aid followed a November 1941, decision by the United States President Franklin Roosevelt to outfit the USSR with an absolute priority over even the competing demands of Britain and the American forces. [2] *Roosevelt's decision held in spite of appalling losses by Allied forces, particularly in the Pacific at the hands of the Japanese, who jumped across Asia to Singapore, Malaya, Java, New Guinea.*

The Soviets, however, gave little credit to the suppliers, and in fact concealed their existence from their own people. The U.S. ambassador grew exasperated at the lack of cooperation or acknowledgment regarding the aid given to the Soviets [3] *All the materials and supplies, in addition to arming the Red Army, added to the industrial base in the Soviet Union East of the Ural Mountains. This area had taken great strides during the thirties with the help of conscripted forced labor. While the USSR built up its reserves, Nazis diverted their strength in campaigns against many races and peoples, especially Jews.*

German MP's marched into the Turkistani compound in back of the lines and hauled off five men, among them Isakjan's medical officer, Sattarov. Isakjan rushed to the military jail to inquire.

"Sir, why are you holding my medical officer Sattarov and other men?"

The MP sternly looked at the lieutenant. "Do you know these men?"

"I know Sattarov and he is a good soldier," vouched Isakjan.

"Maybe, but he is a Jew." The MP never changed expression.

"No, Sattarov is not Jewish," Isakjan lied, fully aware that many of his troops were Jewish and remembering the dark cell for Jews in Gvinsk and the POW Jewish compound. "He is my countryman and a friend. I know he is not a Jew."

"Will you swear to that?" The German sharply questioned.

"I swear to it. Sattarov is not a Jew."

"Then you may take Sattarov with you, back to your company. But first answer another question. Are there any Jews in your company?"

"No, we are all Moslem," Isakjan lied again, for he knew of a number of Jews in his company, but was not about to subject them to the strange animosity of the Germans.

On the way back Isakjan could not understand. "What is between the Jews and the Germans, always the Germans don't like the Jews?"

Sartorov shook his head. "Maybe the Germans are not good for the Jews. It appears that the Germans treat Jews the way Russians treat all minorities."

Isakjan agreed. "Only in a free Turkistan will our people, Jew and Moslem alike, be safe."

Schneider had new orders for Isakjan near the end of November 1941, when he reported to the battalion headquarters, now relocated far back from Yashkul near the Caspian closer to Rostov on the Volga.

"It's back to training camp for you, a break from the front."

So Isakjan moved to another assignment. The train chugged through the winter snow, through the liberated areas, to the switching station where he boarded a German narrow gauge train, and then on to Berlin.

He reported to National Turkistani Unity Committee [4] in the Turkistani Liberation Front offices right in the center of a residential section of Berlin. Commander Hayit gave him a tour of the committee headquarters, which occupied a floor of a building shared by other liberation organizations and exile governments, all with the common purpose of freeing their peoples from the Soviet stamp.

By May of 1942, with 113 Turkistani fighting units already sent to the front, signatures were collected from 130,000 men and a congress called, where the president, Veli Kayum-Khan, pledged the organization to continue to work and fight for Turkistani independence. He had overcome resistance from within the German government and party leaders like Himmler in order to convene the congress. [5]

"Wait," Hayit cautioned. "There is much more."

Isakjan and Hayit traveled across the city, arriving at a multi-level building, formerly apartments, housing other groups of formerly Soviet subjects. "This is the broadcasting department," he explained.

The two ascended, past floors full of Ukrainians, Baltic peoples, Tatars, Armenians, Georgians and others to the Turkistani floor and the office of the chief.

"Please shake hands with the head of the broadcasting department, Dr. Ergash Shermat. Dr. Shermat, please meet one of our officers, Lieutenant Narzikul, from Jizzakh, Uzbekistan."

Dr. Shermat shook his hand. "From Jizzakh? We have someone else here from Jizzakh."

He walked over to a corner. "Do you know this man?"

Yes, he did. He knew the best student in the Jizzakh grade school, Jurabay.

Jurabay hugged his old friend and kissed him on the cheeks, Turkistani style. "You must stay with me for your visit. How did you get here? How long will you be here?"

Isakjan told his story to the broadcasters. When he told of how the Russians at the military School could not pronounce his name and called him Ilja, Jurabay interrupted.

"Isakjan. Now you are Isakjan. I will always know you as Isakjan. You can't fool me," he joked .

"And you, how did you get here?" Isakjan wanted to know.

"The same way you did. Capture, POW, education, reorientation, new job. We all went through the process. Dr. Shermat will tell you his story some day. He spent many years in Tashkent."

"Tashkent?" answered Isakjan. "You know I was there

too, in the Military School. What did you do in Tashkent?" he asked Shermat.

Dr. Shermat laughed. "I worked only a few blocks from the School, at Tashkent University in the law department and also in the Justice Department."

Isakjan marveled at meeting so many educated and prominent Turkistanis so far from home. The Russians had him believing only those from Moscow were prominent and educated. "Dr. Shermat, I am sure you read the newspaper `Red Uzbekistan. My uncle is one of the editors. He took me to lunch several times at the tea house by the central square."

"Yes, I spent many hours at that tea house criticizing articles in your uncle's newspaper and wondering when the Soviets would allow the Turkistanis to write their own articles without Moscow interference."

Isakjan stayed in the rooming house where Jurabay rented from a grandmotherly lady, Mrs. Rogozinski, while taking a more elaborate tour of Berlin.

His conversations with Jurabay and visits with the people in the Liberation Front showed him another dimension of the war and the promise of freedom. The Liberation committee worked for the East Ministry and the Turkistani soldiers reported to German field commanders. These groups actively worked toward the breaking of the Soviet Union into separate states that would naturally be friendly to Germany, as allies and nations with common interests. But this attitude did not come from the controlling Nazi philosophy.

Shermat warned the others:

Before you all get comfortable with the Germans, let me tell you that they can be as bad as the Russians. There seems to be two faces to our friends: one which promises us freedom and another which may treat us as bad as in our homeland. I saw Germans murder many of our countrymen because they were suspected of being Jewish. This was no different from Turkistan where the NKVD kills Moslems and those who do not cooperate. Even though we have no choice but to fight for our liberation, let us beware that the Germans have the same racial bias as the Russians.

The Turkistanis worked under a ministry and an army often at odds with the leadership of Germany. The Liberation Front was not aware of the extent of the conflict, and therefore did not understand the implications of Hitler's racial theories. Unfortunately, the Fuhrer viewed the lands to the Slavic East as areas to clear out for future German settlement and secretly pursued that goal with vengeance. Far from wishing to help the downtrodden, Hitler proclaimed that the "fear of chauvinism is the sign of impotence" [6], and Himmler supported the view of his boss. [7] Hitler unleashed his army on the Soviet states with specific instructions that "It is not the purpose of this war to lead the people of the Soviet Union to a happier future, or to give them full freedom or political independence." [8]

In fact, Hitler and Himmler had decided in secret to destroy all Poles, Ukrainians, Russians, Jews, Lemkes (group of Western Ukraines) by first eliminating the upper class, exporting some youths to Germany for Aryanization while limiting the rest to a fourth-grade education with subjects to include obedience to Germans and counting up to 500. The Wehrmacht did not share the enthusiasm for denigrating allies and wrote an extensive report to protest murders, maltreatment, rapes and looting committed by SS troops, but the commanders who wrote the report were transferred. [9]

The Turkistani Liberation people did not realize that, even though many in the German government wished to treat people in the occupied territories as compatriots, the Nazi top leadership countered at every opportunity. In the Ukraine, where Isakjan had spent many a night hailed as a hero, the Nazis announced no program of self-government and no meaningful breakup of the detested collective farms. Hitler originally refused to reopen the churches, then modified this stance only slightly. Education deteriorated to a condition worse than under Russian tutelage, since Hitler and Himmler thought that knowledge might lead to opposition. German demands on the native food supply created drastic shortages.

A superimposed layer of cold German bureaucrats carried out these repressive policies. While the operating armies pleaded for cooperation with the natives, truculent administrators from Berlin turned a deaf ear. These administrators preferred the theory that Germans came from a superior race and the Slavs were to be exploited.

The turning point in the occupied territories was the German labor program instituted in the late winter of 1941-42. With manpower availability depleted by war, Hitler looked to the East for replacements. Instead of cooperation with Ukrainians, he chose forced labor, subjecting the Slavs to a kind of slavery. Male and female workers were yanked from their beds and from the streets for deportation without notice and stuffed into boxcars.

Almost a half million young girls were conscripted for domestic duties in German homes. This policy had the instant effect of creating a large partisan contingent fighting against the Wehrmacht. [10] This policy extended to other occupied lands.

Isakjan, who had been hailed as a hero in Kiev at one time, could no longer count on even his personal safety. But he did not yet know this. The Turkistanis reported to the sympathetic East ministry or operating officers, and not the Nazi administrators. They did not know the full extent of Nazi deception.

After his stay in Berlin, Isakjan went back to the same training camp he first attended near Lukenwald for a refresher course. From there he rode a train to Skierniewice, Poland, where the fourth Turkistani graduation class needed an officer for the Uzbek company. They already had a German advisor, who introduced him to the German commander.

The troops he viewed this time contained more men with some experience than either his trainees in Latvia or those in his first Wehrmacht company. With them came the mullahs, the German arms, and the new cause. With time to train, another battalion joined the Eastern Army.

They prepared for a special tour of duty to "protect" towns in the Ukraine. After the orders to the population to register for drafts to forced labor, the Ukrainians began to have second thoughts about their liberators. The men preferred partisan activity to forced labor in Germany.

Just before leaving, as the sun set on a February 1943, day, a German officer rushed to their bivouac, sounding an alarm. The entire company responded, grabbing arms. German trucks drove up and the company loaded themselves onto trucks that lumbered into the nearby forest.

Germans ran about excitedly. They came from a special detachment, with black uniforms, chains and emblems about their chests. The German major of the Turkistani battalion accompanied the men, but the officers in black directed the operation.

"There are bandits, partisans, enemies of the government in the forest. We must conduct a search. Stretch out your men every twenty feet and comb the entire area," shouted one of the black shirts.

Rifles in hand, the men began the scouring. With his troops deployed, Isakjan looked at his major. "Who are these soldiers?"

The major looked at him matter of factly. "We call them Gestapo."

The Turkistanis flushed a man in civilian clothes out of the woods and brought him to the Gestapo officers. One punched him to the ground and interrogated him.

They started the questions in German, switching to Polish and Italian. The man, in his thirties, lay sprawled on the ground. One of the Gestapo put his hand in his pocket and brought out a half dozen candies, which he tossed on the ground several yards from the group.

"Pick those up," he commanded his captive.

The man scrambled to obey. As he did, another of the Gestapo took this as a signal, raised his machine gun to his shoulders and opened fire on the prisoner, pouring rounds of ammunition through his body.

Isakjan looked at the man who gave the order in disbelief. "Why did you kill him?" He demanded.

The Gestapo officer walked away, dusting his hands. "He is a Jew."

By this time, other Turkistani troops surrounded the interrogators. They returned to camp in the trucks, complaining about the incident. "In Turkistan, Jew and Moslem live in peace. We consider ourselves one people, and know that Jews in Turkistan have lived with us for many years."

The soldiers agreed, realizing that a number of their members were Jewish. They complained into the night, wondering when they would rule themselves in their own land. A wave of fear and disgust enveloped the Turkistani feeling toward their German allies.

"The Germans seem to treat all others as inferiors, placing liaisons in charge of Turkistani officers, remaining aloof, never sealing a full partnership with the men who risk their lives in a joint battle. With all their power and advanced civilization, how could soldiers of a great nation act so cruelly and cowardly towards another human being? Under what circumstances might the crawling man machine gunned to death be a Turkistani?" These questions bothered them.

"What a waste of soldiers, chasing down civilians and killing them for no reason," they agreed, grew agitated and yearned all the more for a return to their homeland after its liberation. They wanted little to do with the exploitive natures of the nations of the West, be they German or Russian; but for the present, their options were few.

The next phase of their liberation was to blunt the greatly increased partisan activity in the Ukraine. They switched from narrow-gauge German rails to a wide-gauge Soviet train for the trip into the Ukrainian zone. Partisan activity haunted the rails. As if to underline the deteriorated relations, the train hitched three box cars to the front for protection against partisan explosives. Isakjan did not appreciate the enormity of the change as he journeyed through the Ukraine on his way to the outskirts of Kiev, where German repression had eclipsed Russian.

The Turkistanis were charged with keeping order in a little town near Zhitomir, north of Kiev, by a tributary of the Dnieper River. Within the town, a few factories operated, and their production was of interest to the Nazis.

Isakjan surveyed the town with his German advisor, drawing up a plan of protection. They occupied a building next to the school for headquarters and established security procedures. On the street corners surrounding the headquarters, criss-crossed logs shielded machine gunners who guarded their flanks.

He talked to the townspeople, who went about their business, but did not open their homes to him the way others did on his first tour. One day, as he walked out to survey his fortifications, a note was delivered by a village woman who immediately disappeared. The note read, in Uzbek.

Isakjan Narzikul:

I know you are fighting for the Germans although you are Uzbek. I, too, am Uzbek, fighting for the Soviet Union. We know that you are fighting against your will and that you would like to rejoin your Soviet troops. Please meet me outside the town five kilometers West on the road tonight at 7:00. I know you were forced into your situation.

He never went.

Instead, the next day, he led a party of twenty men to rifle practice near a river. Setting the rifles and machine guns in teepee fashion with a couple of men left to guard, the rest went swimming. One man ventured too far into the current and drowned. They searched the riverbed to retrieve his body. The incident shook them, and they further realized that they were vulnerable to a partisan attack, which could have eliminated all of them. Isakjan decided to give the man a proper burial. He invited the whole village to a ceremony in the town center.

He gave a speech commemorating the occasion. To his men, he proclaimed, "You should honor Allah, do your duty, and eventually liberate Turkistan."

Many people from the town attended. He addressed them also.

"One day we would like to be the liberation army for our country, far from here. We will notify this man's family that he died fighting for the freedom of his country."

Isakjan prepared for the regular supply caravan to leave for the base depot a couple of miles away in the larger town of Zhitomir. Feeling a need to promote goodwill with the townspeople, he provided seats for a few women so they could visit Zhitomir and shop. They were not ready at the town edge when the caravan left Zhitomir, so he waited for them, sending the caravan ahead. As he drove to catch up, gunfire echoed ahead. He arrived to find trucks on fire and troops scattered.

Next week, at dusk, Isakjan stood next to the school talking with a woman resident, when two horse-drawn carts piled high with hay approached the intersection where machine guns guarded center base. As the carts passed the armed post, gunfire spewed from the hay, partisans jumped out and began firing. They waited too long to open fire, as they had already passed the point where they could have ambushed the protecting machine gunners from behind. Bullets hit the building around Isakjan. Gunfire commenced from a multitude of hiding places throughout the town.

Due to their delay, the hay riders were shot and killed. Other partisans advanced on the headquarters, but were stopped in front of the same machine gun obstacle. The partisans brought up reinforcements.

Attempts of the Turkistanis to call for help from Zhitomir were to no avail, as the phone lines were cut. Isakjan sent a runner.

The battle raged into the night, with the partisans pushing Isakjan's company back to their central headquarters in the school building. In the darkness, a sudden silence was punctuated with taunts and pleas from the partisans, shouting:

"You should give up your positions. It is a hopeless situation. Why fight for the Germans? We have no argument with you."

Isakjan stood firm, withholding his confusion as to why the countryside, formerly welling up with support for the Germans, had changed.

They could see the nighttime bursts of fire from the surrounding partisans, and Isakjan gave the command to use the mortar gun. The partisans pressed forward, to within thirty feet of his building.

"Raise the mortar gun higher," he yelled.

The gun pointed almost vertically, so that the shells screamed up into the night air, reaching tremendous heights, and then descended while shrieking their battle cry. Any gust of wind in the wrong direction might have brought the exploding packages back to the Turkistani position, but the breezes favored them and the attackers suffered volley after volley of the fierce mortar rounds. The lines held during the night.

The next day, German troops came into town and, with armored vehicles and superior numbers, swept the partisans out. But the partisans made their point and the battalion major ordered Isakjan's troops out of the town as one location that was too indefensible.

Signs of destruction by the partisans became more frequent, and the Germans brought in additional construction detachments dedicated to the repair of roads and bridges. In their march back to Zhitomir, they passed a Hungarian brigade repairing the roads with their charge of forced labor. The laborers were pitiful rag people, driven hard by the Hungarians. One Hungarian company watched over a large group of conscripts, who each wore a Star of David.

The German advisor had orders for Isakjan to head back into Berlin. His second tour of duty over, he caught a train. The ride back was sobering, not like the first. The boxcars in the front of the train, the symbol of the native population changing its mind about their liberators sent a chilly message through his body.

CHAPTER 11

EXILE GOVERNMENTS IN BERLIN

A wise enemy is less harmful than a foolish friend.

----Central Asian proverb often quoted by
Tamerlane (or Timur), Turkistani conqueror [1]

As ominous signs arose concerning the ability of the Germans to win the war, the battle-tested veterans of the Turkistani legions continued to accept new recruits who joined with enthusiasm. They hoped to achieve the same miracle of victory as other warriors from the east had done centuries ago. The Eastern Legion could do as well. The April 1943, graduating class held ceremonies, with several thousand new Legionnaires displaying newly acquired prowess in weaponry. Seventy outstanding class graduates received promotions to positions as officers or mullahs, joining 200 other leaders in the field. A representative of the Liberation Committee promised freedom from the Russian infidels, and then introduced a sixty-three- year-old escapee from a Soviet concentration camp and father of two new legionnaires.

"My sons," he addressed the throng, "the Russians have taken our fatherland and (they) murder and plunder our people and land.... Millions of innocent Turkistanis were deported to the icy wastes of Russia.... and now live in concentration camps. The fight must be merciless..... Keep the Lord in your hearts and rifles in your hands, whether you be priests, workers, or intelligentsia, you are the soldiers of your country. The Lord is with us.... Long live freedom and independence!"

Many graduates heard their national anthem and saw the Turkistani national flag for the first time, a crossbow in front of a field with blue on the top and red beneath. These symbols of independence were illegal in the Soviet Union. They watched equestrian displays and spoke of troubles in their homeland.

One man lamented, "I was arrested in 1931, accused of being a capitalist and an estate owner. I had only a small plot of land and two oxen, from which I supported my family. The others you see here met the same fate. ... We were all put in a concentration camp and surrounded by wire and guarded by the NKVD (the precursor to the KGB). We had to work 14 hours a day irrigating new cotton plantations. We were given thin fish soup, salted and made from rotten fish heads, and 100-150 grams of black bread a day. Many died from exhaustion, particularly women and children.... No one in the world can conceive the life of a slave.... (After years, one day) we heard gunfire and saw airplanes dropping bombs.

"Our group was frightened and dispersed but the NKVD shot at everyone who tried to break away.... one shot my son. I became unconscious; when I recovered I saw soldiers in strange uniforms, who looked after the sick and exhausted.... wearing badges on their sleeves saying `God is with us.'.... One of the Turkistani soldiers said, `Now, dear father, you are free and we will revenge you." [2]

The new legionnaires departed for the front as Isakjan returned to Berlin. For Isakjan, wartime Berlin was the city of the future, the city of power, the city of opportunity, and as a German officer, he received only the finest treatment. Women sought him and he became a man of the world.

He climbed aboard the trolley to the house where Jurabay lived, careful to bring a present to the landlady, Mrs. Rogozinski. He tended to think of her as an elderly aunt and surrogate mother. She evoked the image of home, even though his own mother's style was so different. He never got the chance to become a man to his mother and help her in what had to be a struggle after his father's departure to prison and ultimate death, and so was pleased to call Mrs. Rogozinski "mom."

Isakjan made frequent visits to his adopted city of Berlin, between assignments and during every longer leave. Mrs. Rogozinski informed him that she could provide a room, and he moved into eastern Berlin, the Schonhauseralle section. No longer would he need to impose on Jurabay for a bed when he arrived in town. She gave more than just a room, opening her house and heart to the soldiers who lived with her.

She kept the home in spotless shape. Nothing missed her roving eye. She swept up dirty clothes, returning them promptly with loose buttons and rips sewn and repaired. The meals she cooked rated the highest compliments.

He reported to Hayit, commanding officer of the Turkistani soldiers in the German Army. The Turkistani soldiers in the Wehrmacht formed battalions integrated into the German divisions and looked to Hayit for political guidance while taking their daily field orders through the regular German hierarchy. However, the liberation committee dreamed that one day when the Wehrmacht approached Turkistan, their German patrons would help them transfer their scattered units into one centralized Turkistani Liberation Army. But that dream would have to wait for further victories, and in the meantime the Turkistanis and other Soviet forces who joined the Germans worked to earn recognition for their fighting skill.

Activity reigned everywhere in the Turkistani offices, with over one hundred people working feverishly to ensure the success of the anticipated homecoming. A huge contingent of Soviet

Turkistani troops, numbering over 200,000, had elected to assist the German cause, joining a total of one million Soviet citizens who crossed sides in the war. Unprecedented numbers of Soviet citizens lay down their arms and picked up those of the opposition Nazi forces. They hoped to bring about a military defeat of the Soviet regime. These Soviet-turned-German soldiers fell under the umbrella of the Russian Liberation Movement, which provided political structure to the million foreign recruits in the Wehrmacht. [3] Every Soviet Republic, including the Russian Republic, was represented by Berlin-based exile governments attempting to overthrow the Soviet system. The sub-group of the Turkistani Liberation Movement joined others from the Baltic states, the Caucasus, Cossacks, Volga and Crimean Tartars, Georgians, Ukrainians and countless others, each with its shadow army snuggled into the Wehrmacht.

Isakjan became very friendly with Turkistanis manning their Liberation Committee, among them, Veli Kayum-Khan, President. He also formed a strong friendship with Baymirza Hayit and Dr. Shermat, who had become the chief ideologue for the Turkistani movement. These men reported directly to members of German leadership: Kayum-Khan to von Mende of the East Ministry; Hayit to Luderzin of the Wehrmacht; and Shermat to Oder of the Propaganda Ministry.

Many of the Turkistanis met at the house of Mrs. Rogozinski, who opened her home to their needs and called herself the mother of all the Turkistanis. Whenever one of her adopted Turkistanis wanted to give a dinner party, they hosted it at her house, even if the host lived in another part of the city. After these late sessions, a half dozen guests far from their quarters might sleep on the floor of the living room.

At these dinners, Isakjan learned the histories of all the members of the liberation committee. "Dr. Shermat," he asked. "I understand how Jurabay ended up in the Red Army since he is young and therefore drafted. But how about you?"

"You may be surprised to know that I joined voluntarily," admitted Shermat. "I could not follow the party line in Tashkent, and the NKVD started assassinating my friends. So, rather than subject myself to the same risk, I joined the army.

But how did you get from prison camp to here?"

Shermat continued, "The Germans transferred me from camp to camp in the Ukraine, and always I did clerical work because my law studies had forced me to learn German long ago. Suddenly a number of Turkistanis were selected for transportation to an unknown destination. In spring, I arrived at a camp in Proskurov, a city in the Ukraine, where all the inmates were Turkistani, with good food, even hot showers and rations of vodka. Here the German soldiers who served became friends, conversing with us, playing cards, traveling to Ukrainian cities for tourist visits. I got to know many of our countrymen, made speeches at dinners, and joined in music and dancing among the men. Twenty of us visited Berlin, where Veli Kayum-Khan greeted us and took an interest in me."

`We need men like you in our organization,' he told me.

`Just what is your organization?' I wanted to know.

`We are the National Turkistan Unity Committee, founded by Chokay, our famous nationalist leader,' answered Kayum Khan."

Shermat hesitated in his history for a moment while he refreshed himself with a drink and a snack from Mrs. Rogozinki's kitchen. Then he continued.

You see, I admired Chokay very greatly, and to serve him in the same cause would constitute a great honor. However, when I expressed the hope of meeting Chokay, Kayum Khan informed me that he had died from typhus contracted while searching for Turkistanis in POW camps.

Chokay fled Turkistan after his rebellion against the Red Army failed, and he continued his campaign by publishing a magazine and participating in anti-Soviet groups in Paris and Warsaw. Without support from Western powers and with the collapse of Poland and then Paris, Chokay moved to Berlin and offered his cooperation to the German government in exchange for a hope of liberation of his country from the Soviets. In Berlin he discovered a well-established Soviet community of exiles, rivaling the Paris and Warsaw groups in both size and intellectual production. This resulted in the formation of the Eastern Legion.

`Despite my disappointment over the death of Chokay, the cause still attracted me and I became director of the broadcasting network. Now my only hope is that we can use the Germans. "

Shermat's odyssey mirrored the experience of many others who now filled Europe. Only a few years before the war, the number of Turkistanis in all of Europe had amounted to a handful, but hundreds of thousands had joined in a great cause, published magazines, newspapers, authored literary comments, established a medical department, printed pocket Korans for the legion, and added a secretary general to their exile government. The Turkistani Liberation Front published magazines and newspapers that were distributed to all regiments with Turkistani soldiers.

They concluded the kitchen discussion as Shermat summarized, "Compared with living in the West, Soviet life is hell."

Although the Liberation Committee attempted to foment dissatisfaction in Turkistan as a prelude to civil war, and a number of towns did sponsor riots, the result brought only oppression.[4]

The Liberation Committee sent representatives to the various locations on the front, wherever Turkistanis fought, giving pep talks and watching out for their flock. Even though the Eastern Army had no command hierarchy separate from the Wehrmacht's, they considered themselves somewhat detached, like allies who had given up the right of battle command to the dominant partner. But, in their drive to maintain troop morale, the Committee became a haven for off-duty soldiers visiting Berlin where their building served as social center for thousands of men far from their homeland.

Jurabay spoke on a number of radio programs as a host, broadcasting to Turkistan, advising the people on the status of the war and offering the German interpretation of the unfolding events. In his commentaries, he recited the circumstances of his discovery of the Soviet Union's negative effect on his people. He also translated material from German to Turkistani languages for publication and broadcasting.

Jurabay, Shermat and a man by the name of Karimi formed a broadcasting trio that wrote many articles for transmission. When they did not approve of certain programs given by the Germans to translate and put on the air, they simply altered them as they saw fit and the Germans, not speaking any of the Turkistani languages, never knew.

Karimi, from an old famous Tashkent family, took the office of secretary general. He and Jurabay claimed almost fanatical devotion to the cause of Turkistani nationalism. At the slightest suggestion, Karimi would engage in a long tirade about the evils of the Russians and the need for liberation. Isakjan, however, was less cunning or fanatical, more straightforward like his father. Committee powers did not consider Isakjan extreme enough to be totally reliable. Other soldiers who followed a more strident path, like the popular Alimov, one of the officers from the first graduating class of the Eastern Army, came up for promotion always one step ahead of Isakjan.

Not all of the Turkistanis worked for the Liberation Front and the Army. There was the mysterious Safi Oraz, who held an appointment with German intelligence, enabling him to travel all around Germany and any other occupied area. This made him seem among the busiest of men, but when Isakjan asked, nobody seemed to know exactly what Safi Oraz did.

"The intelligence people never tell you what their missions are," Jurabay confided.

The coloring of Oraz's skin mirrored the dark characteristics of the Uzbek population, while his stature tended toward the short side and his facial features had a Mongol look. His manners and speech engaged all listeners immediately, as he unraveled a huge repertoire of stories.

"Safi, please meet one of our promising young officers, Isakjan Narzikul," Hayit introduced the two.

Oraz shook hands but didn't seem extremely pleased to meet a promising officer. He did, however, agree to join the group on a night club circuit. Oraz entertained the crowd with stories of his exploits while Jurabay shook his head at Isakjan, indicating his disbelief at the exaggerated tales. Isakjan listened intently, then excused himself for a moment to gather some drinks. He returned to witness Safi Oraz asking Isakjan's date to dinner.

Seating himself quickly, Isakjan resolved to watch this sneaky character, although avoiding him proved not so easy, as Safi Oraz had picked Isakjan for an easy tease. Maybe it was Isakjan's young age, maybe the way the boy officer had with people; whatever, but Safi Oraz could never treat Isakjan respectfully.
Jurabay warned Isakjan, "Safi Oraz the braggart sometimes will steal your dates. Oraz always needs to be the center of attention, always fabricating stories. Watch out for him, though, because he can get you into trouble."

Isakjan's life acquired a pleasant bachelor dimension, and his German uniform won him the respect of many women. He learned well that he looked anything but Aryan and needed the uniform as protection on a day that he took a German girlfriend to a luxurious restaurant, dressed in an expensive suit. The occasion called for the best of wine, candles, meat and music. In the middle of dinner, he was interrupted by a hard tap on his shoulder followed by a policeman directing questions at his date.

"Why are you seen with this man? He is not German."

He is a German officer," she responded.

The policeman did not believe her, but restrained himself. He looked at Isakjan.

Your papers, please."

Isakjan drew out his identification papers and handed them to the policeman, who studied them for the longest time. He then placed them back on the table, snapped to attention and saluted

Isakjan.

"Excuse me, Lieutenant. If you please, sir, have a pleasant evening. I apologize for the interruption."

"What a nasty fellow," commented Isakjan as the policeman departed.

His date agreed. "They interfere with everyone. If you weren't German or a German officer you would be in serious trouble, but it is I who would suffer the most. You don't know what they would do to a girl who associates with an `undesirable.' Police are everywhere, especially the informants, so you never know who is watching you, reporting on what you say and do."

Isakjan's girlfriend was no admirer of the Third Reich, and many Berliners shared her feelings. Although Hitler selected Berlin as the capital city of Nazism, the city did not return the compliment. During the thirties, when a number of free elections took place, the city rejected him decisively. Its population followed him begrudgingly and forced him to import storm troopers to stage large rallies. Hitler, in turn, planned to change the name of the city and change its orientation. [5]

Isakjan paid the bill of the nightclub and they walked out to the lobby, even more aware of a displeasing undercurrent in German treatment of foreigners. A prominent sign caught his eye. "Verboten: Jude und Hunde " (Forbidden: Jews and dogs).

The clean streets of Berlin reflected the moonlight. Men in the streets, supervised by Germans and wearing the Star of David with the word "Jude," kept them clean, performing the menial tasks associated with the spotless result. The scene made him realize that back in Tashkent, Russians supervised Turkistanis in the same manner. The myth that Germany befriended underprivileged nationalities and treated them as equal crumbled. How long would Turkistanis hold positions of responsibility in this type of regime? Isakjan's measures of his friends were those he had developed in his hometown of Jizzakh involving friendship, equality, and opportunity. In reapplying his gauge to Germany, the measurements fell lower and lower.

Back in the Turkistani building, other Turkistanis experienced incidents which gave them cause to distance themselves from their German friends.

We must keep our guard up with them," counseled Shermat. "I see signs warning `no dogs or Jews' and it reminds me of the old signs in Tashkent which proclaimed no Sarts or dogs.' We were the Sarts and the Russians to this day still treat us like dogs."

Isakjan admitted, "I have noticed the attitude of the Germans. Here we are fighting with them and helping their cause, and yet many do not like to serve with us. Too often they call their Italian allies `macaronis' and their Romanian allies `gypsies,' which makes me wonder what they call us. They should learn not to downgrade those who are allies and helpers. I like my superior officers, but hear side remarks from others."

"They treat the Ukrainians even worse," agreed Dr. Shermat. "We have no choice but to let them use us so that we may in turn use them in gaining our autonomy. Our country lies much farther from Germany than from Russia; Germany never held historical ambitions to rule Central Asia, whereas the Russians always desired to subjugate us. The Ukrainians are the ones in the middle, desired by both Russia and Germany. They have a very difficult dilemma."

But with all of the insidious side effects, the Berlin government did pay attention to the nationalistic aspirations of the Turkistanis, giving them more access to both their own and foreign culture than they had ever experienced under the rule of Russia, thus delivering what the Soviets only promised. Isakjan spoke with educated people, attended the theater, gained uncensored knowledge, and pursued his love of reading in a city of tremendous publications. He learned more about his native land in Germany than ever was possible in Turkistan.

In Berlin he read free Turkistani newspapers. He started to dream of a career in the government of liberated Turkistan in an economic ministry, or, with his European experience, as part of a foreign ministry.

CHAPTER 12

WHAT HAPPENED IN WARSAW

The political aim was to be achieved by the seizure of the capital (Warsaw) by our own (Polish) forces before the entry of the Red Army. In the liberated capital of the sovereign state, power over the entire country was to be assumed by the legal authorities... The idea was, to manifest to the entire world that the Government was in its place and that there was no need for the installation of candidates imported from the East to govern the country.

--Antoni Chrusciel, commander of the
Polish Home Army Warsaw troops [1]

Isakjan's present mission was in the field and not in Berlin. Orders returned him to the train station, this time with no explanation as to the destination. Once on the railroad, he watched the passing landscape and the city names: Vienna, Budapest, Belgrade, and then the Greek border. Salonika, Greece, overlooking the Gulf of Salonika. The blue waters of the Aegean washed into the bay, with a clarity that permitted the most casual observer to peer deep into the fresh liquid. The fruits grew as plump as in Uzbekistan, while displaying a pleasant foreign variety and greater selection. The weather favored the coast with mild temperatures and cooling breezes.

The respite from the centers of the war made him think of his friend, the Red Army cadet graduate dead in a cold Latvian hole while cadet graduate Narzikul commanded a fully Turkistani company on an Aegean shore of Olympian splendor. Both had just wanted to serve their country in the best manner they knew. Isakjan constantly relived that shooting incident, asking himself what alternatives he might have considered. Since that horrible day, he had expanded his own capacity to act independently of orders and no longer completely merged his personality with his superiors. He mourned his dead comrade, and could see himself in the exact same situation again, ordered to kill a friend and then commit suicide, but was not so sure that he would once more obey such an order.

That agonizing decision never came in Greece. He summoned troops for hunts to rout out partisans in the mountains of both Greece and Yugoslavia, but these turned into pleasant outings and mountain trips. The partisans made sure the Nazi troops never were called upon to fight a battle, disappearing before any approaching German uniforms and declining any invitations to open combat. The arrangement suited the soldiers well.

They spent spring, 1943, in Greece, never firing a gun, relaxing in an easy life, viewing the sea, watching the little fishing boats.

Isakjan watched those boats, and one day saw a man on the boat with a basket, pulling it from the sea. In his relaxed state, he let imagination and curiosity guide him, and ambled down to the beach where the man was docked.

"Kalamar," the man exclaimed.

The strange fish with all the legs squirted a dark ink into the water, but the fisherman gained control, grabbing the animal and dashing it against the stones on the beach. He then proceeded to cut all the funny legs and motioned for Isakjan to follow. In his trim little house, a woman cooked legs of another squid on the stove. The man spoke to his wife, who served some ouzo to the guest. Delicious. He smiled and warmly shook the hand of the man.

The liberation newspaper reported advances of the Turkistani army, and Isakjan read that other Turkistani battalions demonstrated superior efforts in the war and their troops received many honors. The first battalion distinguished itself to the point that it was converted into the first Turkistani SS battalion. This constituted an irony unknown to Isakjan, that the group that sent out hit squads to murder Turkistanis now recruited them. But that seemed so far away from Greece.

The troops did their own housekeeping, with privates assigned to washing dishes and cooking. They did not hire the Greeks, and very little social interaction took place. The Greeks did not like the Germans, and no soldier, ethnic German or Turkistani, could go out with a Greek girl.

But they could visit homes, and many times Isakjan stopped to watch a farmer in his fields and admire the produce. Occasionally a farmer might invite the officer inside and offer him a glass of ouzo with a teaspoon of marmalade, which convinced him of the wonderful hospitality possible in Greece.

Those in charge of the war in Berlin must have come to their senses and realized that the Greek tour could weaken a soldier's determination. New orders arrived: not to end his tour in Greece, but to make a trip to a military school in Alsace-Lorraine. The people in this area combined the attributes of both German and French customs, as Alsace-Lorraine served as buffer and first military objective in the many conflagrations between the two countries.

An elite officers' training camp established classes there, and the Turkistani officers now earned the right to attend. Over the period of a week, some twenty Turkistani lieutenants arrived. A reunion followed, as they had been separated through the expansion of the Eastern Army and their various assignments to many theaters of war.

They met an old friend, the Prussian who originally trained the Turkistani First Battalion, who took charge of the instructions. He came from the old school of Prussian discipline, believing that instruction without very strict regimen served no purpose. They entered the officers' training school for six weeks to learn new tactics, refresh their memories of the old ones, increase familiarity with German Army regulations, and all other matters that would bring them completely into the German fold.

The officers toured the beautiful small city, filled with the best of Germany and France, with good restaurants, dances and shops. At the little cafes and restaurants they discussed the war and the reverses which they had encountered on the Ukrainian front. They sensed that Germany had opened too many operations at once, but agreed that the Wehrmacht could recover and ultimately triumph.

It was inconceivable that the slovenly Red Army could ever deter the Germans. Who was there to challenge the Nazi might? Britain existed only as a thorn while the Japanese allied themselves with the Germans. The United States? An upstart country too far away and disinterested to pose a threat.

They met the females everywhere: dances, stores, even on the streets. One evening Isakjan was invited to the home of some girls, German ethnically, but in an area under French rule since World War I and before 1870. That made them all the more alluring, with their French ideas and their moderation regarding right-wing Nazi politics. They didn't talk much about politics, expressing more interest in where Isakjan's home was and his experiences.

After a couple of weeks, they proposed a party and asked Isakjan if he had a radio for music and dancing, so he prepared for a holiday night as he exited the military compound. In following checkout procedures with the guards, he presented his papers and reported his destination, explaining about the big party.

"Is that why you are taking the radio?" the guard asked.

"Of course," he replied.

Eight couples started off the evening, dancing to the music on the radio, drinking, filling up on the bountiful table of food prepared by the sisters. Isakjan silently thanked the Tashkent Military School dancing class. At about 10:30 in the evening, with the music loudest and the drinks taking hold, a loud knock on the door stopped the festivities.

Isakjan, the most sober of the revelers, answered the door. He faced an instructor from the officers' school and two Germans from the Gestapo.

"Good evening," he said slowly, trying to ascertain the reason for the intrusion.

The senior Gestapo officer answered. "We have a report that someone took a short wave radio out of the camp to listen to enemy frequencies, possibly some from the BBC."

"I brought my radio, as you can see. But we are listening to music."

Isakjan knew his radio could receive stations from afar, as he had listened to Russian broadcasts, but contact with the British was absurd. Notwithstanding the fact he did not speak any English, he never related to the English world. The Germans looked around at the food, drink and girls, giving a cursory search for evidence of subversive activity.

"Why don't you stay and join the party?" asked one of the girls.

"I guess we could do that, in the line of duty," agreed the spokesman.

At least some of the Gestapo could dance, drink and eat.

Orders took him back to Greece, where a new directive placed the Turkistani company under the direct command of a native German sergeant rather than the customary Turkistani with a German advisor, bringing immediate protests from Isakjan. But Major Meyer-Mader, his old commander and protector from his first tour of duty, was not there to help, and instead of a hearing on the matter, the battalion commander changed Isakjan's position to that of adjutant liaison. The other Turkistani officers' authority was similarly switched, and they took the altered chain of command as a demotion.

Isakjan asked why, but was told the Germans could use him better in the new position. A couple of weeks later, five new German officers arrived and replaced the Turkistani company commanders, who were made assistants in a direct command hierarchy from the Germans and not a shadow. Isakjan retained the liaison post through his twenty-first birthday, spring, 1944. (He never knew the exact month of his birth.)

He moved into a small apartment in the town of Salonika, the headquarters city. The Germans always arranged for comfortable housing, giving him no idea who used the apartment before him. He found out that, as liaison adjutant, more privileges flowed. A Turkistani private came to clean the apartment, polish his shoes and cook both local and Turkistani meals. He read about far-away fighting in the liberation newspaper, and learned that his friend Alimov had been promoted to commander of the Turkistani First SS Battalion. The gentle Greek sun provided soothing light in which to read about these events. He had found a delightful corner of the war.

The Greek weather, milder but similar to that back home, made him think of his mother and brother, whom he would not see or communicate with until he marched into Uzbekistan as a freedom fighter.

In late spring, his commanding officer called him in.

"I am sorry to lose you," he started, "but you have new orders, and orders are orders."

He handed Isakjan a piece of paper. He had two days to pack and leave Greece for East Prussia.

The new orders directed Isakjan to report to a German town in East Prussia where he was received by a small unit of three German officers in a tiny office and given a reservation for lodging in a little hotel. Behind the office was a miniature compound. This assignment brought on a familiar feeling of unwanted surprise. He expected to go to a more military area, but here saw no sign of troops, armament or even barracks. As usual, the Germans did not disclose their plans, and the proper behavior for the officer was to wait and obey. Over a few days a dozen Turkistani lieutenants arrived, and all of them were confused. None of the men could make anything of the coming assignment.

Then one day a German captain took all of them about five miles in a van, and they could see a tremendous camp, with prisoners of different nationalities. The compound took on dimensions of great security, much greater than the POW camp Isakjan knew.

The twisted barbed wire looped back upon itself, climbing to heights three times that of a man, with several outer perimeters established. Gun towers were everywhere, only several yards apart, and a small military barracks looked like an entry station or point from which prisoners were taken to work.

The captain told them to take charge of the camp. They speculated it might be for foreigners working in factories. The captain took them back to the small village, but the Turkistani officers did not like the assignment.

One officer expressed all their thoughts: "This is not fighting the Russians for our homeland. This is not a patriotic assignment."

They grew restless and queasy. The picture of the prison made them cold and miserable. They preferred the front to this assignment, and referred the question to Isakjan, who knew the commander of the Turkistani Army.

He called Hayit on the phone, telling him he was in Germany with other Turkistani officers, assigned to guarding some camp.

"We object to the assignment. We want to fight for our homeland. Is there something you can do?" he pleaded.

Hayit expressed surprise at the duty orders. "I was not

informed of this order," he said. "I did not know that you had been transferred there. Don't worry, I will be right back with you."

The very next day, Hayit arrived, unannounced, and took all the Turkistani officers back to Berlin.

He was quite upset, saying, "You are not going to work in this kind of place because this is not our understanding. This is a mistake."

Only in Berlin could they recuperate from the shadow of those towers. They reported each day or so to the Liberation Front, meeting more people of the organization and savoring the pleasures of the magnificent city.

Gradually each officer got a new assignment and departed, until only Isakjan remained. He drew duty as temporary hospitality officer to the raw Turkistani troops on leave in Berlin, reviewing with them the proper manners of the West. His lectures included the same themes as the behavior class he gave to his own company, modeled on the Military School instructions.

"Berlin is a city different than any you have seen. You must bring honor to your countrymen during your stay. The people here behave differently than what you might be accustomed to. Remember to use spoons and forks when you eat, never get drunk, and certainly don't grab women in the streets."

After a couple of weeks, Hayit announced that he planned to leave for another trip to visit his legions. Morale needed boosting, especially with sagging German fortunes in the war. The Red Army had scored a major victory at Stalingrad and pushed further West. The Allies had just successfully landed at Normandy where, much to their surprise, ten percent of the Wehrmacht soldiers they captured were former Red Army soldiers.[2] As the German war effort faltered, the status of their Soviet ethnic allies increased because of a greater need for more supporters.

"Isakjan, would you like to accompany me on a special assignment to Poland?" invited Hayit.

Indeed he did, and so they traveled by train to Warsaw. There they found the first Turkistani SS Battalion had just participated in the routing of "rebel criminals resisting German authority," known elsewhere as the German attack on the Warsaw uprising.

The Polish civilians of Warsaw suffered some of the most horrible atrocities in the war during the uprising and the previous Jewish ghetto rebellion. In the city uprising, the Polish underground, with both Jews and gentiles, attempted to free Warsaw from the Nazi occupation. Freelance Nazi brigades not under the control of the Wehrmacht murdered, raped, looted and destroyed the population. The Red Army stood quietly by on the outskirts, refusing aid and relishing the liquidation of the country they planned to dominate after the war. As the Polish partisans faced incessant hammering from the various German forces, the Soviets denied American and British airplanes the use of their bases, which were essential for airlifting aid to the partisans from Western sources. Some reports claim that the Red Army fired upon the partisans. The city itself lay in ruins.[3]

In that situation, the partisans had to capitulate. Hayit reported that a surrender would take place along a main street, and they drove to a line of waiting trucks and guards to witness defeated Warsaw dwellers and Polish resistance fighters march out in surrender to the waiting German soldiers. They carried flags, some with the Star of David, and marched in a surprisingly bold strut for a defeated partisan group. The soldiers escorted them to a waiting convoy of trucks. Heavily armed men and attack vehicles interspersed themselves between the spaces of the convoy as the trucks drove away.

Isakjan and Hayit continued to the Turkistani encampment, which turned out to consist not of tents, but of luxurious buildings in a wealthy section of the city. The battalion officers welcomed Isakjan as one of the first Uzbek company commanders. The commander of the first battalion was Kamal Alimov, his friend from the first days in the German army, who hugged Isakjan and invited him to a dinner. Alimov had somehow acquired a Russian girlfriend, who stayed with him through a number of campaigns.

The officers sat down to sumptuous dinners every night. Isakjan saw beautiful women with the officers and even the enlisted men, who related to these women as lovers or housekeepers, sometimes two or three to a man. The officers explained: "The battalion was engaged in house-to-house fighting and came across many civilians doomed to die or surrender to the Germans. We realized this, and so did the partisans. Different languages present no problem in this situation.

"The people could see that we were not German, and they wanted to follow us, especially the Jewish ones. We returned home often after a day of battle, gaining only a block in hard fighting accompanied by a date or a housekeeper. Our Jewish soldiers felt especially vehement about saving these people, and they often risked their lives to offer sanctuary."

The girls sat with the men at the table, sharing the feasts.

A few spoke some Russian and expressed their gratitude to the Turkistani officers and soldiers.

Every evening these dinner parties attracted the men, and every night a different group hosted Isakjan. The Turkistanis, by tradition, are very generous to friends and guests, and could not do enough to please Isakjan. The Turkistani soldiers considered the highest form of entertainment to be a festive dinner, to cook great meals, give presents, and engage in clever conversation.

He dined with friends including Alimov, Sattarov the Jewish medical officer, and Nuriddim Qari the mullah. Away from home, everyone became a brother, especially those from the same town. The Turkistanis celebrated their victory over those the Germans called `bandits' with the encouragement of their commander. In fact the Turkistanis had participated in a most infamous brutal suppression of a civilian population and destruction of a city which was not a military objective. The fighting pitted trained and well-armed troops against nonprofessionals. Reports brought back to Berlin by Isakjan and Hayit were not favorable, and criticized the lack of military control that Alimov exercised over troops.

Isakjan prepared to leave for Berlin with Major Hayit, and several soldiers escorted them to the station. As he climbed the stairs for the train, they gave him another present, three heavy suitcases to add to the one he came with.

Upon arriving back in Berlin, to the house he shared with Jurabay and Mrs. Rogozinski, Isakjan met with his friend from Jizzakh. They went out to dinner and traded news and gossip. Back home in Schonhauseralle, he opened the extra suitcases with Jurabay as witness.

In the first, he emptied ten watches, all sorts of gold coins, materials, suits; the second, all kinds of clothing, nylon stockings; the one smaller suitcase, a stuffing of Zlotys, Polish currency.

"What do I want with this? It has no meaning." He was disgusted at the booty.

Isakjan distributed the contents of the first two suitcases quickly, not wanting the gush of tainted wealth. At dinners with German friends and Turkistanis he distributed the contents, saving some material and coins for Mrs. Rogozinski. He then had only the Polish money left and a few coins, most of which he also gave away.

Isakjan occupied his days again as introduction officer to Turkistani soldiers entering Berlin for the first time. He showed them the main attractions of the city. He explained the social manners expected, admonishing them not to get drunk or lewdly accost women, telling them to speak with respect to girls and not to grab; in short, what to do to avoid trouble.

The excesses of war and the arrogance of the Nazis increasingly revolted him, but Germany was the center of his existence. By reading German and Turkistani publications and conversing with the leaders of the government in exile, he realized more clearly the differences between what the Russians said and the truth. He knew that the USSR was not invited into the Baltic States, that Finland did not declare war on Russia, and that the Western countries lived a life superior to that in the Soviet Union. Announcements in the newspaper brought unsettling war news, including the opening of a second front by the Allies. This, combined with increasing stories of the abhorrent practices of the Nazis, forced Isakjan to retreat further from the promises of governments and into himself for fulfillment. He and his Turkistani friends felt increasingly cornered with the possibility that Germany might not deliver on its promise of liberation and they grew angry at their second class status as minority peoples.

CHAPTER 13

TURKS INVADE SLOVAKIA

1932 - The SS becomes a cornerstone of Nazi racial plans as the core of a future Nordic German aristocracy. Members may only marry after special permission, after undergoing extensive biological studies to determine ethnic purity. [1]

1941 - The Nazi SS Einsatzgruppen follow the path of the victorious Wehrmacht with orders to beware of low cunning on the part of Asiatic prisoners [2] *and to liquidate them along with commissars and Jews. Thousands of Turkistanis were executed.* [3]

1943 - Nazi SS battle forces create an Asiatic Turkistani Regiment.

"Slovakia? And a promotion?" asked the skeptical Isakjan in early fall 1944.

"Slovakia may sound like a strange place to you now," answered Hayit, "but it represents a momentous turning point in our battle for the liberation of Turkistan. I know you may be concerned with recent German defeats. In an odd way, that helped our cause because now they need our help more than ever. The SS command, with more political power than the army, has recognized our contribution and invited us into their fighting ranks as the Turkistani SS. They can give us better supplies and equipment than the regular army. We demanded and received permission to concentrate Turkistani troops in regiment strength, rather than the dispersed battalions you are familiar with. The best part is that we can assemble a regiment in Slovakia, far from the worst fighting, subject only to minor partisan activity. Soon we may have a number of divisions to supplement the one we have in the Wehrmacht. "

Hayit was privy to information that early in the war, the SS had formed divisions of Dutch, Flemish, Norwegians, Danes and Swiss into purely fighting units dispatched to the Eastern and Western fronts. As the myth of German invincibility faltered, Walloon and French formations followed. The anti-Slavic theory fell with defeats in the East, and Baltic SS divisions were formed; then Galician and Ukrainian. Even though the SS still distrusted the Wehrmacht, they began to agree on some principles. By late 1943 some of the powerful SS leadership understood what many Wehrmacht officers had from the beginning, namely that winning the war mandated joining forces with peoples swallowed by Russia and treating them with respect. This meant that the Eastern Legions, the name given to Moslem forces fighting for Germany who had previously fought for the Soviet Union, were treated better by the Nazi command.

As months wore on and the ignominious defeats at the hands of "subhumans" blistered the Germans, the SS opened the floodgates of cooperation as desperate, panicked men often do. Ukrainian, Ruthenian, Turkistani, Caucasian, Spanish, Serb and Cossack groups received prompt orders to form SS detachments. With a few exceptions, these SS forces went directly into battle on the fronts rather than perform many of the police and prison camp responsibilities that the SS had concentrated on more exclusively earlier in the war. Aside from SS activities, the Germans belatedly gave the celebrated Russian defector Vlasov the title of general and commander-in-chief of a Russian Liberation Army. This gave new strength and commitment to the amalgamation of liberation fronts, each of which foresaw the beginnings of its own national army for independence. [4] The shift in policy came several years too late.

"We need a battalion commander for this force," Hayit said. "I am sending you there as one of the battalion commanders with a promotion to captain, which, in the SS, is haupsturmfuhrer. This will make you one of the very highest ranking Turkistani officers. You will report to Alimov, who will assume command of the regiment."

"Yes, sir." Isakjan accepted the position with a feeling of renewed vigor. The promotion elevated him to third in the hierarchy of the nascent Turkistani army legions, after Hayit and Alimov. Although a major usually commanded a battalion, minority officers did not receive equal ranks. Alimov received a promotion to regiment commander over the First and Second Turkistani SS battalions.

Hayit had more details. "Your assignment will encompass more than just commanding the second battalion. You should familiarize yourself with the officers, advisors and men of the entire regiment. We may have another change for Alimov, and that will make you regiment commander."

"Will Alimov get another regiment?" asked Isakjan, warming to the idea of a large Turkistan force.

"We are not sure what to do with Alimov," Hayit confided, "and you can give us a report. We receive increased complaints about him concerning drinking, reprimanding officers in front of soldiers, and other conduct not suitable for a commander. The looting in Warsaw was quite unacceptable, as our troops must never behave like some of the freelance German irregulars. We have even been thinking of sending Dr. Shermat down as political advisor. They need to train like the best of the Wehrmacht in order to work for the freedom of Turkistan. We want to move slowly because Alimov is popular with the troops, but discipline is falling under his leadership."

Isakjan reported to his commanding officer, Kamal Alimov, friend and fellow Uzbek. Alimov and all the company commanders continued to report to German supervisors. The new muscle of the Turkistanis did not include independence from advisors. Alimov set himself and his Russian girlfriend up in a splendid house in the little village of Myjava. Alimov, of all the officers, managed to keep a woman through all of his campaigns.

Isakjan met Alimov in Myjava, dressed in the black uniform of an SS officer, with a skull and crossed bones pinned to his hat under the German eagle. The two embraced.

"Isakjan, I am so happy that you were selected. We will give you a promotion ceremony and a dinner right away." Alimov did not sound convincing, and Isakjan surmised that he suspected that Hayit might replace him.

A circle of Turkistani lieutenants and the regiment's German advisors gathered for the occasion. Alimov read the order: "Effective this date, the rank of haupsturmfuhrer is conferred upon Isakjan Narzikul."

He attached the pins of the rank to Isakjan's epaulet.

The attending officers clicked their heels and raised an SS stiff-arm salute.

"Heil Hitler," they chanted.

The men shared a drink to celebrate the occasion, and joined for dinner. Alimov's German advisor called himself Colonel El Rashid, a man who looked and spoke as much like a Turkistani as a German, and who enjoyed the company of his advisees. He asked the new battalion commander what he thought of Slovakia. Isakjan, in fine German, told the Colonel that he thought the new regiment would make a significant contribution to the war effort.

The Colonel looked surprised. "I didn't know that any of the field Turkistani officers spoke German well. I will have to invite you to dinner."

El Rashid invited him to dinner many times, and Isakjan felt that he contributed well in conversations ranging from Hamlet to dancing. The German officers present at the dinners asked his opinion on matters of the world and on smaller subjects like horseback riding. Even Alimov did not take a strong interest in the German language or Western culture, and so did not find as fast a friendship with El Rashid. Further, Alimov could not disguise a growing scorn for his allies due to their discrimination and war loses. As a result, the Colonel had a hard time remembering Isakjan's Turkistani features and treated him like a fellow German.

Dinners with El Rashid were in great contrast to those with Alimov, who drank large quantities of liquor and started to brag about his exploits.

"Those Germans would be nothing without us. I am tired of listening to them," declared Alimov as he shoveled food into his mouth with his fingers.

He had stopped learning German, and had difficulty conversing with his advisors. He stumbled outside to chase a sergeant. Isakjan saw wild arms waving and slaps to the sergeant's face while soldiers gathered for the show. Upon Alimov's return,

Isakjan took him aside.

"Get control of yourself," he advised.

Alimov pulled away. "I can do whatever I want with my troops. Don't forget that I command you. You who dines with Germans all the time, what do you know?"

Alimov screamed out the window. "Damn you Germans. We are saving you. You owe us."

Isakjan grew red in the face, mad at the gross petulance, and he turned Alimov around, fighting to restrain himself and working hard to speak calmly. "You are right. The Germans should treat us better, but drinking and screaming will never get it for us."

Isakjan drove back to his troops, past the German residence with fine china and cultured conversation, past the Turkistani troops scooping pilaf with their hands.

The Second Turkistani SS Battalion bivouacked ten miles from Alimov's offices in the buildings of a local school. When Isakjan arrived, it still needed 500 more men to fill its quota of over 1000. As a battalion in the stages of formation, the group needed much work to resemble a fighting force, and Isakjan wondered if he would ever get a command with fully trained troops. The usual combination of ill-trained Soviet soldiers, former prisoners, and Nazi sympathizers marked his contingent. He always seemed to get the rag-tag rabble, but their presence proved that the German army still captured its share of Red soldiers, in spite of Hitler's interference and sometimes being outnumbered twelve to one on the Eastern front.[5]

He lined up the battalion for inspection. Their special black uniforms plotted out the ground and gave them a certain hard menacing edge, the shoulder patches distinguishing them from other German SS with the "Allah Biz Bilen" insignia. But there was another factor unbeknownst to the Germans, which differentiated the Turkistani SS from others. Their forces included Jewish soldiers, men thrown in with Moslems because of their common Central Asian ancestry. The legionnaires considered themselves one national army, however, with a single common purpose that transcended religious preferences.

The troops stayed in barracks, leaving everyday policing of the town to regular locals. An order frequently came concerning a sighting of partisans, and a squad or a company would dash out to investigate the tip, but the success rate against the partisans was no better than in Greece. The Slovak population itself seemed to have decided to talk openly with neither side, avoiding retribution that both sides could mete out.

Isakjan trained his soldiers rigorously. He detested the laxity exhibited by Alimov and insisted on strict military order with his own men. The confinement resulting from the elusiveness of his partisan quarry gave him time to raise his men's professional standards. The liberation army that entered Turkistan needed to immediately demonstrate their superiority to the disheveled Soviet troops and give reason for pride in a native army. He envisioned his troops as a special unit, and gave them instruction in military etiquette as well as fighting. As the only graduate of a military school, he again strived to translate the materials from many of his old courses, including social behavior, to those under his command. He had stopped following the lead of the government he reported to and instituted his own agenda. The hope of war and the promise of a Turkistani legion excited his ready store of energy. Every week he reported to regiment headquarters in Myjava, surveying maps of the area and comparing the skills of his men with those of the first battalion.

Hayit came for a visit and gave a rousing speech to the troops, trying to assure them the cause would pick up momentum. He did not like the reports of Alimov's behavior. The differences in polish between the newly formed second battalion and the first were too obvious.

The second battalion marched in smart military precision. Their formations stepped out as a large machine, stiff knees cracking, smart boots in perfect cadence, salutes with snaps of their outstretched arms. With one word, that machine could spread out in a low fan and unleash a fury of attacking might, devastating any obstacle in its path. No such obstacle revealed itself, and yet the partisans were active, destroying communication links and railroads, and sniping at convoys. With all the power of tanks and guns at its command, the Turkistani SS regiment spent weeks at a time in camp, overtraining and searching for diversion in the small town. The partisans never consented to a match with the regular troops, and the Germans could never locate the partisans. The hope of war drifted into gentle boredom.

The soldiers strayed into the town, which seemed like anything but an occupied territory. The inhabitants carried on a lively business. Shops were opened and the civilians were relatively unaffected by the course of the war, due in large part to a designation by Hitler of Slovakia as a model country.

Stores contained all kinds of goods, materials and leathers. Alimov's first battalion brought many gold coins and cash from their assault on Warsaw and quickly became favored customers of the tradesmen. Isakjan still carried too much money from the gifts he received in Warsaw and bought beautiful suits. He dated one of the town's few hairdressers.

As battalion chief, Isakjan was given a magnificent house, a Turkistani cook, twenty-four hour bodyguards, a personal servant to maintain his house, a car at his disposal, horses for riding with or without carriage. His valet and cook shaved him, as he then needed a shave every few days. He went riding, and advanced his horsemanship, which had reached its last peak with Eshak the donkey. A German aide of El Rashid phoned him and asked permission to bring his wife over for a horseback ride. Isakjan invited them for a weekend.

The German lieutenant and his wife drove up on Saturday morning. She was Polish, and an exquisite beauty with a flair for Western-style dress. Upon their arrival, willing Turkistani soldiers helped them from the car, nodding to themselves at the decadence of Western women in showing legs and even a hint of breast. After a day's riding together, a social evening and night's rest, the host served Sunday breakfast while horses were saddled. As the three stood up to tour the yard and mount the horses, a phone call came for the lieutenant to report back to El Rashid and for Isakjan to pick up some maps and material from the command room. The soldiers who saddled the horses got to accompany the lovely lady.

Isakjan returned to find the ride over, the woman gone, and an angry husband on the phone. "Captain Narzikul, what kind of men do you have in your battalion? My wife came home in tears after your soldiers tried to kiss her and grab her on the horseback ride."

Isakjan flushed with shame and embarrassment. He apologized profusely and promised to discipline the offenders. Inside he seethed with anger at men he trusted, men he relied on to carry Turkistani honor. He rocked his arms and walked in a small circle for a minute to try and calm his mood before calling in one of the perpetrators.

Isakjan started in an aggressive voice, "What did you do to that lady? How could you do anything to her? They were our guests and you shamed us. What kind of a soldier are you? What kind of a man are you? Don't you know that Turkistanis are as good as Germans? We don't have to act like that. Now tell me what happened." Isakjan's voice rose and his hands shook.

The soldier backed off from the verbal offense. "No. We did nothing. She is lying. We took her for a nice ride. Nothing happened. She is nothing but a tramp, a low Western lady without morals."

Isakjan could hardly hold his temper and strained to hold himself back. "Stand against that wall," he shouted and waved. "Now tell me the truth. Tell me why she should lie to me."

"I don't know what she said. Nothing happened."

Isakjan pulled his pistol out, aimed and fired, hitting the wall several inches from the soldier's head. The man fell to the ground, face white with fear. A full confession followed, corroborated by his accomplice moments later.

Isakjan rolled thundering words at them. "If I report this to El Rashid, he will shoot you. Have you no idea of what you did? Listen to me. You will gather a large bunch of flowers and presents and go call on the lieutenant. Apologize and humble yourselves. Your performance will determine your fate. Do this and report back to me."

As the men left, Isakjan held his head and sat back at his desk. The soldiers were country boys who had never been on a train or in a car before their entry into the war, had seen only a couple of Westerners in their lives back in their little village. The women from their home draped themselves in heavy veils and long dresses and the mullahs taught them that other women were debauched. But he knew that a liberated Turkistan would have to become modern in ideas, and despaired while his offending soldiers made a pilgrimage to the German compound. The men performed well and saved their lives with proper apologies, allowing Isakjan to return to routine and small diversions.

CHAPTER 14

BULLETS WITH THE DESSERT

He (Himmler) then asked if the Swedish Government would arrange for him to meet General Eisenhower and capitulate on the whole Western Front....

Here is the text of my covering message to Stalin (regarding the matter):

Prime minister to Marshal Stalin,

The President of the United States has the news also. There can be no question, as far as His Majesty's Government is concerned, of anything less than unconditional surrender simultaneously to the three major Powers.

-- Prime Minister Winston Churchill [1]

Isakjan's wardrobe flourished with every imaginable kind of suit custom tailored by the townspeople. He made friends with all the storekeepers, who waved to him as he walked down the street. Slovakia emulated the prosperity of Switzerland, and indeed Swiss radios were available, as were liquor and manufactured goods. Slovakia was a showplace.

He took a couple of gold coins with him always, and ordered a leather jacket like the German air force officers wore, down to the knees, in leather dyed blue, delivery guaranteed in one week. The price was in kronin, but Isakjan handed the tailor a gold coin.

"Is this enough?" he asked.

"Thank you. Thank you very very much," the man responded with a broad grin and a warm handshake.

The coat was extraordinary. His friends admired it and complimented him on it. He went to Berlin for a couple of weeks just to show off the coat and immerse himself in more active cultural events.

Back in Slovakia, with food plentiful, the regiment's two battalions did not suffer the rigors of war, especially the first battalion, who lived like royalty, using money from their rout of Warsaw.

They reminisced about the women from Warsaw, and detailed how they presented gifts of money, identification papers and letters of recommendation to them when the battalion departed. They made sure the girls were dressed in Polish peasant clothes and they bragged that no friends were turned over to the Germans.

But they spoke less and less of entering Turkistan as liberation forces when reports of Nazi war miracles turned into ominous excuses. As the 1944 campaigns faltered, events cast a black shadow on the men, and the newspapers and Liberation Front publication could not hide the battles lost and the movements of troops that represented major retreats. Isakjan, no longer an automatic believer of press stories, thought his triumphant reentry into Jizzakh to see his mother began to look ever distant.

The Slovaks understood the direction of the war and were quick to ask what the troops would do when the war was over and lost. Germans were retreating everywhere. Isakjan tried to ignore the inevitable, but the truth hounded him. Every conversation in the town offered theories about the end. At his favorite tailor, the man lectured him sincerely,

"You and your men are not Germans. Now is the time for you to choose what you will do. Save yourselves. Association with the Germans will mean punishment."

He could not deny it. Overhead every morning, clouds of bombers winged their way to Nazi targets in Eastern Europe or Germany, blocking the sun. The tailor pointed out, "Americans. They will eliminate Germany from the map. You are not part of Germany. Escape while you can."

Several hours later the planes again filled the sky, returning with numbers undiminished. Isakjan recognized military power and appreciated more than ever its limitations. Those airplanes did not need to ferret out isolated partisan companies, but proposed to eliminate the cities of the Rhine. He visualized the eventual decimation of the factories and buildings there, even in Berlin. He pictured the collapse of the restaurants, theaters, the liberation building, and the vanquishing of the efficient Germans. Did that mean also the surrender of Turkistani liberation?

"Don't think of military glory now," counseled his girlfriend. "Think of surrendering to the Americans."

"Americans. Who are they?"

"They are the password of the village. We prospered under German protection, and now that will go, but we want to continue our success. That means siding with the Americans," she explained. "Most of us Slovaks would like to be liberated by the Americans, even though some lean towards the Russians. The silly ones believe in pan-Slavism. They think one big nation of Slavs would be better."

As if to make her point stronger, she warned him, "We can't be seen at dances together any more. People are starting to cooperate with the partisans. No one wants to be friends with the losers."

Isakjan struggled with his frustration, hanging on to any possibility for a continuation of the Turkistani, if not the German effort. His most recent relationships with Germans came from personal attachment to special individuals more than loyalty to the German nation, which had demonstrated too often its penchant for discrimination. Nothing could dampen Isakjan's enthusiasm more than repression of minorities. The Nazi element seemed to spoil the German nation.

Isakjan instinctively reviewed the types of help he had received in other troubled moments. No other great power appeared willing to continue his quest for equality and eager to enlist his support by supplying him a uniform and a means of working for his country. He would have to fall back upon his own resources, and so he started to look for someone who could become his mentor, or who needed help with some kind or work. Many kind people had given him hope after he proved his worthiness, but first he had to complete his own studies. He commenced a tremendous effort to learn the Slovakian language, spending all his spare time conversing with the townspeople.

He visited the workers, barbers, leather makers, bakers and asked about the weather, their business, and their health. They, in turn, advised him of the local attitudes on the war in Slovakia.

The police sought him out as the occupation authority. Teachers and the professionals visited him, either because of his position, or his growing reputation as the officer who spoke Slovak. He encouraged this. The school administrators stopped in regularly to check on the school building, ever more sure that classes might start in the near future. They wanted conferences with the man in charge and would express concern to him about what he would do when Germany lost the war, as they too recognized that he and his men were not German.

"We know that you are from some corner of the Soviet Union. You must be fighting to restore your homeland to independence. We have surmised that you are not fighting for Germany, but for liberation," he often heard.

Isakjan sometimes was invited for tea at their homes, and traded gossip for favors. The pan-Slavists and communists who advocated partnership with Russia amazed him the most. He knew the price that such a partnership cost his native Turkistan. But, more and more it looked as though the impossible victory of the Russians over the Germans would occur.

Throughout the Nazi forces, this hard reality crept in, recognized by the liberation committee, and even the hierarchy of the SS, right to up the head, Himmler. The Germans allowed the Russian liberation leader General Vlasov to issue a declaration in Prague on November 14, 1944, forming a distinct army to overthrow the Soviet leadership and calling upon Red army troops to follow him. The declaration made no mention of independence for minority republics such as Turkistan, and therefore met with opposition from the Turkistani committee. Declarations and disputes of this nature might have ensured a German victory in 1942, but in 1944 they represented the last desperate spasms of a dying effort.

Nevertheless, at Liberation headquarters, Shermat grew angry at the announcement and ignored orders from the German chief Oder to broadcast it. Upon reporting to the German's office for a reprimand or worse, Shermat could hardly restrain himself, although the chief spoke quietly with understanding.

"Naturally I didn't broadcast the silly declaration," Shermat defended his actions. "If you insist, I will send out that message, but I will not be responsible for our troops turning on the Germans after they read it." Shermat could always get the attention of his superiors by his understanding of the effects and ramifications of improper statements.

Oder looked at Shermat incredulously. "I fail to understand what you are talking about."

Shermat pursued his argument. "Our men are fighting for independence," he explained, "and the declaration makes no mention of it. It ignores the fate of non-Russian peoples. The troops will smell another trick from the Russians with whom they are so familiar, and will rebel."

The message stayed off the air. The president of the Turkistani committee, Veli Kayum-Khan, did not need to refute the Vlasov declaration.

Kayum-Khan turned his attention toward other matters, mainly a plan to divert as many of the Turkistani legions as possible to the West, where they could surrender to the Americans and British, possibly to live and continue the fight for independence. Surrender to the Soviets meant certain torture and death. Surely the Western powers, with their concern about liberty for oppressed people would aid their cause.

Germany had contacted the governments of the United States and Britain in an effort to convince them to make a separate peace so that the Wehrmacht could concentrate on fighting the Soviet Union, an attempt lobbied for by Archduke Otto von Habsburg, [2] and given the code name "crossword" by Roosevelt and Churchill, [3] Rumors of these negotiations encouraged hope of avoiding total defeat. Britain and America, in any case, were known to be ideologically opposed to the Soviets, and an alliance with them by rebel Turkistanis would be natural.

The Liberation Committee President tricked the Red Cross into delivering a letter to Churchill, divulging his plans and asking for cooperation. The letter explained that they fought with the German government for the liberation of their homeland and not for the Nazi cause. It detailed the committee efforts to switch troops to the Western front for the purpose of allying themselves with the West. An answer never came, but the troop transfer began with clever pleas to the East Ministry official von Mende and the Wehrmacht officer Luderzen, hinting that this would remove the temptation for the Turkistanis to rejoin the Red Army out of frustration at the German defeats.

Back in Slovakia Isakjan worried about his fate if the war ended in defeat for Germany. He intended to falsify papers and slip in with Gypsies for a while. With a German collapse and a Soviet victory, he knew that authorities would not discover him if he could blend in with a meandering crowd. While he tried to perfect this foggy plan and improve his Slovak, he developed a careful attitude, close to paranoia, afraid of orders sending him back to Berlin, and so he visited regiment headquarters less frequently.

Those headquarters, by order of Regiment commander Alimov, moved from Myjava to Leopoldov, ten miles away. The new offices overlooked the Vah River, a tributary of the Danube, and the surrounding hills where a growing number of partisans launched operations.

At the end of December 1944, Alimov planned a party and telephoned Isakjan to extend an invitation. Isakjan at that moment was extremely anxious about possible orders and told his commanding officer that he was sick and felt too depressed for festivity.

Alimov countered, "This is an order. You will attend. I must talk a few things over with you."

Isakjan took a couple of soldiers and left for headquarters.

He arrived about six o'clock, before dinner, and took tea in Alimov's office, talking for a half-hour.

Alimov seemed reserved. "Tonight there will be a small party. Among the guests will be a group of German staff officers." This meant German ethnic, as the Turkistanis never referred to themselves as German officers. "Later in the evening," continued Alimov, drawing himself close and hushing his voice, "they will be killed. Then we are going over the line to the Red Army."

Silence ensued. Isakjan simply could not digest the information. He coughed and struggled to orient himself. He suspected something terrible. "The German officers will be killed and our officers will defect?"

"No, the whole First Battalion," responded Alimov in a

firm and committed tone. "Your battalion will stay behind."

Isakjan could not believe it. Surely Alimov also worried about Germany's coming defeat. Then again, Alimov's Russian girlfriend could be a spy of some sort. He thought that maybe Alimov was just testing him and would listen to reason, so he measured the commander's resolve: "What are you talking about? You are not making sense."

Alimov said simply, "The war is over for Germany, and maybe if we traded sides, we could make things better for ourselves."

The regiment commander showed no sign of wavering, his jaw set hard and his eyes unyielding. Isakjan credited Alimov for exploring vigorously all options and ingratiating himself with every side.

He objected again. "The Russians who run the Soviet government will not treat any Turkistanis who wore German uniforms with anything less than the contempt they showed our nation before the war, and will add a charge of treason."

He quivered at his delicate position, feeling that maybe Alimov was brainwashed or that Alimov's girlfriend pressured him into a wrong decision. Unfortunately, after Alimov disclosed the plan, Isakjan's participation became a necessity. Was he to be a gift from Alimov to the Russians, or was the man just too desperate to make a logical decision?

Isakjan felt that Alimov had considered this for a long time and probably had made contact with the Red Army, remembering the letter he had received written in Uzbek while he commanded an anti-partisan company outside of Zhitomir. Alimov still was a young man, only two years older than the twenty-one-year old Isakjan. Alimov, however, reacted spontaneously to events, a trait that won him many friends but subjected him to indiscretions. Isakjan brooded, studied and considered his moves carefully. He concluded that a Russian system of government capable of shrewdly deceiving large segments of its population for years could not afford to grant mercy to those who escaped the mold and learned the truth. However, he must not upset Alimov. One angry order could put him in serious jeopardy.

Alimov's two most trusted lieutenants came into the room, the holsters on their hips unbuttoned. Isakjan thought fast.

"Do the men of your battalion know about this?" Isakjan asked, stalling for time.

"Only my inner circle of officers. We act for the good of

everyone, but the soldiers can't know," explained Alimov with a disdain that indicated the foolishness of the question.

"Why don't we take my battalion with us also?" Isakjan wanted to know.

"We don't trust them. Some of your troops are not from Turkistan, and those that are Turkistani, I don't consider proven."

Isakjan glanced at the ready pistols of the two assistants and made his decision. He faced Alimov.

"Thank you for the offer. I agree to go, but you should have given me a little more notice. I will run back to my barracks and pick up some belongings: money, camera, and clothes."

Isakjan wanted more time to think, possibly to escape, or even to complain to the Germans.

"I must deny you permission for that." Alimov had thought of everything. "I will send men to fetch your things. Furthermore, you should know that I have invited you along because of our long friendship. Unfortunately, now that you know of the plan, there is no choice except to come with us." Alimov pointed to his two lieutenants, "These men will see to it that you accompany us or that you don't live to tell about our plans."

Isakjan felt trapped, as a few years earlier when his Soviet commander directed him to conclude a killing and suicide. A more mature soldier faced a direct order this time. He paused a moment to gather proper military subordination, and then conceded to Alimov, "I am with you. Only, I want no part of the killing."

"You are a wise man. After the party, these men will stay with you while we finish our work," concluded Alimov as he pointed to his lieutenants.

The German officers arrived in a festive mood, and Alimov served a beautiful meal to the Turkistani officers and the German guests, making small talk and ignoring the war. His girlfriend, the only woman present, kept a low profile. Isakjan was relieved that his friend and frequent dinner host, El Rashid, did not attend. Instead, about ten Germans, the command core of the first battalion "liaisons" together with office and accounting help for the regiment, accepted Alimov's hospitality. The Germans enjoyed the food and managed to get mildly drunk, succumbing to the flattery of the Turkistanis regarding their war efforts and the German race.

Sumptuous plates followed each other, and wine flowed freely between courses. Alimov proclaimed his dedication to the

Nazi cause and apologized for his rough use of the German language. As waiters delivered coffee, the two lieutenants guarding Isakjan stood up and meandered out of the room with their charge between them. Once out of the dining area, they hastened to a rear room and sat in silence. Machine-gun fire and screams erupted from the other end of the house. Then silence.

Alimov appeared with a group of soldiers.

"Time to go."

The lieutenants continued to surround Isakjan, who marched with some of his old associates. Sattarov, the Jewish medical officer whom Isakjan had befriended and helped out of trouble with the military police, marched with them.

The men of the first battalion were called out of their beds for a sudden night mission and gathered sleepily, with no idea what awaited them. They marched towards the bridge that crossed the Vah River, the bridge that held out a one-way passage from the German regime into a Soviet unknown.

Alimov planned to leave Leopoldov with the First Battalion, cross the bridge that was guarded by a few German sentries, and proceed to the mountains. The men of the First Battalion, still without a clue as to the intentions of their leader, believed a routine search was forthcoming. Only part of the regimental staff knew what would unfold.

Barked commands moved the troops towards the bridge, all on foot with the officers, including Isakjan and his escorts, in the front and soldiers behind. Some vehicles and horses followed in the rear. 1200 heavily armed men walked out of Leopoldov.

The German sentry stopped them. Alimov stepped forward.

"I am Captain Alimov, commander of the Turkistani regiment and its first battalion. We are on an assignment to track down partisans," he announced in his broken German.

The sentry saluted. "Yes, sir. And good luck."

The guards stood aside. Alimov, Sattarov and Isakjan Narzikul marched across first. They continued through the night.

In the morning, the soldiers still did not know what had happened, but they dropped their supplies on the roadside and marched into the forest with Alimov leading, the only one knowing where to go. With the supplies abandoned and thin garments on their backs, the men faced the cold December wind. Isakjan pulled his blue leather coat about him tightly, thankful that snow had not yet arrived, waiting for a chance to escape.

Alimov stopped at a clearing where a partisan colonel

and his staff waited. He stopped the procession and addressed the men.

"We know that Germany will lose the war shortly. I have arranged a guarantee of clemency for all of you, and now we will fight as partisans for the Soviet Union."

The December cold did not match the chill sent through the many spines listening.

Alimov introduced the partisan leader, a Soviet Colonel, who continued the address, "I am Colonel Boshinski, commanding officer of the ninth partisan brigade of Slovakia."

The Colonel spoke fluent university Russian. Dressed in a heavy winter coat, he addressed the Turkistani troops in their black SS uniforms, quite inadequate for the cold weather. The men did not have warm overcoats. Isakjan stood to the side in an inconspicuous spot, knowing too well that he held a German rank second only to Alimov and hoping to escape and rejoin his own battalion.

The partisan commander welcomed them.

"I know that you did not willingly work for the German army, but were forced to do so, and that the first opportunity that came, you turned to your countrymen. The Soviet government realizes this and is glad to have you in the ranks fighting fascism."

The men were not so sure that they wished to fight fascism or come back to the Soviet Union, but they followed.

Isakjan did not give up hope of edging his way out of the Russian hug. He surmised that in a few days Alimov would feel secure and not keep a close watch on him, and then the moment to leave quietly and return to his own forces should present itself. He still harbored the zeal of a convert in detesting the Soviet leadership. Isakjan considered that he had elected to secede from the USSR as the constitution permitted, and feared the retribution they might mete out to any one taking their guarantees seriously. Although he understood that he wore the uniform of the losers, he preferred to cling to his old friends or hide with the Gypsies until something availed itself.

Alimov began to concentrate on other matters, but he underestimated the German forces. By the next day, scouts reported sightings of Wehrmacht troops on the prowl pursuing the wayward battalion. Isakjan then realized as a military man that neither the Germans nor the Russians would accept his excuses. Loyalty never needs an excuse; only death can prevent a soldier from accomplishing his mission.

On the other side of the Vah River, Commander Hayit

arrived and personally supervised the disarmament of the Second Battalion, and their transfer back to Germany. Isakjan did not know that, but concluded that reunification with the Germans was out of the question. However, he could expect nothing beneficial from the Soviets either. Maybe Alimov, with his Russian girlfriend, had struck a special deal with the Reds, perhaps had spied for them over a number of years. In that case Alimov might deserve some consideration, but not one who devoted himself to the liberation army and strove to topple the Russian hegemony in Turkistan. But now fate, for a third time, trapped him, by saving his life but withholding a secure destiny.

Alimov divided the regiment into partisan groups, each about the size of a company. Isakjan commanded a hundred men. In order to show their newfound love of country, Alimov named Isakjan's group after General Chapajev, a legendary Red partisan leader during the 1920's civil war. The significance of the name was not lost on the troops. The units stayed in close proximity for the first few weeks, communicating by runner, living in the cold forests.

After days roaming through the hinterland and sleeping on the dirt, the entire battalion "requisitioned" a few houses from a little village cluster. Isakjan's men were packed into a couple of buildings, all hundred of them, but the other companies fared no better. A few nights in the forest made sleeping on wooden floors a treat. Days ago they were like royalty in Leopoldov, and now, hunted down like vermin. Nights under a roof came with great risk of exposure to the pursuing avengers. After a couple of days they planned to scamper back into the forest. The men decided to emulate the ways of the partisans they once had tracked, preferring to avoid contact with outsiders, traveling under cover of darkness.

Overhead the skies continued to fill with American bombers on daily missions. The group chanced upon a pilot who had bailed out of a damaged plane from one of those great formations. He sat wounded by a tree and stirred intense interest among the men. To the men of Central Asia, America evoked more curiosity than anything else, a strange land somewhere between the moon and Mars. Alimov transferred him to the Soviets.

Their new Soviet ally? Never gave direction or joined the group. They might soon claim victory in the war and dominance over the Reich's eastern territories, but could never match the German penchant for organization. Isakjan missed the order and purpose found in Germany, and resented its imminent overthrow. Settling in for a night in a house brought on sentimental self-pity.

In the glimmer of the next morning's light a few men stirred about and stumbled outside to relieve themselves. They were the first to die. Sounds of rapid machine-gun fire permeated the woodland quiet. Germans aimed and shot from an encirclement in the woods, tearing up the flimsy wooden building with thousands of bullet holes. The wounded moaned and the lifeless oozed blood. Isakjan, jostled from an uneasy sleep, pulled on his pants and relied on his most basic animal instincts, leaving his favorite blue leather coat behind. Men pushed through the doors and windows into the crossfire while the other companies burst forth from their buildings. The time for caution had passed and no opportunity for heroics was forthcoming. Only one urge prevailed: to run; run out; run past the bullets.

The chaos that followed exceeded the worst he had encountered in the war, even on his first day as a combat soldier in Latvia. This time he had no foxhole, no order to shoot himself. "Welcome back to the Soviet side," he thought.

He could not hesitate to analyze the battle or predict when reinforcements might arrive. Defense amounted to gruesome mathematical chance. The German barrage slaughtered a few dozen men each minute and a thousand of them bolted into the trees. Some lucky ones passed through the encirclement. The attackers took few prisoners and gave no opportunity for explanation, although many of the troops, including Isakjan, yearned to rejoin their old German regiment.

He ran through the snow and leafless thickets as the German bullets felled his comrades. His former army demonstrated an undiminished power and will to win. Their machine guns filled the air with the thunderous sound of murder. The surrounded men darted like little creatures out of the nest, devoid of all reasoning or feeling, except that required to propel their legs.

Part of the battalion survived, tired, cold, disorganized. They huddled together beneath the forest cover, with no care for injuries. The wounded who assembled were those able to run several miles through snow-laden forest. Others with more serious injuries huddled in the woods to die alone. About fifty men assembled with Isakjan, most of them from his company, but others were from different parts of the old first battalion. The gallant Eastern Army did not look like troops that could liberate

Turkistan.

The pursuing Wehrmacht captured stragglers and some wounded, bringing them back to their headquarters. Interrogation by both German officers and Commander Hayit quickly satisfied them that the soldiers had no knowledge of the traitorous maneuver. Hayit used the event to encourage further transfers of Turkistanis to the Western front.

The captured soldiers also told of the death of Isakjan Narzikul, as they had seen his blue leather coat lying in the smoldering ruins of their encampment. Back in Berlin, the liberation committee organized a ceremony to commemorate his service to their cause and his unfortunate death.

Isakjan Narzikul as a cadet at Tashkent Military Academy, circa 1939-40

Plaque saying "Allah Biz Bilan" (God is With Us) used by the Eastern Legions of the Wehrmacht during World War II

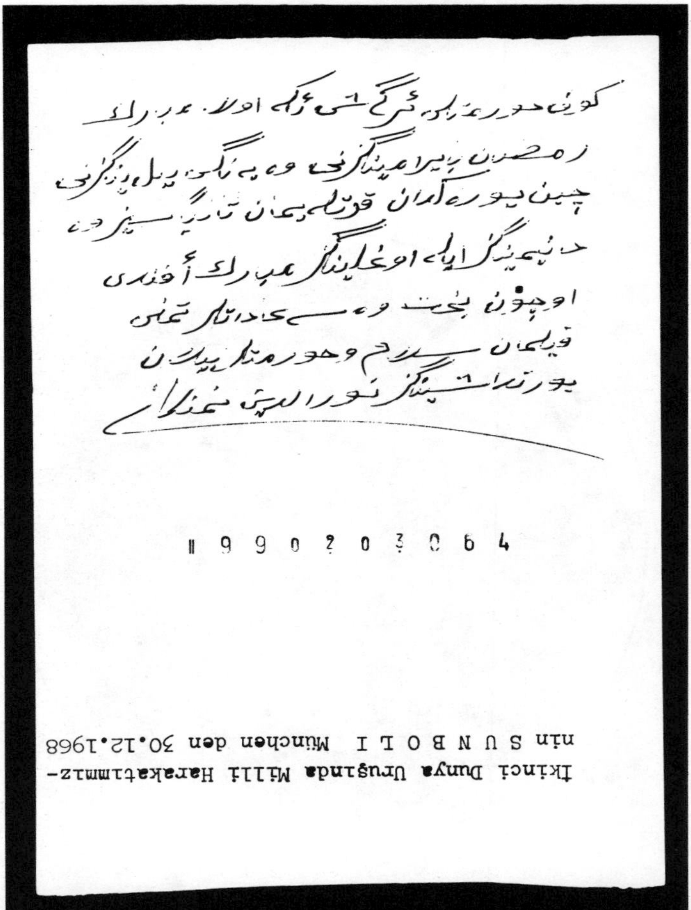

Ikinci Dunya Uruşunda Milli Harakatimiz-
nin S U N B O L I München den 30.12.1968

Note written by Nuriddin Qari, mullah in the Eastern Legions

Isakjan "Jay" Narzikul at a reception for German Chancellor Helmut Schmidt near Philadelphia

Isakjan "Jay" Narzikul in his business office near Philadelphia during the 1980's

PLACES IN EUROPE VISITED BY NARZIKUL

RUSSIA

Astrakham
Moscow
Rostov
Stavropol
Yashkul

UKRAINE

Kiev
Glukhov

Zhitomir

POLAND

Wasaw
Zelonka
Zakopane

LATVIA

Riga

GREECE

Solonika

GERMANY (WWII)

Alsace Lorraine
Berlin
Bremerhaven
Ebenrod
Lukenwald
Munich
Rosenheim

CZECHOSLOVAKIA
(Now Czech Rep.& Slovakia)

Bratislava
Dlona Zdana
Hlinik
Horna Zdana
Klak
Komarno
Myjava
Prague
Priechod

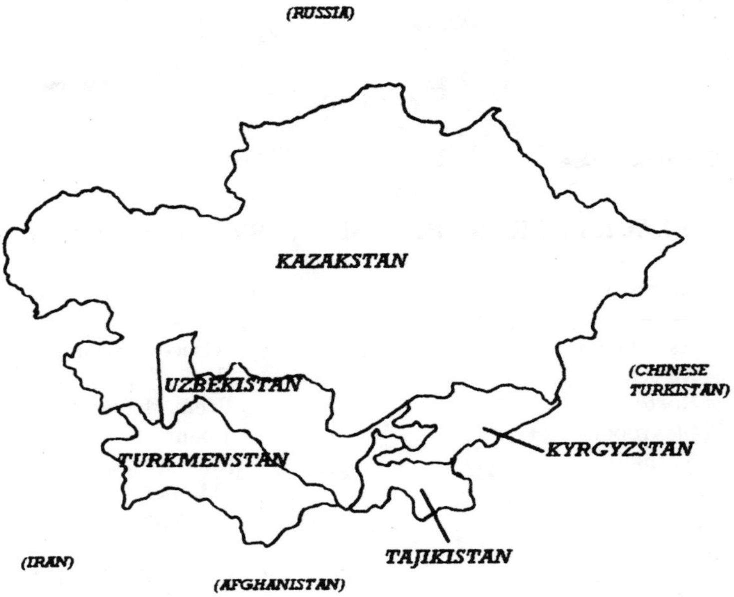

SOVIET TURKISTAN

PART III

CZECHOSLOVAK PROMISES

We, the Czechoslovak National Council....do hereby make and declare this our Declaration of Independence. We do this because of our belief that no people should be forced to live under a sovereignty they do not recognize....

The Czechoslovak State shall be a republic. In constant endeavor for progress it will guarantee complete freedom of conscience, religion and science, literature and art, speech, the press and the right of assembly and petition....The rights of the minority shall be safeguarded by proportional representation; national minorities shall enjoy equal rights.

---The Czechoslovak Declaration of Independence, October 28, 1918.

CHAPTER 15

PARTISAN ACTIVITY

The Great Patriotic War of the Soviet Union (1941-1945) ended in complete victory over fascist Germany. In September 1945, the Soviet Army routed Japan's main land forces and this brought to an end World War II which had taken a heavy toll of human lives and sufferings.

---- Soviet version of the conclusion to World War II given by the Uzbek Society for Friendship and Cultural Relations with Foreign Countries. [1]

Bedraggled men who somehow had escaped the German dragnet filtered into various mountain crevices to assemble. Isakjan found himself with about fifty men, one of whom claimed he had seen Alimov alive. The estimate of the dead approached five hundred -- half the battalion. The survivors formed into little huddles, reassessing their rapid fall from elite and rich German troops to hunted fugitives. Almost to a man, they still would have preferred to take their chances with the Nazi side rather than join the Soviet partisans, but did not expect to get that choice.

The campfires crackled a weak challenge to the frigid night air, and the men discussed the unexpected employment with their old Red Army boss. More urgently, they tried to satisfy their stomachs with snow and their frozen hands with fire. The black SS uniforms did not make the best winter garments. Patches from those uniforms fell into the flames; all the German insignias, including "Allah Biz Bilen," were torn from their shoulders and their minds to be consumed by the lively blaze. No one mentioned the liberation. They prayed to see another day.

The remnants of the battalion never came together again, not by messenger or happenstance. Back at the place of ambush, Alimov's company counted the dead they could find and those presumed so. One of the searchers discovered Isakjan's blue leather jacket. That evidence guaranteed his place in the presumed dead category for the second time in the Soviet army and the coat passed on to another whose cold body needed cover.

Not far away, over a few hills, the presumed-dead Isakjan gathered his ragged band of men into a reformed company. He had evaluated life as a partisan, and it did not suit him. Recalling the partisans he had hunted who were now his allies, he instinctively recoiled from a dislike of crawling out from woods and sneaking into battle, much preferring the direct confrontations of armies.

He thought about the lies of the Russians and the failure of the Germans; the alleged noble spirit of the communist man and the liberation promises of the Nazis. He had served both with strict obedience. Each regime had discovered him when he had been in a state of despair and degeneration, then offered him food, faith and ultimately the hope of war: that battles could rectify the suppression he felt. Neither government could fulfill its prophecies of victory. With the greatest reluctance, his circumstances forced him to cast aside the grand causes of marching militia for the simpler purposes still remaining after armies disintegrate. He had to realize that governments reduce ideals to promises, and the final responsibility for his future lay within himself.

He gave orders with straightforward recognition of their condition, without the blessings of a mullah.

"We will not cut wires, attack railroads, blow up supplies, use guerrilla warfare, disrupt the Germans. With some luck, we will stay alive. That is our goal, only to stay alive, a not so easy task. We will wander the hills until we can find a safe way to lay down our arms and end the war."

But he wanted to retain some discipline to prevent banditry, so he added, "With the grace of Allah we will survive this and join our countrymen in Turkistan, now that we are on the side of victory. However, I will continue to enforce strict military rule. Every man under my command will remain courteous to villagers, not grab or abuse the women, or threaten any civilian. The punishment I give for disobeying this order will be terrible."

They did not contemplate an early reunion with either Turkistan or even their battalion. What they did was meander through the immense forests of the area, spreading scouts out for miles in advance. They observed groups of houses, even villages, watching for signs of soldiers of any uniform, looking for solitude. After sensing that a village was safe, Isakjan would go himself or send a few men into the town to seek the mayor and ask for supplies.

They had no requisition money to pay, but deemed their supposed partisan activity, work to keep citizens out of the war, as sufficient credit. Many bands of partisans used this technique, and a mayor, with little alternatives, usually cooperated. The villages seemed so remote that it was hard to imagine any difference for them no matter who governed the country. Any townspeople not inclined to aid the raiding party needed only to see the guns of the armed men to convince themselves of their duty.

The band grew more tribal, dressed in outrageous combinations of various outfits collected along the way, discarding the German clothes when possible, and picking up warmer belongings. Perhaps a thousand years had passed since exotic warriors from Central Asia roved the mountains along the Vah River. Only the tongue of Isakjan, explaining in Slovak that they came from a remote part of the Soviet Union to fight for their liberation, convinced many villagers that the corps planned no harm or pilferage. He insisted that his men always ask for the head of each town and respectfully request supplies.

After a mayor gave whatever the town could, a few sacks

of flour and a cow or two, the men returned to the forest, cooking on open fires, always on the move, always alert for attack, never staying long, glad every once in a while to spend some time within a town's limits. The unit owned a small supply of horses that gradually dwindled, ending up one at a time in the soup pot.

Isakjan restructured their sentry strategy, ordering his three sergeants to rotate night guards constantly to avoid a duplication of their first disaster. He told them that their first assignment was to save lives, avoid heroics, preserve themselves until a course of direction unfolded.

He took a turn through the winter snow on one of the horses, traveling at night on its back, meandering from one town to the other. The villages nestled in the mountains, separated by five to ten miles of deep drifts and brutal weather. He worried about pursuing armies and leaving tracks in the snow, so they hid at high elevations, looking down on roads. The type of town considered for a few nights' stay afforded a view of all approaches. The desperate situation and the cold nights brought the band close together, as they worried more about each other than careers and possessions.

They reached one town where the mayor realized his defenseless position and invited them to spend the night. As the contingent of the Eastern Liberation Army arrived, the people gazed in wonder. Men like those came out of history books and legends, plundering and pillaging, but now they graciously accepted a cow and flour. A few of the men had Polish money and gold coins, and they asked for trade, seeking personal goods, extra food, clothes or coats. An uneasy peace prevailed, and the men settled down in barns and an empty house for the night.

The morning woke them with sunlight and gunfire. The Germans had circumvented the sentries. Isakjan looked out to see the cook who had lived in his hometown of Jizzakh and was gathering wood for a breakfast fire, suddenly cut down by a German machine gun. Scattered fire raked the houses and barns, instantly killing anyone visible. The noise was less than before, and less than a normal hunting contingent would muster. Isakjan concluded they were ambushed by a German splinter patrol. The attackers did not know how many Wehrmacht-turned-partisans they had surrounded, so Isakjan sent two men to drag the cook's body back to the house, and he ordered return cross-fire, which opened from the Turkistani guards in trees and defensive positions in the buildings.

The Germans dispersed, but the victory made no difference to the cook. The wounded man died as the company prepared to evacuate the village. The shaken men prepared a rapid burial according to Moslem law, by digging a trench and then undercutting it to form a shelf with an undisturbed ceiling for the corpse. The body was washed, covered with white cloth and laid to rest. Isakjan supervised the disbursement of his belongings. Hidden in various folds of the garments, thick fistfuls of American hundred dollar bills and numerous gold coins rolled out. The company split these among themselves, and then hastened from the scene, leaving another Asian grave in European soil.

Once again they had underestimated the Germans, who could find them much more readily than could their Soviet allies. From this they learned to send out the scouts in an even wider circle to avoid a confrontation. The scouts engaged any patrols with quick rifle shots at a distance safe enough that the opening volleys served as warning to the main party, which made successful escapes. The company stayed in isolated mountain areas to avoid confrontation.

In times of danger and stress, men learn many strange skills. Isakjan thought it could never be done, but he learned to sleep at night on the back of a horse, holding the neck, ignoring his freezing feet and hands, dreaming of a warm fire while branches of trees flailed his iced face. The winter snow, which had declared its allegiance to the Soviet cause, declined to make an adjustment for those former German allies. It drifted high and blew fiercely, only allowing the slowest progress. When the band of men settled down for a rest, they crossed branches of evergreens on the snow and went to sleep between blankets of green needles and cold fluff. He was reduced to eating what had become a white enemy, scooping it into a body already racked with hypothermia.

By March 1944, their status edged lower. Still cold and hungry, they found the roads and towns more dangerous. Germans from the East retreated rapidly, and those from the West still hunted them down. They slipped into a town only at night, or stole lodging in an isolated barn.

They disintegrated into renegades, running from everything and afraid of their own misty breath, trying to save their miserable lives with no friends to help, and no shelter. Occasional forays late at night into towns to collect the partisan's debt of food amounted to little more than expropriations, and contributed only irregular stock for the soup.

From the high peaks and hidden corners, they watched growing numbers of retreating trucks filled with German troops on the highways below. The partisan fervor never seized them, and they felt no desire to challenge the withdrawing army, defeated but not docile. They wanted only to disappear.

Instead they prowled the mountains between the Nitra and Hron Rivers, skirting the numerous little villages with their strange isolation from the events of the world. As they initiated a stay for a few nights in one town, scouts departed through the forests to the neighboring towns, both to seek room and board for a future night and to assess the German troop activity in the area. They brought the world and the war to these people of Priechod, Dolna' Zdana and Svaty Kriz. They traded smiles, threats, and promises for food and berth. Some towns became regular stop-overs, and the inhabitants, aware that the Russian empire would shortly win the war, cooperated. In the middle of winter, the company requisitioned a small house, sending the occupants to live with neighbors for a few days. Lookouts searched the surrounding area.

One scouting mission brought a sergeant and three men to the town of Horna' Zdana, where past visits taught them the village layout and the homes most likely to contribute. The officer pointed out houses for each man to solicit and picked one for himself, ignoring the standing orders to report to the mayor of the town. The sergeant walked through the yard of his designated house to the barn in the rear, opening the latch and walking in unannounced.

A girl was raking straw at the end of a short row of stables with short strokes, concentrating on her work. She didn't look up, as she could not hear the door. She was deaf. In any case, she would not have greeted him with other than a smile because she was also mute. The sergeant knew this, and had selected the house for that very reason. He closed the door behind him and rushed towards her, unbuttoning his pants as he charged.

She fought with surprising vigor, and he beat her against the barn siding. Her attempts at screams caused her to gag. He ripped the clothes from her back and breasts.

The scuffle caught the attention of family members outside, and as the sergeant tried to finish his business, they entered the barn. Between their shock and his alertness, he forced his way past them and into the street. He brought no food from that house.

The following day, the mayor of Horna Zdana requested an audience with the partisan captain.

"Bring him in," ordered Isakjan. The mayor walked into the parlor of the home Isakjan had "requisitioned" for a few nights, where a convenient table combined with a couple of chairs to serve as an office.

"Captain, we will continue to comply with your requisition

orders for supplies and lodging, as we wish to celebrate your victory over the Nazis soon," spoke the man. "However, we would like you to help us also. Certain matters come to mind."

The mayor chose his words carefully, not wishing to offend the captain, watching his reaction to each sentence.

"You know that we supply you with food and shelter."

"Yes, yes." agreed Isakjan, perfectly willing to dispense with the formalities and get on with the favor this man obviously wanted. The mayor hesitated, and then proceeded with this most unpleasant task which he, as mayor, was compelled to complete.

"Last night an incident occurred with your scouts. They came to our village to get food and we were glad to give it to them. They attempted to rape one of our citizens."

The mayor stopped for a breath. He could see Isakjan's eyes widening and anger rising which gave the mayor courage to add details. "One soldier attacked a woman, who couldn't scream or call for help. She is a deaf mute. Fortunately some men heard a scuffle and came to her rescue. This is very bad for both you and us."

Isakjan pushed the table from in front of his seated position and leaped out of his chair, ready to punish the culprit immediately. He fumed. Even as wandering misfits, his troops were not going to rape and plunder. He addressed the mayor with fervor.

"Sir, you can rest assured that the man responsible will be punished. We are not like other partisans. My men know how to behave. I will do absolutely everything in my power to guarantee that nothing like this will ever happen again."

The mayor took his leave. Isakjan summoned the suspect soldiers into the house. They lined up sheepishly in front of him. He wasted no time, calling them to attention with angry roars.

"Give me a report of your activities yesterday," he demanded.

They fumbled over themselves, each agreeing that they scouted the town, picked up supplies and returned.

"No, no," Isakjan insisted, with great agitation. "The truth." His normal nervous pace in times of action grew into a frenzied walk. He pointed to one of the privates.

"You, stay here. The rest of you, out!"

Once the room had cleared, he continued, "The truth, that's all I want to hear," he screamed at the man. "If I don't get the truth you will be punished severely, with no mercy."

Each private broke down and related what he knew of the

rape.

Confronted with the evidence, the sergeant admitted his crime. He fell to his knees and begged, "Captain, I made a mistake. I lost my mind. Please forgive me."

Isakjan breathed fire.

The man cried, "I will never do this again. Please forgive me."

"You will dig your grave. I want nothing more to do with you." Isakjan assigned two men to accompany the sergeant under machine gun guard to a field.

A few hours later, he received word that the ditch was completed, and called all troops except for the sentries to witness. His assistant then called the men to attention. The guilty sergeant knelt on his knees in front of the hole, sobbing quietly. Isakjan stood several yards away, in line with the guards with their machine guns cocked and ready.

"According to military rule." he addressed the assembled, "This man has committed a grave crime. We are guests in this country and want to show an example of how Turkistanis treat their friends. His actions hurt the local people who give us food, and gave a bad name to our troops. For your punishment, I sentence you to death by a firing squad."

The crowd froze in silence, afraid as though they each had performed the crime. Isakjan continued, confronting the sergeant, "Now, tell me and your fellow soldiers, what we should tell your mother and father when we go home after the war, when we are victoriously marching back with our Soviet allies and you are missing. What should we tell them when they ask what has happened to their son?

"Should we tell them that you tried to rape a girl who couldn't talk or hear? Should we tell them how you disgraced our country? What do you want us to do?"

The sergeant fell on the ground and broke into wails and moans, groveling in the snow, begging for mercy and for his life, promising to become a good soldier and do justice to his fellow soldiers.

Isakjan turned on his heel and walked to the side of the formation. "Take aim," he commanded the guards, who raised their machine guns.

The man begged again. "Please give me one chance, on behalf of my mother and Allah, to make good. I will not fail you."

Isakjan looked disgustedly at him for several long silent minutes. He held up a hand as though he needed to quiet the formation. "In consideration of your mother and father, who wait for you in our country, and for your fellow troops, who would like you to improve your deeds, I have reconsidered. You have a second chance."

Isakjan turned and departed. His lieutenant dismissed the troops.

Late in March, they commandeered a few houses near the town of Klak, immediately surveying the greater area for future stops. The erratic wandering of the forward patrol happened to place them outside an ideal small town: concealed, back to the hills, an open view of the valley and road below. The scouts canvassed the road, able to see for over five miles. They watched the road for the better part of the day, waiting until after nightfall to enter what became their next town, Dolna Zdana.

Isakjan decided to approach the town himself with a couple of men. That afternoon, he shaved carefully and arranged his attire in the neatest possible manner. Then he inspected the two men selected to accompany him, anxious about possible reaction among the villagers regarding the rape. He wanted to live in harmony with the people who, if aroused, could make his survival a much more difficult undertaking.

He and two assistants knocked on the door of the outermost house in the village of Dolna Zdana. A light shone through the window. Rifles in hand, thickened snow on their coats and stiff in military bearing, the men breathed violence and panic into the night air. He spoke Slovak.

"We are partisans. Can you please let us in?" As many questions, this one was rhetorical. The woman who answered the door opened it. In walked the war.

"We will not hurt you," he assured them. "We are partisans fighting to free Slovakia. We come from far away. Our homes are on the other side of the Caspian Sea, and we need a little help. Please, would you take us to your mayor?"

Another rhetorical question. The woman called across the parlor and from a room to the left emerged a couple, and Isakjan assigned his soldiers to accompany the man and retrieve the mayor. He watched them dissolve into the night, and then looked around the small house, typical of many in the villages, with bedrooms surrounding a central parlor. He could feel the warmth on his face from the wood stove, but knew that much time would pass before the heat would soothe his bones. He stood uneasily in the house, so untouched by the chaos outside. Indeed, the whole village seemed peaceful and unaware of the horror that stalked the land.

A careful gaze at Captain Narzikul showed a man living in primitive conditions, but recently groomed. His rifle hung from his shoulder, far enough away from his hands to give an impression of power, but not immediate menace. He held his hat humbly, did not move from the entry area, and spoke gently in a most pleasant voice. The terror of a man at the door with a gun melted.

The woman, for her part, moved gracefully, a product of careful upbringing, with piano lessons and education not available in such a small town. She had traveled to the cities of Czechoslovakia, Austria and Germany.

"Do you speak German?" she asked in Slovak.

"What a strange question to ask a Soviet partisan," he countered, and then answered in German, "Yes, I do."

The lady smiled, convinced she had found a friend. "Some tea?"

She offered him a chair and went to boil water. He stood very still, shocked by what seemed to him outrageous behavior for a woman facing a stranger with a gun.

"She must be from one of the families who sympathized with the partisans," thought Isakjan. It was so hard to tell. Some favored the Germans, and others the partisans, but most preferred to avoid the war altogether. The tea brought a glow through his body, and soothed his cold hands when he wrapped them around the cup.

The lady continued her smile. "We have never seen partisans so close, you know, but have heard so much about them."

The noise in the living room caused a stir from another room in the house. From the right side of the living room came three beautiful teenage girls in long nightgowns. Months of subjection to bullets and attacks by blizzards had repressed his memories of kind people and loving homes. Only people not inured to war, those still living in a civilized state, would permit three lovely girls to greet a wild trooper of the night. The family was so delicate and innocent, so exposed to a fateful visit of renegades. He had forgotten that most people live very well without grand causes, mass movements and the might of armies.

Isakjan sipped his tea and sat down on a comfortable sofa.

"It has been a while since I could talk to someone familiar with culture and education," the mother confided. "The last year has been one of terrible times. I even had to suspend piano lessons for my daughters."

The woman showed such a lack of discretion, or was it the courage of conviction? She determined that the young man in front of her, despite his rough clothes, rifle and Central Asian features, deserved respect as an equal.

Isakjan looked again at the girls. Moments ago he felt crusty and old. Suddenly he became a young man once more.

"These are my daughters," she laughed. "Which do you think is the prettiest?"

He relaxed for a moment, no longer the hunted stranger, but the neighbor dropping in for gossip.

"This is Eva, Elena, and Mayna," she introduced her daughters. "Which do you like the best?"

All of a sudden, his relaxation turned to arousal. He felt elevated to a plane of eligibility and respectability. He focused on the girls. Lovely. A German touch gave them light hair and blue eyes. Eva, the oldest, just about his age back when the Soviet Army catapulted him into a world without values or gravity, rekindled a spirit that had shriveled within him.

"Eva." He didn't realize that he answered the question.

The mother kept the interchange going. "Have you fought the Germans?"

"Yes, but now we avoid them. They are defeated."

The mother agreed, but could not say anything negative about the losing side.

"We do not live here, but are visiting because our house is right near the road of retreat. We could see them leaving through the woods. Where are you staying?"

"Right now in Klak," he spoke like a tourist on a trip. "But we are on the move all the time."

The men returned with the mayor. Isakjan warmly shook his hand and praised his village.

"Your hospitality is much appreciated by all the partisans under my command, and when we win the war, your help will not be forgotten. Please spare us a cow, flour and tea."

"We can do that. We wish to cooperate," pledged the mayor. He went back out into the night with the soldiers and Isakjan remained, transfixed by the hostesses, who wanted to hear about the war and the dark stranger who commanded partisans.

The girls, shy at first, followed the mother's lead and wanted to learn all about the band of soldiers and how they fought.

"You are the first partisan we have had in our house," confessed Eva. "And certainly the first from so far away. Tell us about your home."

"You probably never heard of it, a town called Jizzakh not too far from India in the part of the Soviet Union they call Turkistan."

"That sounds like an exciting place," she said, referring more to the man than the place.

Isakjan began to enjoy the visit. He felt no rush to leave and forgot about the outside, someplace where the mayor, the owner of the house, and his men rounded up supplies.

"Have you girls ever seen a partisan squad?" he joked and the three sisters giggled.

Eva spoke, "No, no, we stay far from everything."

As the visit extended to a couple of hours, he kiddingly asked, "Then, would you like to come with me to visit and meet some partisans? If you do, get dressed."

To his amazement, she agreed, and slipped back into the room to gather warm clothes as the mother nodded approval. The father seemed not to be present.

A knock at the door by his soldiers, supplies in hand, ended the visit. Isakjan and Eva exited the house.

"Are you crazy?" his assistant asked Isakjan.

"I want to go," answered Eva, a girl with spunk.

They went to the house near Klak where they intended to spend another night or two, depending on reports from scouts. They shared a dinner of gruel with the adventuresome girl and put her up in a separate room.

In the morning, a scout ran back to the house with a breathless report for the commander. A lone person approached the town with a gun, maybe a madman.

Frank Fridrich was no madman, but a mad father. "I want my daughter!" he demanded.

The tough renegades stared at the preposterous demand. Men accustomed to killing, men with death at their door do not have to listen to fathers. The family and village did not understand their precarious situation. A slight misunderstanding and Frank Fridrich could lie bleeding on the ground. Isakjan opened the door to the father, who marched over to his daughter, face red with anger. "Never leave the house without my permission, Eva. This is wartime, and you are young. You will be punished for this." The father yelled, oblivious to the partisans as he scolded his daughter and escorted her home.

CHAPTER 16

WHILE ISAKJAN DANCED

All Soviet citizens liberated by the forces operating under United States command and all United States citizens liberated by the forces operating under Soviet command will, without delay after their liberation, be separated from enemy prisoners of war and will be maintained separately from them in camps or points of concentration until they have been handed over to the Soviet or United States authorities, as the case may be, at places agreed upon between those authorities.

-- Article 1, Agreement Between the United States and the Soviet Union Concerning Liberated Prisoners of War and Civilians, signed at Yalta, February 1945. [1]

Three days later, Isakjan knocked at the door of the same house in Dolna' Zdana, escorted by two of his soldiers. Mrs. Fridrich opened the door and burst into a wide grin upon recognizing her visitor. She had expected him.

"Come in. Come in," she beckoned, and then called out to the rear of the house. "Eva, our partisan has come to visit."

As tea brewed, the guards rotated sentry duty outside, and the women prepared for a bit of entertainment from their champion partisan, the cultured dark foreigner from the exotic East. Isakjan sat on a soft chair, opposite Eva on the sofa.

"What is it like in your country of Turkistan?" she asked.

By the time Frank Fridrich came home from work, dinner for extra guests simmered in the kitchen. The master of the house forced out a reluctant and gruff "hello." He swallowed his meal in absorbed silence and announced that he had work to attend to and would come back later.

The women paid him little heed. After dinner, they turned on the record player. "Do you dance?" asked Mrs. Fridrich.

"I learned with a broomstick," he remembered.

Isakjan and the Fridrich ladies danced into the evening. He planned to return often.

Through April and into May, the Germans were preoccupied with leaving Slovakia, and had no time to pursue their complaints with the Turkistani battalion, or what was left of it. They stayed on the roads leading directly back to Germany, and the General Chapajev partisans hugged the roads and towns leading in circles about the mountains.

Isakjan let down his guard, and stayed longer in occupied areas. He learned the paths and roads, and which ones led back to the Fridrich house.

Frank Fridrich owned the lumber mill in Hlinik, only a few miles from the house where Isakjan had met the family. Frank bought trees from woodsmen and loggers and reduced them to lumber. With the Germans in formal retreat, the girls moved back to their house in Hlinik, and Isakjan made it a habit to enjoy their company. His men worried no longer about attacks, and villagers openly helped them, not wishing to be interpreted as parsimonious by the victors.

His visits with the Fridrichs rapidly grew longer, and in April he remained in their house for two and a half weeks. He spent much of the time exploring the area on walks with Eva, but remembered the angry father, and tactfully submerged any ideas of courting the lovely girl. A town boy already claimed that honor.

The father began to calm down as visits became more frequent and his wife and daughters remained uncorrupted by the ruffian partisan. Frank usually departed when Isakjan arrived, disappearing without conversation until late at night. Finally, after months, he stayed for after-supper dialogue one day.

"Where did you say you were from?" he asked.

"Almost on the other side of the world, a place called Turkistan," Isakjan answered. The two men spoke in German, as Isakjan related his odyssey.

"Well, you do speak German well for someone so far away. Have you ever been to Berlin?"

"Yes, many times."

"Well, my family is German, and I always liked the German way of doing business." Frank spoke very kindly to the partisan who claimed to be the enemy of Germany. "Tell me, how did you happen to visit Berlin?"

Isakjan swallowed hard, realizing that Frank had displayed a great amount of trust in espousing a love of Germany. He decided to return the confidence.

"I was a captain in the German army."

"Well," mused Frank. "I didn't give you enough credit. Eva tells me you enjoy the theater." All of a sudden, Frank approved of his daughter seeing this partisan.

"Yes, very much so."

"Well, what about hunting? I have a little lodge and invite friends once in awhile. Do you think you might like to join me next week?" Frank gave Isakjan a small opening, a chance to show his worth, which was all he ever needed.

One morning, he sat on a log at the mill when helpers came to work buzzing with news: "The Red Army advanced past our town yesterday. We are now behind Soviet lines."

Isakjan went to Frank, explaining to him, "I must get back to my troops."

Frank's position in the town and his liking for Isakjan

became apparent. "Let me help you. I can borrow a motorcycle for you to use."

Isakjan drove the motorcycle to the last village of bivouac, Sklene Teplice, and hailed the first person on the street.

"Have you seen the Chapajev partisans?"

The man obligingly answered. "They went a week ago to the another town, Svaty Kriz."

Luckily Isakjan had the use of a motorcycle. He repeated the same question at the second town.

"Have you seen the Chapajev partisans?"

"The Red Army came, disarmed all the partisans and put them into trucks under guard. We don't know where they went."

Isakjan grew alarmed, remembering Alimov's pledge that no soldiers accompanying him would be arrested, and had guaranteed immunity. He scoffed at the promise, exposed as another opportunistic lie. Some Red Army soldiers patrolled the town. He had seen so many Soviets killed that it was difficult to imagine so many more, but there they were, with enough men to patrol even small villages. He drove to the town where a Red Army command post was established.

"I am Captain Isakjan Narzikul, of the Chapajev partisans. Can you tell me where the partisans went?"

"Someplace in Poland," the Soviet officer answered.

Isakjan continued, asking another Russian, an officer, "What about Commander Alimov? Where is he?"

"We sent Alimov and the officers to a place across the border in Poland, very close, near Zakopane. Go outside of Zakopane to Osak, where the headquarters of the Third Army is stationed. Marshal Konev commands it. Someone will help you there."

He revved up the motorcycle and drove back to the Fridrichs' house.

"My troops, I must go to find my troops."

Finding his men became an obsession, a link to all that represented his life in the recent years, a group to associate with. He felt responsible that they were arrested and tried to think of what he could do to help them. Frank took a more practical approach. He, and his father before him, ethnic Germans, managed to survive waves of pro-German and anti-German sentiment.

"Stay with us and forget the army. The war is over, and there is plenty to keep the Soviets busy. Let them forget you, while you make a new life with us," he counseled.

Isakjan could not believe that Frank meant what he said.

His wife must have put him up to the offer, thought Isakjan, for what did he, a nomad soldier, have to give in return?

"I cannot hide. At least I want to get some information, whether they are looking for me. The Red Army will win the war and I have to live with that. Some consideration might be given if I contributed to the end of the war."

"I disagree, but take the motorcycle if you have made up your mind."

Isakjan did not trust his own words, and wanted Frank to debate him into a corner, where he would be forced to stay. Frank did not. He must be ambivalent about the offer, concluded Isakjan. At that time, Isakjan could not conceive of a generous offer to himself, unless it came with his own pledge to join a momentous cause and meld his personality into its goals.

Isakjan hugged the family, one at a time, and mounted the motorcycle.

"I still have time to run if I need to," he reasoned, and drove off on a seventy-mile journey to Zakopane.

The Soviets knew how to demonstrate control of land. About thirty miles, from Hlinik, their soldiers manned a checkpoint in a small town.

"Dismount." Back to the Russian language, a jolt after so many years. The soldier performed his function with no regard to the rider. Isakjan obeyed while other soldiers held the motorcycle.

"Let me see your papers," he demanded.

Papers, more items of control. Papers paved his way to prestige in Jizzakh and Germany and he could see they would now create his downfall.

He answered the command, "I have no papers, sir. I was with the partisans. I am a Soviet citizen, an Uzbek. The Germans captured me and sent me to a labor camp, but I escaped and joined the partisans. The partisans had no time to issue papers. I am going for a meeting with the army."

The soldier conferred with his mates on duty.

"Go, get out of here," he yelled.

"And my motorcycle?"

The soldiers were wheeling it away. His questioner grew mad.

"I told you to leave. Do you want to be arrested?"

He hitched rides with farmers, and after a couple of days, he arrived at the town of Osak, where the number of Soviet soldiers exceeded the number of civilians. Obtaining directions to headquarters proved no challenge.

He walked to the center of town where the army established its offices. Asking about, he was astonished to find two Turkistani officers, both of whom he recognized, and one he knew well.

"Sattarov. Sattarov. I don't believe it's you."

Somehow the medical officer from the first battalion had survived the transition and ended up with a responsible job. Isakjan was excited to see someone who could be trusted, and the two embraced and kissed on the cheek. Perhaps he was wrong to doubt. The Soviets might be capable of forgiveness.

"Sattarov, where are the others? What is happening?"

Sattarov returned a grim face. The man he had saved from the Gestapo knew about these matters. He stood up from his desk and asked the other officer to leave the room for a few minutes, walking alongside the departing man and thanking him for the privacy. Sattarov closed the door and sat on his desk, very near Isakjan. He spoke in a hushed voice.

"Jail," he replied with a vertical motion of his hands signifying bars.

Isakjan reeled back. "Jail? and Alimov? Surely Alimov, with his Russian girlfriend and his delivery of an entire battalion, is in good stead."

Isakjan's tension mounted. He regarded Alimov as a test for his own situation. Sattarov never changed his expression.

"Jail also." He seemed apologetic. "I'm sorry."

Stunned, all of a sudden vulnerable and threatened, Isakjan could not bring himself to face the repercussions.

"Who would do that?"

Sattarov knew. "SMERSH, military counterintelligence."

Isakjan had much to learn. "I never heard of SMERSH."

"SMERSH means death to spies, and is made from the elite of the KGB and others."

Isakjan repeated the words, "death to our enemies." He was one of those enemies for whom death waited. Sattarov pressed him.

"Why did you come? Are you crazy?"

He produced the weakest of answers. "Everyone told me to come here with the other officers."

Something did not make sense. Sattarov sat in a desk of authority. Alimov wasted in jail.

"Why are you here?" he asked Sattarov.

Sattarov did not tell him the truth, that he was a KGB agent himself and had reported during the war. Now his job was to breathe the cold winds of revenge upon the enemies of the Soviet Union. But Sattarov placed value on the service Isakjan had performed, saving him from a Jewish fate in Germany. He answered Isakjan, in a friendly manner. "For you, there is no problem," he explained. "I have told the truth to the authorities and mentioned your name with the highest of praise. Everything will work out fine. You have nothing to fear. Just tell the truth."

Isakjan knew that, if a Soviet agent, Sattarov would not disclose his identity, and he sensed a power from Sattarov never apparent in the German Army. Here stood a man who obviously played a more sophisticated game than Isakjan could imagine, but the man would not harm someone who had saved his life. If Isakjan judged the man correctly, he could rely on the promise that no harm would come at this time. But what about the next time, when Sattarov could not come to his aid. That question struck new fears.

"Tell the truth, and that will save you. You are a valuable man, one we all admire. Just tell the truth," Sattarov repeated. "They will ask your life story, so prepare yourself with the details. Then the next day you must tell it again, so think about it and don't change what you say the second time."

Sattarov then motioned Isakjan very close to him, and, whispering in his ear, continued. "Say that you always wanted to rejoin your comrades and that you planned with many, including me, to come back to the Soviet Union as soon as you could."

Isakjan immediately thought of his future and not his past. He didn't like the shuffling that Sattarov and Alimov accomplished, bouncing back and forth between loyalties.

"Maybe I should disappear," he suggested.

Sattarov countered. "No, now you are in the system. You have nothing to fear, though, since I have given a recommendation. I will arrange for a barracks you can stay in while you are interviewed. The others are locked up, but you can have a standard military bunk."

Sattarov kept his promise and supplied a barrack bunk, not a jail cell. A captain interviewed him the next day. .

"Tell me all about your life," the captain started.

Isakjan recalled his days in Jizzakh, his training by the Red Army, his capture. He admitted to fighting for the Germans, but said he and the others had been starving, and would have been shot if they had not fought. Naturally they had not wanted to fight against the motherland, but had been forced, and had come back the first time an opportunity presented itself.

As the words piled out of his mouth, Isakjan held back

disgust for his own story. He knew that an officer should never take arms against a country he loved and suspected that the interrogator believed the same. Once he stood ready to sacrifice his life for the Soviets, and had killed for their cause. Now he wanted to risk his life for their defeat.

The following day he faced the same captain.

"Today, we will repeat your interview. I have studied what you told me and suspect a few discrepancies. Tell me all about your life, in a little more detail, but this time with the truth." The captain stretched out his notes. Isakjan had prepared, and added a few anecdotes, but did not deviate from his previous statement.

The next day he received orders and traveling papers to report for duty with a Red Army division in Western Poland about to enter Germany. He took the papers and thanked Sattarov very much. Sattarov had delivered, but even he could not erase the past, or the thousands who had read about him in the Liberation Front newspaper and had served under him in the many campaigns. His past lay open, like rich loamy soil, for continual harvest by a vengeful bureaucracy.

He reported back to Sattarov, showing him the military orders and thanking him. He worried about the others.

"What will happen to Alimov and the officers?" he asked.

"They will pay. There will be punishment."

Sattarov knew more about the impending punishment. He knew much more than he would ever tell.

Isakjan realized the limits of protection; that others more powerful could override a well-meaning offer, and that perhaps a time might come when Sattarov might need to use the Narzikul information for his own purposes. In addition, Isakjan could never hide in the USSR. Somehow the secret would out.

Isakjan saluted Sattarov and walked to the outskirts of Osak, where the clusters of houses opened up to farmland.

At the time of Isakjan's encounter with Sattarov, the United States and England had launched an aggressive campaign to return Soviet citizens who had fought for Germany back to Soviet jurisdiction per an agreement finalized by the allies at Yalta. At no other time in history did powers such as the English-speaking nations carry out the desires of a vindictive third power, namely the request of the USSR to take custody of its ex-soldiers, extending efforts well beyond those required by the treaty to include forceful repatriation.

Liberation troops from many countries under Soviet

domination, hoping to ally themselves with the Western armies, struggled to capitulate to United States forces. Those that surrendered to the Red Army faced firing squads or worse. Many of these men found themselves forced to surrender to the Soviets, who then occupied vast stretches of Eastern Europe. The Red Army had accomplished this occupation with their own vast army, with American aid, with industrial capacity developed before and during the war, and with conscripted labor.

Having helped build the Soviet war machine, the United States watched while the Soviets pushed the Germans out of the USSR and then replaced Nazi occupation with Soviet occupation in Rumania, Bulgaria, great parts of Hungary, Yugoslavia, Poland and Czechoslovakia before the big three conference at Yalta began. At the same time, former Soviet Army personnel who had fought with Germany found no respite in the American zones.

American and British soldiers forced at gunpoint Turkistanis, Cossacks, Ukrainians, Baltic and Ruthenian soldiers into trains which rumbled eastward to Russian agony and death. Thousands slit their wrists or hanged themselves during the passage. The western Allies searched hospitals and scattered groups throughout Europe, even in France, for the helpless volunteers, and turned them over to the Soviets. They continued this policy even years after VE day with very few exceptions. [2]

Various precautions were taken in returning Soviet nationals to Russia, as an excerpt from a United States Army order shows:

"As little publicity as possible will be given to their forced repatriation...

`Guards will be thoroughly oriented that these prisoners are desperate characters...

Every effort will be exerted to insure that adequate anti-suicide and escape measures are taken...

A showdown inspection will be held in which all possible weapons, knives, razors, glass, etc., are confiscated...

Train guards should be equipped with normal weapons except as follows: Rifles or carbines will be substituted for pistols...

Prisoners will be loaded as quietly as possible. Not more than one hour advance notice should be given prisoners and they will not be told where they are to go..." [3]

One of these soldiers turned over to the Russians was the famous General Vlasov. After the secret trial of him and his assistants, and torture of the group too gruesome for witnesses to tell, they were hanged from a gallows with piano wire and hooks through their skulls. [4] Others who were not executed joined the millions in Soviet forced labor camps, where they found people accused of crimes such as escaping from the Moscow siege and spreading rumors that rations were meager, that the Germans had excellent equipment, and that people were dying of starvation in the Leningrad blockade. Not only were those who fought for Germany guilty, but those who had lived under the German rule or among Germans were subject to imprisonment. Even those conscripted as German forced laborers were arrested. They knew too much about the outside world. [5]

The Liberation Committee itself, in an effort to surrender in an American zone, escaped Berlin in all directions. The city edged toward panic, hoping for occupation by the Americans, but listening to the details of the Red Army advance, and fearing the mass rapes and plundering officially encouraged by Moscow. Citizens stockpiled suicide rations from rat poison to cyanide, for use in the event that Berlin was to be captured from the East.

Hitler's depraved interference with the Wehrmacht aided the Soviet advance towards the city, an advance that would have to be checked in large part by youths under fifteen years of age and by retirees. American planes daily made two bombing runs over the city, and Soviet planes began to make appearances, arriving without warning and strafing the civilian streets with machine-gun fire. [6]

In preparation for a retreat from Berlin, the Turkistani broadcast director Shermat asked Isakjan's friend Jurabay to accompany a small party of Liberation Front officers. "I will follow you," Jurabay answered. Shermat, Major Hayit and President Kayum-Khan took a train to Czechoslovakia, still under German control in the border areas. The tracks were bombed between some stations, and they walked these stretches. Kayum-Khan, Hayit, Shermat and an entourage stayed in a town West of Prague where General Patton's troops occupied the streets. American tanks lined the roads with G.I.'s marching everywhere. The Turkistanis stayed in a hotel across from where the Vlasov generals were quartered. They celebrated their good fortune, expecting that the Americans would help them.

A red flag appeared above a neighboring building, which the Czech Communists requisitioned. Across the street, Soviet police entered the hotel housing Vlasov's officers and dragged them into waiting trucks. The Vlasov men screamed for help to the

American G.I.'s, who stood their distance, chewed gum and smiled at one another. They smiled when the Soviet army entered the Turkistani hotel to capture the members of the Liberation Committee, but the Committee was gone.

The only English-speaking member of the group, Mrs. Kayum-Khan, had gone to arrange a meeting with the Americans. United States officers followed her to their hiding place and arrested everyone. All possessions, including 4,000 marks were taken. The officers transported Veli Kayum-Khan to an undisclosed location.

"We protest!" they exclaimed. "We are friends of the Americans."

The military men knew only one answer, "Yalta. Yalta.

Allies searched for potential enemies of the Soviets, which included locking the remaining members of the Liberation Committee in a basement for three days. Finally, one by one, a soldier called them for interrogation. A guard led Dr. Shermat from the cellar into the office of a young American captain with the CIC, military intelligence. Shermat sat down and the captain bellowed, "Who are you?" in perfect German.

Shermat explained his position with the Liberation Committee and his activities in the broadcast department.

The captain looked angry. "So you collaborated with Hitler?" he demanded.

Shermat answered simply, "Yes."

"Then you are a Fascist," concluded the captain.

Shermat rose to incensed defense. As chief ideologue for the Turkistani National movement, he wanted to argue the simple application of that label. "If I am a Fascist, you are a Communist," he countered.

The captain moved backward, as though struck in the face. A look of surprise flashed across his face. "I am no Communist," he declared. "What do you mean by that statement?"

Shermat had waited for that question. "I gave not one mark to Hitler, and certainly no weapons. What did you and your United States do? Millions of dollars to Stalin and boatloads of weapons. You talk of collaboration. I will tell you of collaboration. America collaborated much more with Stalin than Veli Kayum-Khan did with Hitler. Furthermore, the United States had a choice, and did not have to work with Stalin. The United States was never an occupied country. Our country was occupied and subjugated by Stalin. We were caught between two devils, the Soviets and Germany. With Germany we had a chance at freedom."

The captain thought for a few minutes. He cleared his throat. "No, you are not a Fascist, and I am not a Communist. You are free to go. How can I help?"

Shermat responded, "We want to get to the West, out of Soviet jurisdiction."

"We can point you in the right direction."

The CIC officer returned the belongings of the group, including their money. He added another 6,000 marks to their cash.

Hayit, Shermat and two Turkistani soldiers marched on foot back to Germany, traveling at night and hiding in woods during daylight. As they approached Munich, they revealed themselves during the day, identifying themselves as Turkish students who were caught in Germany during the war. An army jeep drove them the last few miles to the United Nations relief agency.

They had avoided Berlin and the horrible battles there. But Jurabay stayed in Berlin and never attempted to join his friends in the committee. He remained in the house of Mrs. Rogozinski and awaited the arrival of the Red Army, for he was a spy for the Soviets and needed to report to his contact person. He did not wait long, for its troops rapidly fought through the suburbs into the city itself.

Jurabay dressed and went to greet them. He met his cell chief and was assigned to a Soviet captain, traveling with the captain on secret missions boding ill for the Turkistani legionnaires. His intelligence activity did not entirely give him a pardon or a permanent job with the Red army. After making use of his information, the Communists sent him to Siberia.

The United Nations Relief Organization put Shermat and Hayit up in a barracks, where they shared a room. Down the hall, Uzbek music spilled out of another room, and they hastened to find its source. Inside a merry group of German Jews danced and sang.

"Where are you from?" asked Shermat in Uzbek.

The music stopped for a moment. "We are Jews who escaped to Tashkent during the war," came the reply.

Two stood to the side, and upon seeing Shermat, ran to him and embraced him tightly.

"You saved our lives. We are so grateful," they fussed over the man. "You were the one who told us to tell the Germans that we were Moslem and to recite the prayer way back in the POW camp in the Ukraine."

Shermat had temporarily forgotten, and hadn't recognized their faces, but, with memory refreshed, he joined the merriment.

The next day, the Swiss consulate was kind enough to

believe their story and issue them Turkish papers. They could then walk the streets safely and not fear the many military police of the Allies who were searching papers and delivering Soviet citizens to the Red Army.

Meanwhile, leaving the Polish headquarters of the Red Third Army, Isakjan sensed the enormity of disaster. The man who had walked beside tanks into machine-gun fire did not fear death. He who had survived near-starvation and deprivation in Jizzakh, in POW camp, in Slovak blizzards did not dread a prison term. But he trembled, soaked his clothes with sweat and couldn't digest his food over the possibility that he might debase himself becoming a donkey for a Russian master. The panic first experienced when selling milk to a Russian returned ever more severe each time he encountered the Soviet political system.

His feet refused to walk in the direction of the orders he carried. The Russians once taught him how chauvinism and exploitation combine to produce poverty and discrimination. They instructed him well, in order to win his devotion, all the while transporting the cotton and gold of Jizzakh to Moscow and the trade and prayers of his father into dusty crevices. Isakjan did not want to mumble his deepest thoughts and bury the products of his trade. He cringed in fear at that prospect.

As his stride took him away from the Soviet encampment, he noticed Polish farm houses. He approached the first, and addressed the proprietor.

"Can you give me a ride to Slovakia?" he asked.

"These are not times for a man to leave his family," responded the farmer, and the second one he approached gave him no better satisfaction.

The third got curious.

"What is the pay?"

Isakjan shoved his hand deep into his pocket and brought out one of his American hundred dollar bills from the cook killed in action.

The Soviet headquarters at Osak shortly faded into the past.

"Why are you going to Slovakia?" asked the farmer. Isakjan dug his hands back down into his pocket again, and presented his komanderovka, waving it without giving the man a chance to read it.

"Orders," he answered.

A couple of days traveling brought him back to Hlinik. The town had its advantages, which he had appreciated months ago as a roaming partisan. Its isolation and the welcoming Fridrich family, so far from the Russian magnifying glass, could only help. Frank hugged him with a firm fatherly embrace, matched only by the sweetness of Eva's kiss. Neighbors happened by to show respect. He showed the Fridrichs his papers.

"I am off to a new assignment," he said, but made no move to leave.

"You can't be serious about rejoining the Soviet army," stated Frank. "We both know the risk that would bring to you."

Isakjan paused, collecting his wits. With great difficulty, he made a momentous decision for himself and decided to trust a man and a family, forgoing the security of a government and a cause.

"I think you may be right," he allowed. "I should have taken the advice that people gave me when I was stationed in Myjava, and escaped to the West. Maybe it is not too late. If I can get across the Danube and into Austria the rest will be easy."

Several days passed, and Frank took him aside. "Have you given any thought to my suggestion, Isakjan? I have no son, and could use a willing hand, someone to teach the business to. Your help would make my job easier. I'm going to show you everything I know. It's a good life. Think about it. I say this in the most sincere way, and worry that any other decision might bring you harm. You should not go to the West when you have a home here."

Isakjan didn't need to think farther, finally convinced that Frank genuinely wanted him. He waited a respectful time to accept. Eva jumped for joy and kissed him.

Mrs. Fridrich hugged him and repeated her first inducement, "Don't forget to pick one of my daughters. They each need a good man."

VE day followed after just a few weeks. The war's end brought much celebration. Isakjan greeted everyone in Hlinik, and realized that the Fridrichs' had introduced him as a son to the entire town. He returned to the comfort of close living, with plenty of food and no guilt in pursuing a livelihood. It felt good, and he looked to Frank as a leader and patron of a new type of life, one without guidance from mass movements. Frank did not mince words or rely on trickery to conduct his affairs. He walked with head high to the local church, displayed pride in his business, and needed only a one-tier accounting system, unlike the manipulative tallies required to balance books back on his old collective farm.

Isakjan made a decision to switch his name back to the Russian appellation, to avoid attracting attention. He once again became Ilja.

Mrs. Fridrich cleaned out a room for him, and Frank, true to his word, started him in the business. He did more; he took him into the forest to his secret hunting places, sometimes with local friends, including the mayor and the local priest. He soon invited Ilja to learn the management part of his business, and as apprentice he fit into the routine rapidly, measuring timber as it came into the yard, and lumber as it was shipped out. Isakjan kept track of the boards and tree trunks, writing everything carefully in his ledger.

This amounted to a promotion, compared to brigada talbilci back in Jizzakh, and it sat well with him. He concerned himself with the accuracy of the books, as never possible in Jizzakh, determined that Frank should know every last detail about the flow of his money.

In Hlinik, Slovakia, he lived the ideal that had escaped him through two regimes and their opposing armies. This family was different from its neighbors, both in achievement and in the use of privilege to open hearts and minds. He felt more secure than in many a year.

CHAPTER 17

DON'T RETURN TO PRISON IF YOU CATCH A COLD

Reaction of people is that at Munich,
Czechoslovakia was sold to Germany, and at Yalta, to Russia.
While the former
was temporary, they fear the latter will last.

----American diplomat [1]

When the Czechoslovak government passed a proclamation declaring its intention to reimburse the population for anything taken in the war by Nazi or partisan troops, the citizens of the Hlinik area naturally looked to their local resource: former partisan captain of the Chapajev company Ilja Narzikul. As an officer of the partisans, he could attest to conscription of supplies from civilians.

First the mayor of Dolna' Zdana came on behalf of those who had contributed cows and flour. Ilja rewarded his effort with a certification that his company indeed did "borrow" supplies, and added a cow to count for interest. Then others came: Jews who had suffered confiscation and had no documents, peasants who had lost livestock, and entire villages wanting compensation for lost supplies.

Ilja journeyed to a nearby town where a workman specialized in stamps. He purchased a hard rubber one with the words "Skupina Chapajev (unit Chapajev)." When people came to him asking for proof of their losses, he appraised the situation and generously attested to partisan usurpations of materials. They came and he signed, always remembering to add generous interest.

He rediscovered the pleasures of distributing government favors, so easy, so pleasing, and so popular. Ilja was recognized in the street and at monthly dances. Gossip buzzed about this newcomer with the eastern accent, walking to the hall with one of the prettiest girls and living under Hlinik's most stately roof.

Eva spurned her local suitor in favor of Ilja, and the lad in disfavor started a slander campaign against his successor. As a result, Ilja discovered the eyes of discrimination lurking in Slovakia, prying into his affairs. Eva's former boyfriend counted himself among the most vociferous in this tawdry enterprise, causing Ilja to wonder if his adult life would continue in the same pattern as before, never able to please people born with advantages. But the campaign against Ilja had no groundswell of support beyond some of the youths, although it affected him out of proportion to its severity.

Eva walked with him to the town dances. Youthful peers avoided him, edging him into a corner of solitude. After one dance, constricted by the ostracism, he felt a wave of social claustrophobia and rushed home to pack and leave. He scarcely had opened a drawer when Eva burst in his room.

"Where are you going, Ilja?" she asked, showing her concern.

"It just won't work. I don't fit in here. I have to rely on you too much. "

"But I want you here, don't you see? The others mean nothing. You are special. Don't let their pettiness bother you."

He stopped packing, unable to deny the woman's plea. She must mean what she said, must like him after all and not just as an unusual diversion. Her support for him came as a sign of acceptance. It was hard to understand why this family wanted to adopt such a renegade so completely. If he had been part of a victorious army or a prestigious family he might consider himself worthy. But then again, he had entered a new life, one built on personal relationships and trust, and so he placed the incident in the back of his mind.

That weekend he accompanied Frank on a hunting trip attended by the parish priest.

"But you are an individual, with value apart from your family and your memberships in organizations," explained the priest.

Ilja liked that reasoning. It sounded like what he had strived for all his life, and did not require enforcement by a powerful government. Perhaps his mentors over the years followed the same reasoning, but why didn't more people look at him as an individual?

The Father said that God regarded each man separately, and that made up for the people who didn't, and he preached the message as he administered Catholic services which Ilja attended with the Fridrich family, sitting next to Eva. For the first time, religion became a personal word rather than a secret or political cult.

The priest expended extra effort on behalf of his new parishioner, initiating long conversations on religion and philosophy. Ilja's lack of knowledge regarding Islam, the religion of his boyhood household, embarrassed him. Before, he had experienced religion only as something his father had practiced secretly, something that caused the mullahs to deliver rousing political speeches, something that gathered masses to the hill outside of Jizzakh to chant in mesmerizing cadence, something that his teachers condemned.

"Did you ever wonder about the origin of man?" the priest wanted to know. "How about the effect of materialism on faith? Did you read of the Pavlov experiments with dogs? You have a whole realm of learning to uncover."

The priest, in his mild coaxing way, ignited Ilja's interest, and reminded him of a hunger for knowledge.

"Well, I am ready to learn," Ilja stressed.

"You were born into poverty. Now you have food, culture, money, freedom, and yet you are still in poverty until you gain the faith of religion."

Ilja did not take that lesson entirely to heart. "There is one point I can not agree with you on," he insisted. "When you describe to me the wonder of belief and the satisfaction that it brings, you talk of things I admire. But you can never point out exactly how God works, can never arrange a meeting for me with Him so he can prove Himself."

"Ah, and that is where you must accept the fact that you are human and He is not," responded the clergyman. "Religion is not philosophy or a point of debate, nor a club that brings you political or social means to salvation. You ask too many questions. There comes a time when you must stop sparring with words and make a leap to belief."

Ilja could not make that leap. "I pledged myself to the promises of several governments, and only after much suffering found them to be lacking. Now you ask me to place my belief in a regime in the sky on the merit of testimonials."

Even though he did not make the leap of religious faith, he did make one of personal responsibility, taking the example of Frank to heart and learning that people can decide the kind of life to lead rather than have their government decide. This differed from his experiences in the USSR and Nazi Germany, and he savored the freedom and self-determination it gave him. The discovery was at once exhilarating and devastating, for it made him realize that he had often blindly followed orders and suggestions from political leaders which worked against him and his country.

By the fall of 1945, Eva celebrated her seventeenth birthday, still too young in the opinion of her father for serious courting, but ripe for some formal education. The family traveled by carriage for a half-day's trip to the nearest operable train so Eva could attend the conservatory in Bratislava; use of the closer Hlinik train station awaited reconstruction of bridges exploded by retreating Germans. In Bratislava, she could refine her skills in piano and harp. The entire family visited the city.

Bratislava, a beautiful active city and Slovak headquarters for the Red Army, became the center of her studies. The war had been over for a half year, but legions of victorious Soviet soldiers still strutted thick in the streets. Ilja grimaced at the sight of them. He worried that they might include his name on a list of war criminals, and he flushed with anger that their troops included men from Turkistan, the country he had once sought to liberate which was now doomed to interminable subjugation.

"When will they leave?" asked Frank, wistfully breaking Ilja's thoughts.

He did not respond, and so Frank continued, "The Germans brought Slovakia out of a long depression and treated us well. Hlinik never prospered so well as with them. Those crazy people who welcomed the Russians are already regretting it. Pan-Slavism is a misguided dream."

Ilja still did not answer, absorbed by the soldiers he saw. Hundreds of men in Red Army uniforms mingled in the streets, and a fast-beating heart and a mind trying to hide his identity paralyzed his faculty of speech.

Eva enrolled in the conservatory, majoring in the harp. She planned to continue her piano studies also, with the encouragement of a number of instructors. Frank had arranged for a room with a Bratislava family, and her five-year program began.

The two settled into a routine: Eva learning music; Ilja training in the lumber business. What could be better activities for children of a prosperous merchant's family in Hlinik? Frank spent days with him at the lumberyard, detailing the business. Sometimes he dispatched Ilja to another lumber mill to trade supplies. Often, the other local lumber merchant drove to the Fridrich's house to visit.

The two lumbermen belonged to the ranks of the very few who owned cars, as horses and carriages supplied basic transportation to the area. The remarkable visitor ran the neighboring lumber operation. After the Nazi government in Slovakia nationalized the visitor's saw mill because he was Jewish he convinced them to allow him to run the company. Under this arrangement, he continued to prosper under the Gestapo snoops as though he still owned the place. After the Soviet victory, the new government declined to return his property, but the man managed to remain in de facto charge and extended his success.

Prosperity in wood products affected everyone associated with that trade, so Ilja no longer wore the shabby clothes that marked him as an old SS trooper turned partisan. Frank donated a more suitable old Czech uniform for daily wear, and escorted him to a tailor who prepared a fashionable suit, something for church and his frequent trips to Bratislava. Ilja replaced the local lad as the official escort of Eva, recognized by the family as such, but continued to draw menacing stares from his former competitor.

But life was too busy in late fall 1945 to worry about such petty rivalries, and so he merrily enjoyed an excursion with Eva in the family carriage back to the train station on her return to Bratislava, taking her sisters along for the ride. With the family servant holding the reins, Ilja sat in the back with the girls. As the train whistle signaled its impatience, the young couple kissed on the platform. Halfway home with sisters Elena and Mayna, the carriage passed through a small town. Czechoslovak police stood in the street, waiting for them to pass again. Upon the appearance of the surrey, they snapped to action, halting the carriage and following excited orders from their leader.

"You, out. We have questions to ask."

Ilja, confused, climbed down from his seat and the girls started to follow. The policeman had other plans and held up his hand.

"Girls, stay in the carriage. This is none of your business."

He pointed at the driver.

"Take them straight home. We have things to do that do not concern you. Go now."

With a surprised voice, Ilja protested. He guessed they were rounding up all non-Slovaks for routine questioning, and tried to bluff, figuring that a story about a captured POW who escaped would give them an excuse to dismiss him.

"You can not do this." he claimed. "I am a citizen of a socialist state, and equal with all others."

The police knew better.

While the driver whipped the horses to continue the journey home, the police called the Red Army post nearby, and waiting soldiers came within a half hour to accompany Ilja to their command center.

Ilja broke into a cold sweat and his stomach cramped. He preferred the tension and fear of battle to this uncertainty.

The soldiers pushed him into the building they still occupied over a year after the war had ended. They stripped his new suit from his body and shaved his head.

"Put this on." An old German uniform.

They instantly reduced him from adopted protégé of a pillar family to POW again. But what war? What enemy?

Sweat kindled his brain. After reviewing the possibilities, he realized that the Soviets were not so organized as to track him down in Hlinik. Eva's old boyfriend. Yes, he could do this, and all because of jealousy. He prepared for a different type of bias, one emanating from his success rather than his misfortune. Any person who viewed him as a false claimant could call upon an active exterminator of strangers: the Soviets. In retrospect, it seemed all so simple. Eva, so beautiful, and the police, so informed as to when he crossed their station. The jealousy of a spurned lover had led to his misfortune, something hard to avoid. If he freed himself from this crisis, he must repress any sign of pomp or pride, and give no reason for covetousness.

A lieutenant questioned Ilja right away.

"What are you doing in civilian clothes?"

Ilja swallowed. "I am visiting friends."

He had not noticed the soldiers on the side of the room that stood in line to approach him. With malice in their eyes and bats in their hands, they rushed forward in battle formation. The bats resembled those horrible weapons carried by German guards at the Ebonrod POW Stalag. They had learned their trade as effectively as the Germans, beating him about the face and body until he bled. The lieutenant, indignant over the interruption, continued.

"Now, tell me your life story."

He remembered Sattarov's advice, to tell a convincing story that does no damage, then stick to it, and even though the man was not there to protect him, the advice would guide him.

"I am an Uzbek, and I attended The Soviet Tashkent Military Academy. The Germans captured me in Latvia and sentenced me to forced labor in the coal mines. I escaped to join the partisans and stayed after the war. Since all socialist countries are equally wonderful to live in, I chose to live where my friends reside, Czechoslovakia.

The lieutenant rubbed his face, tired from listening to sad stories. The day drew to a close early as the fall sun set.

"We know you do not belong here. You will tell us what you have done."

It was obvious that the Red Army did not have a dossier on his life. Encouraged by this observation, Ilja gathered they were curious because he was a Turkistani in Slovakia, a most unusual circumstance and therefore suspicious. Familiarity with their methods gave him confidence that the Soviet interrogation machine could not transfer central documents to all areas. The notes taken back in Poland after Sattarov's coaching were lost to a file.

As the questioning went on, Ilja gained some confidence as his speculations unfolded just as predicted, and asked, "What do you intend to do with me?"

The lieutenant stood up from his desk. Prisoners did not need answers, and the officer saw no reason to deviate from that rule. He brought the session to an end. The bat patrol pushed him down the basement stairs and locked the door. Alone in the dark, he nursed his injuries.

Then, during the night, the door opened and another body rolled down the stairs.

"I am a Russian, and my countrymen treat me like this. I fear they will kill me," the new arrival lamented.

"What have you done?" inquired Ilja.

"I was captured by the Germans, and they forced me to fight in the Vlasov army."

Ilja related his story, true to the version just presented the day before. Hopefully, his cellmate would have an opportunity to corroborate what he had said.

"I hope they will realize I had no choice," said the other inmate. "They have forgiven others."

In the early morning, a soldier called into the basement for Ilja's roommate. An hour later, Ilja was taken upstairs and there, in Soviet uniform at the front desk, sat his inmate friend of the previous night; he had been a plant.

Reeling from the deception, Ilja watched the lieutenant emerge from his office. "We see no reason to charge you with a crime at this time," he concluded. "But, you do not belong here in Slovakia. Our government wants you back in Uzbekistan."

The soldiers led him to a grouping of other Soviets who had been forcefully interned by the Germans for labor. This band numbered about twenty-five people released after the war, who by various coincidences ended up in the Slovakia area. They were all placed in a large house near the Red Army station, with no permission to leave, even to the yard, without approval of the sentries.

The soldiers prepared to escort them under light guard out of Slovakia and back to their ethnic homelands. Since many train tracks remained unrepaired from war, Ilja's group assembled for a march to the nearest operating railroad for shipment to a transfer station.

Ilja considered the chain of events that pointed him back to Turkistan. He enjoyed the life in his new adopted town, finding life away from the excitement of Berlin surprisingly satisfying. Small towns did have their advantages. Hlinik shepherded its community in a manner similar to its poor distant relative, Jizzakh, also ruled by Russia. Why wouldn't the new rulers want their citizens to live in a place of their choice, either of two similar socialist towns? The Soviets must not want nationals of one republic living in another, since this would encourage communication and information exchange inimical to their plans. In separating non-Slovaks from that country, they could probably distinguish and punish people who fought against the system.

With two soldiers guarding them, the group marched twenty miles per day towards the railroad. All the other people were Russians, Ukrainians, or Byelorussians. As they walked he gravitated to the center of control: one of the guards. Getting close to power in order to understand it had worked so well and so often that he unconsciously tried it once more.

Ilja concentrated on the guard, walking by him every day. Each evening they requisitioned a few houses from the mayor of the respective town, meeting in the morning to continue, and Ilja stayed in whatever house his friendly guard selected. Very few of the marchers spoke Slovak, least of all the guards.

"Let me help you get supplies," offered Ilja.

Soon the guard merely directed him, "Go and get some vodka, eggs and potatoes."

In an old German uniform issued by the men who had taken his suit, Ilja went to gather food for the troupe and vodka for the guards. As he chatted with townspeople he learned the locale of the train station and the schedules. He noticed the Soviet guard carried a big sack of suits, booty of war.

"You know, I have trouble getting supplies wearing this German uniform, even though it has no insignias. Do you think I could borrow one of your suits?" he asked.

The Russian agreed.

Ilja, with money for the supplies in pocket, walked into the town of the day to run his errands.

"Don't forget the vodka," called out his guard.

Ilja forgot the vodka -- and the supplies. Out of sight and around the corner, he raced to the train station to catch an early coach, and headed for Bratislava.

In his new suit and shaven head, he disembarked from the train in Bratislava and proceeded to the house where Eva stayed.

She had just returned from classes.

"Ilja, oh Ilja, I worried so. Is that you with the shaven head? And you're here, in Bratislava. What happened?"

He told her the story.

"I can never go back to Uzbekistan. My tale will never stay unchallenged there. I cannot claim indenture as a forced laborer there. Sooner or later someone will recognize me. I think about my old friend and commander Alimov. Maybe they shot him or, in a fit of mercy, gave him ten years in Siberia."

He was in a trap. How good a hiding place was Slovakia?

Eva worried with him. "How can you be so sure they would do that?"

It was all too obvious. "Close to a quarter million Turkistanis fought for Germany. I was a well-known person whose picture appeared in many papers."

"I am just so happy you are here and well."

He stayed the night and contacted her parents on the phone, discussing the problem with Frank. "I agree," said Frank. "your arrest was probably the result of jealousy. It is the old boyfriend. I will take care of it."

Ilja stayed in Bratislava, cowering before the omnipresent Red soldiers, and at the same time enjoying the time with Eva.

"You know my friend Kata?" she said. "Kata is marrying a German, West German and moving. Imagine that. Her married name will be Blitz."

Ilja expressed surprise. He knew Kata slightly as a conservatory student in the vocal arts with a great voice.

"She can have a job there if she wants." Ilja knew the night clubs, if they still existed, would welcome her in Germany.

After a week's stay in Bratislava, Frank suggested that Ilja could return to Hlinik in safety and greeted him at the station.

"You were right," agreed Frank. "Eva's old boyfriend is the culprit, but I don't think there will be more problems. He has made enough trouble now. Besides, the Soviets are moving from the area, back towards Bratislava. I heard they have given back the post where they interrogated you."

Ilja had to believe that the incident was an oddity, as the alternative was too miserable to contemplate: a life as a Gypsy wanderer fearing every city and every face. Frank and Hlinik Police Chief Stefanik believed that no more problems would brew.

Frank did better than his word with regard to teaching Ilja a business and giving him a home. He showed him a world where a person could make his own way in life, without bonding his future to a sacred mission, be it communism or liberation, whatever those slogans meant. In his isolated valley town between the mountains of great political powers and anarchy, Frank lived where leadership and individuality could control events.

"And I have more good news," he added. "They fixed the rail bridge, so the station in Hlinik will open. You can visit Eva more often."

That news made him forget the unthinkable. He walked the quarter mile across the Hron River bridge to the station often, as the November weather turned cold in preparation for the coming white blankets of snow. He dashed about the lumberyard probing every corner, sometimes making mistakes, but in the end dusting himself off and prevailing. Late that month, he got off the train, returning from a trip to Bratislava to visit Eva.

Elena and Mayna waited for him and he rushed past the benches on the platform to hug them. Frank's friend the police chief sat on one of the waiting benches.

"Hello, Chief Stefanik," called out Ilja, a little nervous at the sight of any policeman.

Stefanik had held the position of chief for many years, long before Soviet domination. He belonged to the village, taking an interest in everyone and going hunting often with Frank. But Stefanik stood next to a young Communist Party man, sent with him to assure proper compliance with orders. This especially surprised Ilja and pricked his nerves. On hunting trips, Stefanik had assured him that more slip-ups would not occur.

"I really must apologize to you," The man stammered. "But I must ask you to come with me down to the office for a few questions."

The safe house in the little village collapsed about him and Ilja's anguish returned. Mayna and Elena stared in disbelief. For a second time, they watched a raw abduction made all the worse by the use of Stefanik, friend of the family and mainstay of the town. The Soviets had succeeded in breaking down the fabric of the community.

"Get your father and tell him what has happened," Ilja urgently told the sisters. Maybe this would be easier with Frank to help.

An ethnic Russian lieutenant and a soldier walked from around the station building. The safety of the small town disappeared completely and hope died. Ilja feared his turn in front of the executioner would come next. He reverted to Russian, addressing the officer.

"Good day. What is going on? What are you doing here? I am not charged with anything."

The lieutenant showed no interest in his questions.

"You must come with me."

Ilja persisted. "You cannot do that. You are only a lieutenant and I am a captain. Only a superior officer can arrest another officer."

The lieutenant did not look amused.

"We are not going to bother with formalities. I am arresting you anyway and you are going back with us to Bratislava."

"May I fetch some clothes and things at my house?" Ilja asked, resigned to the first defeat but still looking for room to maneuver.

"I will send the police officer to the house. You will come with me."

In Bratislava, the secret police occupied a big stone house with a dark cellar and no sign on the door, an arrangement familiar to Ilja. The persistence of the Soviets in pursuing anyone who stood out from the population as being a little different unnerved Ilja, for it showed the determination with which the Red Army pursued defectors. After a hair shave, guards brought him to an interrogator who displayed a professional air about his grimy work. The procedure was virtually identical to that of Ilja's previous interrogation.

"I want to know about your entire life. Everything!" demanded the questioner.

The same questions from different men, all glaring with their eyes, all wanting details, facts to further their careers.

"Who did you know in Jizzakh? In Tashkent? In the POW camp?" The Russian repeated himself incessantly.

All day, every day, they brought him up from the cellar with a questioner and a guard, but no beating, just horrible food. After five days of the same, he still didn't remember all the names, all the places, which angered the men with pencils and quotas.

The questioners put him in a truck, the kind used for delivering furniture and potatoes, for five hours. The vehicle had no sign to identify it as "KGB," or "Internal Prisoner," and so the transfer added insult to the kidnapping. Like a vegetable he moved to another market, with never a disclosing signal from the interrogators, never a proclamation of the reason for internment or what he might expect.

At the end of the journey, a huge camp with barbed wire loomed like a city. For his first night in Baden, Austria, he stayed in a small locked room in a building next to the wire. The men in Bratislava turned their quarry over to another; evidently, the Soviets had no shortage of interrogators.

"We will review your life in every detail." announced a major. "Let us start with where you were born."

The major loved details, and insisted on the most penetrating small ones, day after day. He also prided himself in "double backs."

"You told me that one of your friends in Tashkent Academy was Krasinski, a Jew. You said he had dark hair and was about 5' 8" in height. "

Ilja admitted that.

"Think again," cautioned the major. "Krasinski is 5' 11", not 5' 8". Furthermore, his hair is light."

Ilja tried to look cooperating. "Sorry, sir. When I knew Krasinski, he was 5' 8" and had dark hair."

The major was about 35 years old, a White Russian with a big title. He instilled a fearful anxiety with his sessions, which continued every other day and caused Ilja to sweat and turn without sleep at night. During the day he could not eat.

The major tossed his papers around. "You are not telling the truth. We know about you. Confess!"

The major must have known that many Soviets served with the Germans, and that a Turkistani hiding in Slovakia would be a likely candidate for something mischievous.

As the weeks passed, Ilja started to fear that a trump card would be played, condemning him irrevocably. After thirty days, the major finished.

"Get your belongings. I have other orders for you."

Ilja looked at his belongings: the same clothes that lay on his back for the last month, the same unchanged underwear, and the ever-longer beard. A soldier took him to the railroad station, presenting him with a loaf of bread for meals in transit, which he put under his arm.

The soldier, with rifle slung over his shoulder, escorted Ilja, still covered with a month's dirt, to the station. They joined people who waited for trains that did not run on time, that might arrive a day late without notice. The same trains had run on time under German tutelage. Many soldiers milled in the station, as though forming for another war. Could there be any soldiers back in the Soviet Union, with so many in Czechoslovakia?

Across the station hall, a captain watched them and Ilja thought he recognized him. The officer approached.

"Good afternoon." he addressed the guard. "May I talk with your prisoner?"

"Yes, Captain."

"What is your name?" the captain asked Ilja. "And what happened to you?"

Ilja told his story.

The captain gave his name, one that sounded to Ilja of Tatar origin, a supposition confirmed when the man said he lived in the Crimea. The officer explained that he was a captain in communications and planned to take a train to Budapest, Hungary, downstream on the Danube from Bratislava. Ilja liked this man, one who might have become his associate if he had not discovered the truth about the Soviet Union. No need to try and enlighten this officer, a good man trying to extend a bit of comfort, a man he would have shot a short while ago. Now he struggled only to determine his own destiny, to separate it from the dictates of Soviet doctrine.

"You will be stationed near my adoptive family," exclaimed Ilja.

He then told about the Fridrich family. The Tatar agreed to deliver a letter to the Fridrichs, and provided paper and pen.

Ilja composed a quick heartfelt note.

"Thank you for everything. I am indebted to you all. You are my family and I miss you. My future is uncertain, but if I get out of this I would like to marry Eva.

Whatever happens, you are on my mind and heart. If the worst happens, I may be taken back to Turkistan and only hope that I can see my mother before any punishment is meted out."

With love,

Ilja

He handed the letter to the captain. The assembled hopeful passengers in the station slept on the benches waiting for trains to arrive. In the morning the captain asked to take Ilja for a shave.

As Ilja shaved, he looked through the station, and mentally formed an escape route. Did the captain mean for him to go? He could strike the captain and then run. But where? Although he thought of a breakout, his despair overcame him.

The train came at last and the guard led Ilja, who followed like a child to the destination. They disembarked at another immense camp, with high barbed wire and much more security than

Ilja had ever seen. It intimidated him.

He followed the guard to a side building with administrative offices. The sentry checked in at an office. Other detainees mingled about and he talked with them.

"What is this?"

One man answered, "The camp was built by the Germans and the Soviets are using it for a transfer point to return Soviets who were in German forced labor brigades back home."

Possibly the camp was the destination of his aborted first trip. But his access was restricted and he could not leave the building and its porch to approach the main camp where the forced labor people waited. He could talk only to others within the administration building. His status no longer designated him as a mere transferee.

For half a week he nursed anxiety, twisting at night and fighting gnawing cramps. He reviewed his life over and over, and dwelled on his conversations with the Hlinik priest. He started to pray.

"Dear God, please help me. I have done nothing evil. Is it wrong to strive for freedom and equality for all people? You are mighty and can influence events. You healed the lepers and parted the water for your people. I did not understand this until now. I doubted and I am sorry. You have given solace in dark times to many people. Please show me the way. I will forever be in your service," he prayed.

He made the leap of faith referred to by the Hlinik priest and it brought him a measure of peace, but he withheld a little room for himself to exit or doubt should the leap find him in mid-air over a cliff. Then a soldier escorted him into an anteroom.

"Someone wants to see you," the soldier explained.

The anteroom made him even more nervous, and he paced back and forth. Another soldier brought in a Turkistani, who took a seat. Ilja panicked since he recognized the man.

"Salaam," he called under his breath.

The man nodded, but showed no sign of recognition. Ilja could not place the man in his mind, but, before he could pursue further thoughts, the guard directed him to a closed room.

A dark complected man, maybe Turkistani, Georgian, or Azerbaidzhan, with the rank of major sat at the desk.

"Hello, Captain Narzikul. Sit down. I am here to listen to your life story."

The man listened for days, patiently jotting down notes and punctuating the discourse with thoughtful questions. After a week, he grew restless and pushed a pile of paper to the corner of his desk.

"You are very consistent, but don't waste our time; tell me the truth."

Ilja pleaded, "Do you want me to lie? I do tell the truth."

"You don't understand," the major explained, "I want the truth. I know that a man like you was probably captured by the Germans, and after a short stay in some prison camp was taken out and invited into the German army, fought for Germany opposing the motherland against his will, and at the first opportunity during the war, came forward and joined the partisans. Men like you tell the truth. In consideration of the truth, the Soviet government takes everything into consideration, and the government believes in mercy.

"The government realizes what happens in time of war, and even brings people back into its military ranks. So if you have a fear, don't worry, because anything you did was against your will. Think about it because I would like the truth."

The major stayed calm and spoke softly. He withdrew from the room. Ilja imagined that he went to question the other Turkistani. He held his sore stomach and tried to envision how he could escape misery. The invitation to agree with the interrogator's suggestion, and admit that he fought for the Germans under threats tempted him, but he remembered the many tricks used by other interrogators and feared that any admission of culpability would lead to a worsening spiral of self-incrimination.

Shortly the interrogator reentered the room. On his return, the major wasted no time.

"Did you think about what I said?"

"Yes sir," he responded. "There is nothing to think about, as I told the truth. I can go over it again if you like."

Ilja surmised that the interrogators liked plenty of detail, days and days of it.

The major abandoned his use of the Russian language they had been using, switching to Uzbek.

"Upon my mother's honor, may Allah strike me dead if I lie. No harm will come to you if you tell the truth."

Words of faith, words of bond. The words were pledged years ago by Veli Kayum-Khan, before deliverance from POW camp.

"Come on now," said the major, continuing in Uzbek. "Tell the truth. Let's not play games. I am going to help you, not hurt you if you tell the truth."

Still Ilja did not budge. "I told you all."

Silence ensued, and the major flipped through a stack of papers in front of him while Ilja worried about the man he saw in the waiting room. The major looked at Ilja.

"Now. Who is Veli Kayum-Khan?"

A general question. Ilja did not get perturbed. "The president of the Turkistani Liberation Committee."

"You know him?"

"No."

"You know Alimov?"

"No." He said it fast, too fast. Ilja never had mentioned Alimov, but claimed he reported to the Russian Colonel Boshinsky during his partisan activities. Alimov signaled danger, someone who could crumple his stories. He did not want to talk about Alimov, whom they had sent to jail.

The major again swore. "Nothing will happen to you. I know about the Turkistani divisions in Germany."

Ilja fidgeted, sweating as the questions came closer to him, wondering what the Major really knew and what the man in the other room might say.

Somehow Ilja saw the outlines of a competition. He suddenly feared that the more the major had to disclose, the more of his time Ilja took, the more he would suffer. The major played increasingly large cards, face cards now, and soon aces. If he caused the major to play an ace, he, in turn, received the joker: death in Siberia. The pressure became too much. He looked for a window to jump from, and there was none. He needed to relieve the bursting fear, and finally jumped to the only ledge remaining: surrender to God. If beneath the interrogator's stern exterior, a man of faith who honored pledges to Allah dwelled, Ilja would be safe. The alternative now seemed to indicate a cold cell in Siberia. Ilja placed his trust in God and only hoped that his adversary placed more faith in Allah than in Moscow.

"I first saw Veli Kayum-Khan at Ebenrod. He asked for the officers and educated men to step forward, and promised us something better than the prison camp."

The terrible truth poured out, with compulsion, with details, with conviction. The major sat back, not even bothering to take notes, as though he knew all along. Ilja told everything, right up through his stay with the Fridrichs and his hope to marry Eva.

The major stood up. "I will see you tomorrow."

He walked out.

Then Ilja really convulsed, couldn't sleep, couldn't eat,

couldn't pass time. He sweated and agonized. Two days lapsed, and he got faint and delirious, thinking that he had signed a passage to Siberia and unimaginable torture. Would the interrogator honor his promise before Allah or his pressures from the Soviets?

The major finally called him in.

"What will happen to me?" Ilja cried.

"Nothing. We will send you back to Uzbekistan."

Uzbekistan today, Siberia tomorrow. By now, the lines of Russian domination were all too clear and he understood that they wished to separate all of the supposed brotherly republics into isolated spheres of ignorance unable to communicate with one another, and to return all of those individuals who had spent time out of their homelands during the war, so as to limit discussion with the outside world. He could hardly concentrate on the major's words in his contemplative misery. Surely a return to Uzbekistan was not what the Lord had in mind.

"I have a girl friend, and want to marry her," he sobbed. "I have belongings, and things at her home that I left when I was arrested. These people were nice to me, and I never got the chance to thank them and say goodbye." Ilja hid nothing, exposing his deepest feelings as well as his history.

The major listened. "I will consider that and will call you in a couple of days."

Again the tension, the prayers, the cramps. The major compared his allegiances. The couple of days amounted to four before another session.

The major seemed uncommonly friendly. "I will send a soldier with you, so you can say goodbye to your girl friend. Get your possessions from Slovakia and then you will be going back to Uzbekistan, to home. "

The major looked out the window. "The weather is cold this December. Take care, because if you get sick, you cannot travel and get to your home."

Ilja had lost all count of the days. A calendar on the wall said December 6, 1945, before the celebration of St. Nicholas. Of course the weather was very windy and cold. Who cared if he got sick? There were no doctors in Siberia.

The major leaned over and stressed, "You must be very careful in the cold weather, because if you get the least bit sick in the cold weather, you cannot travel and the plans will be disrupted."

Ilja could not believe the major's cruel concern, asking him about a cold as he sentenced him to death. The major dismissed Ilja. "Remember, if you are sick you cannot travel."

Ilja coughed.

"That is a bad sign. I fear you might not make the trip." The major winked. He coughed again, and the major touched his finger to his mouth. Ilja finally understood. He walked out of the room practicing his cough. God and Allah were the same, and could inspire two men of faith to reach a private peace.

A young Ukrainian soldier accompanied Ilja in an army truck going to Bratislava. He knocked on the door of Eva's rooming house on December eighth.

"Ilja, Ilja, Ilja," she cried. She hugged him. They embraced. She rubbed his shaven head, his mark of unscheduled vacations. She presented him with St. Nicholas presents kept for his arrival, gifts of cigarettes and clothes.

"St. Nicholas has given us the most precious of presents -- you."

They were so happy, and called the Fridrich house in tears. Frank jumped into his small brown, square car, a Skoda-Rapid. He immediately drove to Bratislava, picked them up, including the soldier, and drove back home. They attended special services at the Catholic church in celebration, where the priest hugged the returnee, who made a confession on the spot. "I didn't fully believe before, but I have made the leap and am truly converted."

Then back to Bratislava to a doctor who wrote a letter attesting that Ilja was sick and was not able to travel. They told the soldier that the unfortunate sickness ruined the plans. They related the message of the Turkistani major to the guard, who had orders not to return a sick man. Frank bought the guard gloves and other presents, and then gave him gifts for the major. After a few days the soldier took his leave.

CHAPTER 18

DOES CITIZENSHIP PREVENT ARREST?

The ways of acquiring or losing nationality are regulated by the law of each State.

-- International treaty signed at Rome, typical of citizenship agreements [1]

"You should become a Czechoslovak citizen," Frank advised. "It's the only way to avoid Soviet madness. The time has come to straighten out papers and make things legal. Now that you are marrying Eva, who already is a citizen, the process will be easy." As a man accustomed to making decisions, he wanted Ilja to become a solid part of his family. Ilja knew that in the world of uncertainty, only a father with influence could protect a family and preserve the peaceful home necessary to nurture love and understanding. Back in Uzbekistan, Teacher Saraf and Nora Melkakse's family had demonstrated that long ago.

Frank had done some research, and explained to him, "In order to apply for citizenship, first the town must grant approval for you to stay."

In a small meeting the town approved his application. With that accomplished, Frank moved the application process to his friend, Judge Chernov, who promised quick action. After a month, the Judge invited them to his chambers.

"I am ready to issue the citizenship, but first: one detail. I must get the permission of the Soviet Government, because they have decreed their review must precede any new transfer of citizens from Soviet to other nationalities."

Frank and Ilja didn't move. The silence embarrassed them.

"I will get the permission," volunteered Ilja, giving them time to think.

Frank could hardly talk. Eva cried. The family prepared to relinquish hope, but Ilja had no intention of letting so important a moment pass for lack of a piece of paper. He remembered his childhood and the Tashkent Teacher's School records. Forging records again seemed a small risk to take, and so he sat down with pen and paper and wrote in his best Cyrillic script a letter to himself and those concerned.

To Captain Ilja Narzikul and those interested:

Ilja Narzikul served as commander of the Chapajev Company in the Partisan Army against the Nazi invaders. He served well, fighting in the Slovak province of Czechoslovakia under the military authority of myself, General Boshinsky.
I have interviewed this man and approve of his desire to become a citizen of the country he fought in. Permission is granted to Ilja Narzikul to become a Czechoslovak citizen.

Colonel Boshinsky
Soviet Army
Ninth Partisan Brigade

After signing the Colonel's name to the Russian language document, he wrote a translation in Slovak and signed it again. A notary attested to the translation, giving an indication of legitimacy to both the translation and the original.

"Colonel Boshinsky, if you are alive, I thank you," he thought.

The Judge hardly glanced at the letter. He put it aside and expressed his pleasure at welcoming the new citizen. The ceremony lasted only a few moments.

"Do you, Ilja Narzikul, swear to uphold the constitution and laws of the great country of Czechoslovakia?" asked the judge.

"I do," swore Ilja.

"Congratulations and welcome as our newest citizen."

They all cheered. Ilja added a piece of paper to his resume, along with the accounting system of the Jizzakh kolkhoz, the Soviet constitution, and the German army induction. Uniforms and papers had figured so importantly in his life, but up to now, he thought, they only helped temporarily. The engaged couple caught a train back to Bratislava, planning to stay a few nights.

"We are going to have a baby," she told him.

Ilja was shocked, and then delighted to seal the upcoming marriage with a child, the dearest sign of family. Frank and the village priest arranged for the wedding. The bride and groom were interviewed and given favorable recommendations from the church. A short ceremony officially converted Ilja to Catholicism.

Frank threw the biggest wedding remembered in either Hlinik or Dolna Zdana. The beautiful bridal gown and the exquisite groom's suit rivaled styles in Bratislava or even Prague.

Everyone in the town plus friends from all the Slovak river and mountain villages attended the February event. They spent a few nights in the house for a honeymoon and the baby came in May 1946.

Ilja worked full time in the lumberyard, and when Frank went on business trips or retreats to his hunting lodge, he assumed charge, collecting money and keeping the books. The couple moved into a room in the house, newly furnished with the best available. Eva's grandmother also resided there and took charge of the baby.

Eva resumed school, usually taking the train in the morning and returning in the evening, but sometimes staying overnight. Her sisters also started lessons at the conservatory.

One day a man walked into the yard and asked to see Frank. Ilja went to fetch him.

"Who is he?" Ilja asked.

"A Jewish lumber merchant. He used to do a lot of business with me, name of Martin Suezz. Suezz did business with me right up to 1943, when the Germans cracked down on Jews in Slovakia."

Suezz had left a large wooden box with Frank at the time the Germans transported Jews out of Slovakia to Germany. His wife and two daughters were lost in the holocaust and he had come to claim his belongings, trusted to Frank's safekeeping. Frank took out the box, and Suezz opened it, showing Persian carpets, ornaments and jewelry.

"What now, Martin?" Frank wanted to know.

"A new life. Canada. Freedom has departed from Europe and I must go to the Americas, where it still breathes."

"Why do you have to leave?" Ilja asked.

"You don't know what happened." Suezz seemed reluctant to talk, introspective and sad. "The Germans rounded up Jews and sent them to death camps. They killed us in big gas chambers, thousands and thousands, even millions. I lost my wife and children and can never forget, can never stay. They almost killed me."

Ilja couldn't answer. He knew that the Germans didn't like the Jews and had witnessed horrible treatment they received, but this was too much to comprehend. He wanted to hear more, to fathom this dark secret. Suezz could not talk and held his hands up to discontinue the conversation. This was a second blow to his veneration of Germany: first losing the war, and now terrible accusations. Some horrible demon lived in Germany unexposed.

Then Ilja read the details given at the trials at Nuremburg, revealing the truth about a schizophrenia that lurked in wartime Germany. He realized how false were the hopes that Germany had given him for the liberation of his countrymen.

Suezz had to leave Czechoslovakia for freedom, and Ilja had to stay there in order to find his own. He felt less secure than ever, with the two self-proclaimed liberating countries of his life compromised. But only one of those, Russia, pursued him still, and kept him awake at night.

In July, 5:00 one morning, a knock brought Ilja to the door where police, Chief Stefanik wanted to see Frank.

"Frank, we have a problem, a mistake. Every year or so the Department of the Interior sends out a questionnaire demanding to know the names and addresses of all people born in the USSR and living in the area since 1915. I always return the paper blank, but it came unexpectedly last week while I was on vacation. My assistant filled in Ilja's name."

Stefanik realized only part of the problem. Stalin issued clear instructions to bring back the maximum possible number of Soviet citizens into the Soviet Union. He did not want so many witnesses against the Soviet system available to the rest of the world and he could use more forced laborers for his prison society.[2] He was successful in gathering over five million of them back into his grasp. [3]

Ilja bit his lip. What of his theory that the paperwork of the bureaucracy never catches up with itself? That may have been correct, but he missed the point that once the Soviet dragnet was cast, the intended prey would always need to run and would still stand a chance of getting snared. The central government might not be capable of tracking down a single man, but they could very well repress whole segments of population.

Chief Stefanik felt very dejected.

"I'm sorry to disturb you but I have to take your son-in-law."

"Isn't there any other way?" queried Frank.

Stefanik answered. "I hate these lists. The Soviets sometimes use them for arrests. They are looking even for czarists and old Bolsheviks who escaped after 1918. They like to catch up with their old enemies."

That didn't cheer up Ilja, who still suffered nightmares and cold sweats from his multitude of interrogations.

"What are your orders, chief?" Frank wanted to know.

"Take your son-in law to Komarno, and turn him over to

Russian puppets."

"How should you do this?" Frank asked.

"Through our police there."

The city of Komarno straddles the Czechoslovak Hungarian border, separated by a bridge across the Danube.

"I am a citizen now," Ilja complained.

"I have my orders. It is no use." reasoned Stefanik. "You have your papers and I have mine. I am the police, however."

Stefanik reasoned that he had done his best to prevent the unhappy incident, but who was he? An ordinary man. Those with power ordered ordinary men, who obeyed, seeing the inevitability of a greater force and the fruitlessness of refusal. Ordinary men are so sensible, so willing.

Frank broke a thick silence. "I know the chief on the Slovak side. He grew up nearby, and roamed the woods with me. Let me drive."

As the police guarded the family, Ilja hugged and kissed them all, his wife and in-laws. The chance that he might never see them again haunted everyone. He kissed his wife and baby boy again. Everyone cried. The memories of his past arrests flooded his head and he retreated into submissive defeat, unable to respond to the enormous danger with the guards and guns so close.

They arrived together in Frank's car. The police commander tended papers in his office and interrupted his work to greet a friend. At last, Frank's active life in the town gave them a wedge. After appropriate salutation, Frank related their story.

"This is my son-in-law, married to Eva. He is a Czechoslovak citizen now. Have we no pride? Do we surrender our sons to the Soviets?" Frank summoned all his powers of kinship and persuasion.

"Wait a minute," the commander suggested. "Let me make a phone call."

He called department four, a part of the interior department. The group from Hlinik waited outside his office, and after a while, the commander opened his door and came out to them.

"I talked with the head of the department, who could not locate the order." He informed them. "I have good news for you. You can go home."

Their happiness and relief stretched beyond words, as did Ilja's devotion to his extended family.

A year of peace ensued, and a second child arrived. Perhaps a new life was possible.

The mill ran at full capacity, quickly increasing its employees to over fifty people, the largest concern in the area. Frank spent more time on business and other journeys, leaving Ilja in charge. He could afford his hobbies, as his money accumulated into wealth.

"Father," Ilja called Frank. "I am disturbed with the books your superintendent keeps." He had discovered that the superintendent often wrote down that some people who bought lumber still owed on credit, but Ilja knew that many had actually paid. The superintendent had pocketed the money. Furthermore, many people abused their credit, obtaining goods and not paying for indefinitely long periods.

"I contacted your credit accounts," Ilja pressed on. "Many didn't want to pay because they already had."

Frank quietly told the superintendent that he wished his son-in-law to learn the business by taking charge of all books. Another position was found for the man. A new credit policy followed: no credit. Profits leaped, and Frank's wealth catapulted.

Those preferring the old sloppy way of doing business never failed to ask for Frank to place an order. Frank managed to keep himself too busy for such matters.

The rebuilding of Czechoslovakia proceeded, and goods became so scarce that the government saw fit to institutionalize a ration. Ilja recognized the system, known to him in several other countries. Two prices prevailed in Slovakia; one with ration cards and one without. The rationing system gave the mill another surge in cash.

Frank's fame grew. He sold his Skoda and purchased a new Mercedes, which he loved almost as much as his children.

The mill's steam generator, fired by scrap wood, ran all day throughout the year. The fire never stopped, driving three saws on a long shaft.

Frank regularly invited Ilja to join him on his hunting trips. It served as base for a little club of Frank's friends, including their priest, the most frequent visitor, the town doctor, and the mayor; a leadership club.

The Communists brought changes to the club after seizing power in the country. They appointed a new mayor, suspending elections and placing a street sweeper loyal to the Party in the office. The new mayor was not invited to the lodge.

There, eating a dinner of freshly killed boar and deer,

Frank liked to talk, drink and review the past years. After enough liquor, inevitably, the conversation turned to the past war.

"After the first war," he remembered, "Slovakia joined with Bohemia and Moravia to form Czechoslovakia. Because Slovakia was held for centuries as a vassal of Hungary, the rest of the country promised to help us out. Rubbish. What they did amounted to new domination. All of our teachers and administrators came from the West, with no sign of improvement here.

"Only after we split from the rest, with the help of Germany, did Slovakia start to prosper."

Ilja recalled his last days in the Nazi army. "It's true," he attested. "The shops in Leopoldov and Myjava brimmed with goods. I bought beautiful suits and an exquisite leather jacket."

Frank continued. "During that time, my lumber business came to life. But things are not that bad now, if only we can stay free of the Soviets."

Ilja worked with a strong devotion to Frank, the strong father figure he had always wanted. Frank in turn, granted a fountain of help for his daughter and son-in-law. A maid came for the household work, and the babies slept with their grandmother, who took primary care of them. Eva had few duties in the household, a spoiled girl who played piano and harp, continuing lessons in Bratislava a few days a week with her sisters. On the weekends, they went to church.

At night Ilja and Eva huddled in their bed. The house of brick and wood met the highest of rural standards in any part of the world, with a pump in the well delivering running water to the kitchen, a coal stove in the living room, and graciously appointed furniture on both floors. Heat from the coal stove rose to the second floor, but did not succeed in defeating the winter cold.

They did not lack in entertainment commensurate with their status, and would go to Zvolen, twenty-five miles away, known for its mineral hot springs and big hotel. A weekend or a day, it didn't matter. Often their priest joined them, replacing his collar with a tie, and enjoying dinner, wine, dance, opera, and plays. The Father was a handsome man six years older than Ilja. The priest's mother sent wine from the family vineyards for all of them to taste.

He ran the local school as he had done before the war when the church was the only source of schooling. The Communists changed this soon enough.

On many weekends, Zvolen did not suffice, and Ilja and

Eva met in Bratislava after her lessons. She liked the city theater, restaurants and parties. Frank made sure Ilja had the money for their outings by heaping krona into his wallet. Ilja never took a salary, and otherwise had all of his material needs taken care of.

Ilja sometimes heard Frank in his office arguing with tax officers, as disputes from ten years back always surfaced. Frank managed to push them under, temporarily.

Ilja calculated the payroll, and each Thursday or Friday, Frank drove to one of the towns with a bank and withdrew cash. All transactions were cash, and they never thought of robbery. Ilja then put the pay in envelopes, subtracting the amount withheld for taxes, and distributed them to the workers.

Frank beamed with satisfaction at the relationship. He saw to it that Ilja received his ultimate status symbol, a driver's license.

CHAPTER 19

ESCAPE

I just have a hunch that Stalin is not that kind of man. I think if I give him everything I possibly can and ask nothing from him in return, noblesse oblige, he won't try to annex anything and will work with me for a world of democracy and peace.

-- Franklin Roosevelt, [1]

We Bolsheviks, or you can say communists, have another idea of Slavism. We wish that all will be allied irrespective of whether small or large, but every nation will preserve its independence and arrange its life according to its ideology and tradition, be they good or bad.. It rests with each state individually to determine how it arranges it.

-----Joseph Stalin [2]

Frank often slipped out for rides by himself in his beloved Mercedes, as Ilja deduced he must have done on a payday, winter, 1947. He finished the calculations in anticipation of his father-in-law arriving by mid-afternoon. At quitting time he still waited for Frank and told the workmen that some foul-up must have delayed Frank, promising to send a messenger through the small town to call the workers when the payroll cash arrived.

Darkness and no Frank. The banker, reached on the phone at home, said Frank had picked up the regular payroll on schedule. The list of possibilities narrowed to the most unpleasant, causing the family to sit together near the living room window in sullen silence before finally reaching a consensus that Frank had gotten drunk and either had an accident or had fallen asleep on a side alley. After searching the nearby roads, they retired to start again in the morning light.

In the morning as they prepared to launch a major search, Frank's brother-in-law, the lumber mill's factory mechanic, crossed the dirt street in front of the house and mill. Not yet informed of the rising panic about Frank, he passed the house to a brick building in the rear which served as tool shed and garage to get some repair items for the steam generator.

He parted the garage doors and a tide of smoke rolled out. The car, its engine quiet after consuming a tank of gas, sat quietly with Frank slumped at the wheel. Efforts at revival came too late and the doctor pronounced him dead from asphyxiation, with a theory that he must have been drunk and passed out before turning off the engine. The funeral procession stretched the length of the town on its way to the large brick monument on a plot that Ilja purchased for the whole family.

Neighbors talked about the lucky Russian who inherited the largest concern in the area, missing the fact that he was not Russian, and that he greatly longed for his adoptive father and protector. He had to jump into complete charge of a large company for which he still apprenticed; it all created another nightmare for the young man. Like a nervous cat, he pounced on every aspect of the business and each of its problems.

The building expansion continued gathering even greater momentum and people came from as far away as Prague to buy materials. The mill initiated shipments by the train carload and still the prices were fixed ever higher, with a hundred percent bonus for sales without ration cards. To comply with regulations, a bill went out for two cars, but only one was delivered in order to demonstrate compliance with the set government price. Tremendous amounts of lumber were consumed.

He never had so much attention as a business clerk, even back in his Jizzakh tabilci days. Strange men drove into the yard and offered to buy large quantities of wood. Bank accounts grew ever fatter.

Work and business were so plentiful that the residents of Hlinik didn't want to bother with their traditional backyard farms. Eggs, milk and good meat became expensive and hard to obtain. Ilja, an old farm peasant boy, bought chickens, pigs, and a few cows so the family could eat the best food possible.

The cows produced milk bountifully; so much milk, so much butter. He bought corn, mixed it with the extra milk and fed the pigs. The pigs got so fat they could hardly stand on their feet, yielding excellent meat. The butcher, after shooting or axing a pig, prepared bundles of ham, smoked ham, sausage, and kolbasa.

Ilja's duties as head of the household covered setting allowances for Mayna and Elena, who felt that the family's new fortunes should entitle them to large sums, unhindered by an unofficial successor to Frank. Eva and Ilja continued their social rounds, widening them to Prague. They also heard from friends who had departed for the West, including one of Eva's friends, the singer she knew from Brastislava Conservatory. That friend wrote of her acceptance by West German audiences and a thriving nightlife in Munich.

Ilja traveled to Prague on business, frequently with Eva. He loved to visit beautiful Prague, which supplanted Kiev as his paragon of cities. The Narzikul couple regularly stayed in the luxurious house of Mr. and Mrs. Clepak, elderly aristocrats whom they had met at the opera. The Clepaks never missed a chance to rail against the Communists and took a special interest in cultivating the friendship of a man besieged by them. They always kept one of their guestrooms available to the couple.

Also among their friends in Prague was a couple engaged in acting and entertaining, whom Ilja had met years ago when he had first started to learn the lumber business. Ilja had spent a night in Prague alone, relaxing in the extravagant Phoenix nightclub watching a show. As he watched the entertainment, a beautiful girl dressed in white minks sang sweet melodies as the man next to him drew a butt of a cigarette and asked for a light. Ilja gave him a rare whole cigarette and lit it.

The singer kept looking at their table, smiling. At intermission she ran to the table and kissed the man.

"This is my wife," he proudly announced to Ilja.

A friendship began with Ilja driving them back to his hotel and showering them with gifts of almost nonexistent items like cigarettes, kolbasa and wine.

"You are our first Russian friend, and we thank you for liberating our country from the Germans," they toasted. Ilja just smiled. They invited him to their home.

When Ilja drove up to their home the next day, a large Soviet flag flew outside to greet him.

"Please don't fly that flag on my behalf. That is my old life." He laughed just a bit nervously. "I am not Russian, but Turkistani."

They laughed in return. The singer said, "I thought you would see the flag as a gesture of friendship." In 1947, the couple often recalled the flag-waving incident as they complained about the continual presence of the Red Army in their country and Soviet interference with politics.

A constant topic of conversation among their friends was the pressure from the Soviets on the Czechoslovak government. It seemed that every facet of life suffered: theater, culture, freedom, religion, education, taxes and politics. When the Soviet government forbade Czechoslovakia the right to participate in the Marshall Plan, they realized the country was fast degenerating into a vassal state without its own history or culture. As pressure increased, more friends became entangled with the Communists and escaped to the West, including a frequent host at dinner parties and the theater named Andrej.

At the mill, letters from the internal revenue department revived Frank's arguments with the taxmen. Ilja drove to the city of Banska Stiavnica where the revenue office housed the representative for Frank's account.

"My name is Ilja Narzikul. My father-in-law, Frank Fridrich, passed away, and I am trying to straighten out his affairs. Please help me to set the numbers right with the government." Ilja bowed his head as he talked, presenting his most humble and polite manners.

The agents were ready to help. "Let's start with Frank's pending cases, how much he made over the years, and, if you are his helper, how much you made." The young man in charge of the case brought out a pack of papers.

"I just want to do the right thing," declared Ilja.

He repeated this at dinner when he treated them. He repeated this over and over; over dinner, over the nightclub table when he invited the wives and men to dance, and over a weekend vacation at the mineral springs in Zvolen. He kept repeating his pledge and his entertaining until they accepted a favorable settlement. Frank's neighbor lumberman inspired Isakjan in his interaction with the officials. If the Jewish lumberman could prosper under successive repressive regimes of the most lethal type, Isakjan could at least settle a little tax matter with the same bureaucrats.

"How did you do it, Ilja?" asked his mother-in law. "Frank tried to reason with them year after year and never satisfied them. The settlement is so small."

"I just kept telling them I wanted to do the right thing," he answered. But he fretted over other developments in the government.

Back in 1946 the election could be described as almost free in Czechoslovakia. An active Communist who had stayed in Moscow during the war became the prime minister, an old Czechoslovak parliamentarian became the president; and a man from a Czechoslovak political family became the foreign minister. There were many parties: Democratic, Communist, Agrarian, Labor and others.

The constitution provided for a division of responsibility among the parties, but the Communists found excuses to forestall the change of power, and arrested members of the Democratic Party under false pretenses. Wielding the club of Soviet troops in Czechoslovak barracks, the Communist Party took important posts in the national government, including the interior ministry, education, defense, information.

The other parties received unimportant posts, and Ilja worried about the Communist advances. While parliament protested their infractions of the law, the Communists, who well knew the difference between law and power, instructed the Interior Ministry to search houses of other parliament members. In protest at the Communist actions, the Democrats resigned their positions in the government. According to the constitution, the Prime Minister and other officials then had to submit their resignations and order another election to establish a new government. The Democrats thought this would rectify the abuses, but they had not studied the Russian treatment of constitutional law in the Soviet Union.

The Communists did not resign. Instead, they appointed Communists to all the emptied positions, put President Benes under house arrest in the presidential palace, arrested government advisors and did not allow them to make statements.

Then one after another, the Communists issued directives

regarding nationalization and collectivization of farms and factories.

In 1949, Ilja opened a notice he had received in the mail:

"According to the directive of the government, your lumber mill is being nationalized, and will be run by a worker's representative for the good of the proletariat."

Ilja rushed to his banks. Already, those financial institutions had orders to impound all cash. Back at the mill, a man appeared at the door with an official paper.

"I have been appointed to be in charge of this business," he said waving his authorization. The new manager of the Hlinik lumber mill was only one locust in a plague that descended over Czechoslovakia. They ate everything in sight: the will to produce, the right to decide, and the heritage of a people.

The Communist took the car keys and told Ilja to continue working at a low salary. Ilja's family was instantly reduced from leadership to government worker, but at least he kept the house and a small animal farm in the back. Another generation of Narzikuls experienced nationalization.

As Ilja should have expected, as in Uzbekistan, the Communist-appointed head of the factory held credentials amounting to obedience to the Party slogans. Otherwise he was a lackey and a drunk, sometimes not showing himself at the mill for days at a time. He appropriated a house fifteen miles away, driving Frank's car to work when he decided to appear. Ilja sought guidance from the fellow lumberman in the next village, who advised him, "Treat the manager well, and he will be happy to leave you alone."

Ilja introduced his new boss to cash bonuses, which he put in his pocket, in addition to whatever the party granted him. Management of a business now became illegal, just as his father had discovered. He planned not to repeat the mistakes of his father, whose forthrightness made for easy detection.

It seemed, since Ilja refused to return to Jizzakh, that city's spirit came to him, appointing him tabilci to the Party head once again. But, unlike the grateful boy clerk, Ilja built up an unaccustomed resentment. He paced about, looking for a way to work out of the impossible path fate had taken.

"This rascal never knows what happens in the mill, barging into the business, telling everyone what to do, driving the company car, and contributing nothing. Just taking over, now you work for me." He yearned for the efficiency of the German state.

The Communist manager combined the worst

characteristics of usurpation, incompetence, absenteeism and drunkenness. He had no idea of the operation, from books to trees. Ilja saw that the mill could still collect some profits, which he siphoned to a secret spot under the house foundation, an action similar to his father's years before. He commiserated often with his fellow lumber merchant from the neighboring town, who still retained his own car. "I can try and help you if you get into trouble with your manager," he promised.

But Ilja, already disadvantaged as a foreigner, could not find the same magic as his fellow lumberman. The degree to which he excelled over his father in unapproved side activities did not eliminate the basic danger that moved ever closer to him. Every time Ilja extended his hands for a handshake he offered the undeniable skin of an outsider. Authorities noticed the differences. His attempts at assimilation and humility were too obvious and open, like the man himself.

Only with great difficulty did he ever get to sleep due to a constant dream that haunted him. After setting out his clothes, ready for instant dressing and escape, he wrestled with enemies in the night. They came, in great coats with rifles pointed at his head, and he ran miles before he jumped from the lonely bridge of his dark nightmares a thousand times, waking up more tired and exhausted than the evening before. The Russian menace in the basement of Czechoslovak culture moved to his own cellar.

Very early one morning, in summertime, 1949, three policemen from Bratislava knocked on the door.

"Ilja Narzikul?" they asked, and not waiting for an answer, continued. "We have some questions to ask you. You must come with us to Bratislava."

Eva wanted to go with him, but they didn't let her. In Bratislava they proceeded to the ministry of the interior, and locked him in the cellar, this time not shaving his head. In Czechoslovakia, the police in all towns form a national hierarchy, not a local one as is common in many Western countries. After three days, an officer brought him into a questioning room.

"Mr. Narzikul, please tell me about your life, from the beginning."

Ilja tussled with him for a few days, and then was assigned a police escort for a transfer to Prague by train.

At the Prague station where he had stood many times before, a car waited for his delivery to take him, like a major criminal, for a leisurely drive past the buildings and streets he had visited so regularly. The dark sedan pulled into center city Prague and stopped at 4 Bartolomicka' St. Police led him to a fourth-floor room just over twenty feet on each side, converted into a cell which held six people all dressed in suits like himself. The Soviets were forever converting buildings into cells, with never enough for their purposes. The other men were Czechs and Slovaks, each arrested for a different reason. One tried to escape to West Germany; one received broadcasts from the West. Leaving the country or listening to the wrong radio station had become crimes.

The room contained no furniture, and the men stretched out on the hard bare floor to try to sleep. Within a few days, twenty men occupied the room, straining the capacity of a human body to function. Stench from the unbathed sweaty men, healing wounds from beatings, and the toilet pot overwhelmed the small window and its little contribution of fresh air. Paper and pens sat in the corner. Every morning Ilja wrote to protest his arrest and demand an explanation for his internment, but he received no answers. Downstairs, Eva, who had located him, was denied a visit. The food and cigarettes she brought never made the journey to the fourth floor. She stayed with their friends, the Clepeks, for weeks waiting word, and then returned intermittently.

Every day or so police removed one or two men from the room, but not Ilja. What departed as a man returned as bloody flesh and black bruises, dragged by guards since he was unable to stand or talk. The broadcast receiver and the escapee encountered this treatment every week. With painful groans, they removed their shirts and exposed the red meat of their backs. The most pitiful were those who had made a successful dash to the West and returned to help a relative escape before their capture. Ilja, without change of clothes, spent a month with no signal or indication of his fate.

The converted prison building had frontage on Bartolomicka' St. Next to the building, a huge garage door for deliveries led to a court, with a small door next to it for pedestrians. Each week the inmates were permitted to take a walk in the courtyard behind the two doors. A guard always stood by the small door, an inspector without weapon. One room at a time, prisoners trekked to the court and into a bathhouse. Each week, still more men crowded into the cell. A warm August sun ensured discomfort even in sleeping, for those who could throw off their anguish long enough to lapse into unconsciousness.

Like a man bent on trouble, Ilja befriended the broadcast receiver and the escapee as people to be trusted. They formed a group, including another inmate. Suspicion in the cell thickened the hot air with sultry speculation on the identity of the Russian plant. Ilja whispered in the corner, "We must take a chance."

They talked, concocted, and planned. Each was young and afraid of the long prison sentences sure to follow, not to mention the beatings and horrible living conditions also guaranteed. The plan they developed was to wait for a walk in the courtyard. Ilja suggested the method.

"As we march around in our circle, walk in order, coming very close together at the door. The first in line can hit the policeman. I will go second and open the door. Everyone then run out and turn left at the corner onto Vaclav Street, the biggest street in Prague."

The broadcast receiver lived a couple of blocks from the office, and they agreed to regroup there. Ilja expected to proceed to the house of his friends, either the Clepeks or the entertainers. A former escapee to the West contributed his research.

"If we can get to West Germany, there are refugee organizations in Munich. None of us can stay in Soviet territory."

The words shocked them. "Czechoslovakia is Soviet territory, spoils of the war."

The planners prepared for a morning dash. The guard guided them to the court and gauged his watch as they paced around. Ilja lined up his men, looking casual.

"Today," he whispered.

They circled into position, in front of the door. The broadcaster stepped out of line and suddenly stopped in his tracks to the complete surprise of the others. Four police officers marched through the small door. The plan aborted.

"You, get in line," shouted the guard.

The next walk glimmered like a dream, a week away.

Three days later, the morning call for bodies included that of Ilja Narzikul. His knees grew weak and he felt light-headed, afraid of a beating, and afraid of a transfer to Uzbekistan and Siberia. His eyes were red from lack of sleep, nightmares of chases and jumps from countless bridges, recurrent dreams of torture, yearning for his wife and family.

The door opened and the guard motioned him inside. Ilja spoke first, in Slovak. "Good day."

The man behind the desk answered in Russian, "What are you doing in Czechoslovakia? Why don't you go home?"

Ilja nearly collapsed.

Ilja tried to speak. He had obeyed the constitution, become a citizen of Czechoslovakia, spoke the language like a native, married and raised children, contributed to the life of his town. He saw that these details amounted to inconsequential pieces of paper, that his efforts were little aggravations to the Russian monolith. He had succeeded in fooling only himself with dreams of equality, achievement, family, friendship. These were mere games, while his nightmares spoke the truth.

He fumbled with his lips. "All socialist countries are the same, equal in their cause. I met a wonderful lady, got married and ...."

The interrogator, sounding rebuffed and impatient, stormed, "I want the whole truth, your whole life."

Ilja gave his story, slowly. While he talked they did not beat him or send him away. He planned ahead in sequences of only minutes. The interrogator had no time for the usual formalities and techniques, cutting the visit short with a curt conclusion.

"You can not stay. You belong in the Soviet Union, in Uzbekistan, but after a while you can send for your family."

A guard followed him back to the cell. He had to find out about transfers eastward.

"When will I go back to the Soviet Union?" he asked the guard.

"Every week a big truck comes and takes out ten to twenty Soviets to Austria, and then back to the USSR." The guard must be referring to the Austrian camp that Ilja had unfortunately inhabited before. He had no desire to visit the Uzbek interrogator once again.

Weekly transports didn't leave much time for the escape to work. If the next truck rounded him up before the next walk, all planning would end up unfulfilled. Each hour thereafter loomed with threatening signs of transfer, and he spent hours in the corner, hoping that each guard opening the door would not call his name. Three days later, a soldier ordered them to the court. Ilja noticed the policeman next to the door, an older one, half-asleep.

"Today."

After once around the court, another whisper. "Go."

The lead prisoner swung hard at the guard, and he tumbled. Ilja yanked the door and the men ran out.

Someone from the office yelled, "Catch them. They are escaping. Two pedestrians tackled the first escapee. Ilja, the second, was grabbed. His attacker twisted and grappled with him.

Ilja struggled and shouted, "Politicke', politicke' (political prisoners)," and the pedestrians backed away. Around the corner he bolted, then stopped suddenly to straighten his hair and suit. He joined the pedestrians and the broadcaster, who opened the door to his house.

"This is registered in my girl friend's name," he explained.

That night they slept in the girl friend's attic. In the middle of the night, heavy knocks sounded on the door, and the police broke into the house. They brushed aside the girlfriend and routed through the house. In the attic, the two fugitives froze while the search continued. The police had the right lead, were smart enough to reach the right house, but not to check the attic.

In the morning the girl friend gave Ilja some money and he decided to search for other friends. A streetcar delivered him to the house of his entertainer friends. He furtively made way to the door and knocked. No answer. In exasperation, he rushed next door, to her mother's house, where the elderly lady greeted him enthusiastically and gave him food.

"I was in jail," he told her. "I escaped."

She turned cold.

"What will happen to us? You can't hide from them."

"Can you take me to my friend's house?" he begged.

He didn't want to go by street car and risk additional public exposure. She walked him to the gate of his other friends, the Clepeks, and ran back down the street as Ilja walked through the gate praying for an answer to his door knock.

"Ilja. Welcome. I am so happy, so glad they let you go. Have some tea."

Ilja sat down, but motioned for her to wait before making tea. "You might not welcome me when I tell you this. I escaped from jail."

Her face wrinkled in concern, but the worry was for Ilja. "Don't fret about that. Tell me what happened."

Ilja told her everything. She called her brother, also a very strong anti-Communist, on the phone. He arrived in fifteen minutes with a car. He wanted to get Ilja out of her house quickly, because a connection would be made between the new escapee and his friends.

The brother drove to a lovely house on the outskirts of Prague. For a couple of days they talked, and came to the decision that the house was not safe. The brother gave him money, even clothing, and made arrangements with another friend they could trust. A middle-aged couple stopped with their car and drove him to still another house.

"Do not worry," the husband assured him. "First, we will send a telegram to Eva, saying that you will travel to Kosice, which is close to Hungary. This will lead to some confusion among the authorities "

In Czechoslovakia, every morning at 7:00, the authorities sponsored a criminal broadcast by the police, and the announcement went forth. Eva and all of Hlinik and Dolna' Zdana knew he had escaped and thereafter, all telegrams would be read.

The wife went to visit Eva, with precautions, and returned bringing money, his gun, bullets and suits. Ilja settled into a routine of hiding in the house, where the couple had moved their daughter to the grandmother's house so the child could not talk to friends about a stranger.

Eva came, staying in Prague with friends.

"Why did you come? You might be caught," Ilja admonished.

She gave him money, his wallet with driver's license, his gold watch fob, and other personal possessions. They made a plan for Ilja to escape to the West. Eva hesitated, believing that things would get better.

The trains going west were subjected to additional policeman for the last few stops. Guards checked the passengers thoroughly and reviewed papers to make sure people did not try to escape. The police rounded up suspects by the carload.

Ilja read during the day since he was alone and bored. His hosts took him to movies at night, and even asked him to a public bath, since the washing facilities in the post-war house were primitive, but Ilja was paranoid, seeing a policeman in every face. He declined.

"I will stay dirty."

After a month, the husband came home excited. "We have found a connection. You will leave soon, when we get a message. Then we travel, taking the first train in the morning. We will get off several stops before the last, because police walk through the train to question suspicious or unfamiliar people. After that, we meet a man with a car, who will take you to the border and freedom.

The telegram arrived. "Please send a basket of fruit."

Enactment of the plan began.

The hosts and Ilja boarded the train. A man waited with a truck at the appointed stop.

"Better than a car," thought Ilja.

Greetings and signals were exchanged. The entourage proceeded to his house, ten miles from the frontier, where the man outlined the escape path.

"I will take you to the forest and show you the stone where Germany begins."

Ilja handed him 50,000 rubles, keeping his pistol, bullets, a handful of chocolates and a dark raincoat.

Later that night, the host couple returned to Prague, and Ilja followed his guide into the forest under the cover of an overcast dark sky. Ilja watched cars on a road in the distance but could not determine if they were German or Czechoslovak. Their headlights peered like fireflies through the trees, and the guide offered no explanation.

Pondering his fate, he realized that he could never find peace within the Soviet Union and its puppet states. The best he could hope for was a long prison term and then stifling work as a sweeper. Like his father, he would then come home to mumble prayers, too fearful to transfer his beliefs and history to his sons whenever he might be permitted to see them, too cowed to hug them and know them. He could not live without those basic human expressions.

He had fought on both sides of a great war for the right to those expressions and still encountered the evil that had racked his life from birth. Gone were the days when he turned to mass causes, and armies to resist. However, he finally knew that armies and ideology alone could not guarantee his freedom.

Worries about the risks of escape interrupted his thoughts, and he envisioned dogs, guards and machine-guns, but he feared dogs most of all. Other than the right to run, the pressures on him allowed only two more alternatives, and he invoked them both. First, he prayed. Then he made a pledge not to be taken alive. He refused to set himself as an example of surrender to evil in front of his sons. Gripping his pistol, he vowed to kill himself before capture, and not miss as he had in Latvia.

The guide pointed to the cars. "Go across the street and proceed another quarter mile. You will come to the stone."

Ilja, confused, retorted, "Why are you explaining? Won't you go with me?"

The man pointed again. "You will see the stone, then houses on the German side. Goodbye."

They stood next to the truck and the guide jumped back in. Ilja ran after the rolling vehicle.

"Wait. You are supposed to accompany me."

The guide stuck his head out of the window. "No, No. Good bye."

Fear again, always fear and then happiness and then fear. And then, fear's turn once more. He ran military style, fifteen yards slouched, fifteen bent low to the ground. He crossed the road and crawled along it, noticing a path. The accursed moon came out full, like daylight. He sweated pounds, running, crawling, wriggling, with a dark raincoat on his back and a pistol in his hand, living his nightmare of running from guards and soldiers.

Night noises panicked his escape, and he held himself motionless, waiting for a dog. He drew his gun forward, preparing to dispense a couple of shots at an enemy before committing one to his head. Nothing but the moon, laughing. He spotted a rock, but still did not believe the silly story about a stone marking the line of West Germany. The woods opened into a field. He inched towards a house on the far side of the field. The sound of a quiet conversation drifted through the night air, and Ilja decided to crawl to within hearing distance.

A man and woman spoke. He slithered closer and closer. They were young lovers, kissing and unaware of the figure squirming very close. Within fifteen feet of the couple, he slowly stood up, folded his hands about the pistol handle and placed it in his raincoat pocket. Taking a step forward, he cleared his throat and greeted them in Slovak. "Good evening."

His trigger finger twitched. The man, startled, turned to the dark figure.

"Vas sagen sie?"

Ilja switched to German. "Could you please tell me where I am? Is this Germany?"

He struggled to keep his balance, almost fainting. The couple stared, wondering what was the matter with him.

"Germany?" the man answered suspiciously. "This is Germany."

Ilja reached into his other pocket and pulled out the chocolates he had forgotten, then extended his hand.

"Do you want a chocolate?" he asked, tears in his eyes.

The couple stared at the seemingly mad interloper. He cried.

"I have just escaped and want to get a train for Munich."

The couple shook their heads. "All of the trains for the day are gone. We will take you to someone."

Ilja had no money remaining after making the payment to the guide. He offered their friend his coat, pistol and bullets in exchange for a ticket to Munich. The deal was struck, and he stayed at the house waiting for the morning. He rode to Munich and asked for directions to the IRO, International Refugee Organization.

PART IV

AMERICAN PROMISES

Give me your tired, your poor,
Your huddled masses yearning to breathe free,
The wretched refuse of your teeming shore,
Send these, the homeless, tempest-tossed, to me:
I lift my lamp beside the golden door.

Inscription for the Statue of Liberty,
New York Harbor, USA
Written by Emma Lazarus

CHAPTER 20

THEY SHOOT OFFICERS

----A blind man loses his stick only once.

-- Uzbek proverb

In the fall of 1949, the Western Allies -- England, France and the United States -- still devoted considerable efforts to the postwar refugees. An immense array of organizations, public and private, under the umbrella of the International Refugee Organization (IRO) attempted to sort out separated families, people without homes or countries. The refugee achieved a degree of distinction by receiving a new appellation: displaced person.

The Soviet Union also devoted considerable energy towards the refugee question, although through markedly different means. Within their realm of control, covering the USSR and Eastern Europe, the Soviets gathered up hordes of ethnic groups moved by the vicissitudes of war. These people were returned to pre-war homes, willingly or not, while others attempted to escape the net of Soviet control. Many other groups, like Tatars of Crimea, who remained in their homeland during the war and aided the German cause in an attempt to dissociate themselves from Russia, were forcibly turned into refugees by coerced relocation. Finally, Moscow attempted to stem the tide of refugees fleeing Westward to escape their Communist dictatorship.

The most recent escapee from Soviet Europe, Ilja Narzikul, found his way to a city of low wooden former military barracks outside of Munich. The grief and disorientation caused by the sudden separation from his family was only slightly eased by his returning to Germany, a country that once welcomed him as a distinguished ally.

Munich did not compare with wartime Berlin, now in the middle of the Soviet zone. Somewhere in that city still stood his adopted house and the kindly Mrs. Rogozinski, his landlady. He tried not to dwell on all the people who meant so much to him in order to concentrate on the business of establishing a refugee status. He reported to the processing department of the IRO, where he found a bed and waited several days for a turn in the processing office. A number of Czechs and East Germans occupied bunks next to him.

"Where are you from?" they asked the new roommate.

Ilja answered, "I escaped from Czechoslovakia, but I was born in the Soviet Union, in Central Asia."

A German drew close, getting interested in his story "Central Asia. How did you get to Czechoslovakia? You must be one of those forced labor people from the war or an ex-Soviet soldier."

Ilja patiently explained, "I did serve in the Red Army as an officer, but was captured by the Germans."

The German grew concerned. "Stop right there." he commanded. "Do you know what the Americans do with ex-USSR soldiers, especially officers?"

Ilja, surprised by the strange question, kneaded his brow. "No, what do the Americans do?"

"The Americans drive up in a car accompanied by an ethnic Russian KGB or SMERSH officer and stand by while the KGB man places the ex-officer in handcuffs. The Russian KGB then drives off with the poor man, and we never hear from him again, even though we know what happens. The Soviets beat him up and send him to Siberia or worse. They do shoot officers, you know."

A couple of days later, the camp office called Ilja for a formal entry interview.

"Name," the clerk, a Czech DP himself, asked.

"Ilja Narzikul."

"Citizenship," he continued.

"Czechoslovak."

"Place of birth."

"Dolna' Zdana, Slovakia."

Ilja gave the answers routinely, using the strategies learned in Slovak interrogations, he created a new identity for himself. He needed a resume that would prove uninteresting to prying authorities. The clerk copied his responses without interest in the details, allowing Ilja to relax just a bit. He shuddered, thinking of his former soldiers and how answering questions incorrectly might lead to his sharing their fate. He did not slip out of Czechoslovakia to be packaged up by the Americans and handed over to a Soviet delegation.

"Identification," continued the clerk.

Ilja handed him his Slovak driver's license.

He muttered to himself, "Thank you, Frank."

After a night's sleep in one of the barrack dormitories, he returned the next day for a more complete interview. In sweaty nightmares and during the day in paranoiac imagination, he ran from Russians, repeating his tortuous dream, running from pursuers in great coats and rifles until Ilja jumped off a bridge.

At a follow-up session, a different clerk opened the just-started file.

"We need to know much more about you," he explained; "Where you went to school, your address in Slovakia, your life history."

Ilja wove a Slovak story, relating his knowledge of the countryside around the Hron River. Unlike his past Soviet interrogators, the clerk merely listened to the answers and jotted them down. Also, in contrast to the procedure of his Soviet interrogators, Ilja suspected that the record might end up in a central file accessible for future reference. That central file should remain as innocuous as possible, as he had a hard enough task ahead of himself reestablishing a trend to life, and hopefully reuniting with his family. Without the uniform of an army or the patronage of a powerful mentor like Frank, Ilja knew he needed to rely solely on his own resources for the next difficult phase of his life.

"Please stop back again tomorrow for further processing."

Ilja went back to the same barracks. The people there, from a number of countries and with different stories, had one common goal, explained by a recent escapee: "We hope to go to America."

"What is this America?" he wondered. From the time he entered Slovakia, the United States and its call to the world became more intriguing. Now he determined to take the American pull more seriously. If it was such a great country, he would go there too, and if he entered as a Slovak, he could escape whatever dragnets the Americans placed at the behest of the communist secret police.

The next day, he returned to the processing station.

"I understand that Czechoslovaks are housed in compounds together," he commented to the housing officer.

"Yes, that is true."

"I have a friend, Andrej, who escaped a while back and is in a camp someplace near Munich. May I get transferred there?"

The office issued him a housing voucher for a camp about fifty miles outside of Munich, and he prepared to depart with a travel allowance, but first he found a telephone book and visited Eva's friend Kata Blitz, the singer from Bratislava conservatory who had married a German. After she gave him tea, dinner and a gift of money, he climbed a streetcar back towards camp.

Directly across the aisle sat a fierce looking older man in a turban and robe. The two stared at each other.

"Nuriddin Qari," gasped Ilja. The mullah from the First

Turkistani Regiment nodded in disbelief.

Ilja jumped to embrace the man, who stood shaking badly, turning pale, barely able to stand. He met the embrace, but hesitantly. He thought Isakjan was dead.

"Isakjan?"

"Yes, it is me," he replied in Uzbek.

"You are dead."

"I am alive and here in Germany."

They hugged wildly.

"I performed a ceremony for your death in Slovakia. After the gun battle our troops found your blue leather jacket," Nuriddin protested.

"No, I ran too fast to put on my coat after the ambush."

They got off the streetcar at the first station, went to a coffee house, and there Ilja related his story from the Slovak forest to 1949.

The arrival of Isakjan Narzikul, commander of the second Turkistani SS battalion, in Germany made one of the biggest news events for the small surviving Turkistani community since the end of the war. The shock caused happiness, surprise and rumors.

They remembered very well that Isakjan Narzikul the military leader had lived in a house with Jurabay. They also knew that, as the Soviets entered Berlin, their forces used the services of Jurabay in finding records, places and people. While others hid in basements and tunnels to save their lives, Jurabay turned traitor and sided with the enemy.

The Turkistanis asked themselves, "Was Isakjan in Slovakia, or maybe in Moscow? And did he escape or is he on a mission for the KGB?"

Ilja, oblivious to all the speculation and unaware of the role Jurabay played for the Soviets, transferred to the Czechoslovak section of the DP camp in Murnau. He had explained to Nuriddin the dual roles of Isakjan and Ilja, and hoped to reunite with those Turkistanis still alive and in Germany. He tried to contact some of those mentioned by Nuriddin, but his calls went unanswered, and those he spoke with were abrupt and declined to extend the most minimal invitation.

The relief organization directed him to the Czechoslovak barracks where his friend Andrej lived. The two embraced, speechless with happiness at seeing each other, but shocked at the circumstances. Andrej had not yet given up his DP status and was trying for emigration to the U.S.

Andrej explained the machinery of emigration: "Australia

and New Zealand will take anyone, with few questions, but the U.S. and Canada are more strict, requiring, among other things, a sponsor who can guarantee a job and housing. But, if you can get to America, that is the best."

Ilja moved into a new home, a big open room with twenty-five people on metal cots. Meals were given at the mess hall. In the morning he walked to the camp office, where a couple of Americans and Swiss were in charge. Some Czechoslovaks waiting for émigré status obtained jobs as assistants. On the bulletin board he read publications about which countries accepted refugees, and what qualifications each required.

A candidate for admission to a particular country filled out a form and waited to see if that government chose to pursue the application. If so, a representative called the applicant in for additional screening. Every day there were places open in New Zealand and Australia as predicted by Andrej, provided the DP accepted a two- or three-year contract with a company that offered a sponsorship.

Andrej continued his explanation: "A lot of people, especially those like Jews and Poles, do not need to apply to New Zealand and Australia. They get into the U.S. with the help of relatives who have immigrated years ago."

Ilja adopted Andrej's position, "I would like to go to the U.S."

"That is such a rich, good country that gold practically lines the streets and money practically grows from trees," agreed Andrej. "For Czechs and Slovaks it is possible, but hard. If they find out you are Uzbek, forget it. There is some kind of a law which says that Asians are forbidden to immigrate."

Ilja fell for many immigration scams. He gave money to a number of people departing for the United States who promised to find him a sponsor as soon as they got there, but he never heard from any of them.

He tried to widen his contacts, but feared writing to Hlinik just yet, as that might endanger Eva and his family. But other refugees in the Czechoslovak compound became friendly.

His efforts to renew relationships with old Turkistani friends moved slowly, as they continually appeared too busy to see him, and didn't give out their home addresses. As Ilja settled into the camp life, a messenger from the gate ran to summon him.

"Some strange-looking people want to see you," reported the messenger.

Access to the camp was restricted at the entrance to those

with passes. When Ilja went to the gate, he could make out the flowing garb of Nuriddin, who brought his old commanding officer, Hayit. The Czechs and Slovaks were amazed to see this foreign man with a beard and turban.

Hayit gave him a warm Turkistani hug, and they departed to a restaurant in Munich. Hayit, with his ever-neat suit, looked him over carefully.

"Is it really you? You are alive?" he asked.

But Hayit acted distant. "What is this I hear about you in Slovakia?" he asked. "Where were you married? What did you do at the lumber mill? When did you visit Brataslava? How many times did the Soviets jail you?"

Ilja shrugged, almost sensing an interrogator's approach. The day passed so quickly that Ilja had to leave and hardly could ask about many of the Turkistanis in the Liberation Front.

"I will come soon and visit again," promised Hayit.

He honored the promise, and several months later, Hayit returned, this time exhibiting his old warmth and friendliness.

"Isakjan," he addressed him in his Turkistani appellation, "you alarmed us when you came back from the dead. Much has happen since the end of the war, and many horrible things have transpired. Do you know about Jurabay?"

Ilja did not.

"Jurabay ran to the Red Army at the end. We saw him in the streets with Soviet troops. He pointed out places and people. Alimov is in Siberia. And, for his reward, Jurabay also lives in a Siberian prison working on his rehabilitation.

"When you came, we thought you might be a spy because of your friendship with Jurabay. With your most unusual disappearance just after deserting the German army, I had to check out your story."

"How did you check out my story?" asked Ilja, very displeased with the thought that his word needed checking.

"I work for British intelligence, and Safi Oraz, the Turkistani who did secret police work with the Germans, now works for American intelligence. We confirmed your story."

Ilja sat, shocked. "So that is why the Turkistanis I met were so cold and reluctant to give me home addresses."

"Yes, that is why, but that should now change."

"Most of the Liberation Front Committee works these days with the British, continuing to publish our papers and distributing them about the world where Turkistanis are scattered. Our president, Veli Kajum-Khan, was held for a possible trial at

Nuremberg, but was released over the objections of the Soviet prosecutor after a couple years of internment.

"Some German friends from the old days are still in good jobs, and fortunately, one of them is our old German political supervisor from the East Ministry, von Mende, who works with the British and entered West German politics. We made contact with other old liberation groups, especially the Ukrainians, who are very well organized. The umbrella organization is called the ABN, for Anti-Bolshevik front of Nations.

"Von Mende introduced us to the British Military Government and we met a representative many times. At each meeting, the English envoy reiterated an admission about the enormous human and political error the Western Allies committed by turning over millions of Soviet expatriates to the Red Army. Possibly to make amends, the British sponsored a plan to generate research on the situation behind the Iron Curtain, and we resumed the publication of `National Turkistan.' Kajum-Khan was freed to join this British effort. All expenses are borne by the British." Hayit added, "Jurabay is a traitor."

Other Turkistanis then visited Isakjan. They told him to watch out for that old devil Safi Oraz who worked for American Military Intelligence and wrote reports on people. He had the power to make it hard on those he disliked. Ilja remembered him well and decided to keep him at a distance. He didn't want a negative report on his emigration file. All the concern with files bothered him, but he always inclined to the cautious side.

Ilja's old commanding officer returned several times with many others of the approximately 100 Turkistanis in Germany, and they often speculated about Germany's defeat, guessing what went wrong.

Hayit had thought about the subject often and wanted to present his conclusions in his often-rehearsed sequence. "Why did the mighty German army meet defeat? We can now look back and assess the reasons. First they fell into the error of believing in their superiority, deceiving themselves into a delusion of invincibility.

"Next, the Nazis spent tremendous efforts perpetrating atrocities against the Jewish people. Many Jews, especially in the Soviet Union, would have helped us were it not for the horrible acts committed against them. Also, they established a two-front war, and finally, the policy towards the East. Instead of accepting help from all of the Soviet republics, Hitler punished them with repression. The Ukrainians welcomed the Wehrmacht with gifts, and a year later the Nazis returned bullets. They treated Soviet laborers like slaves and kept their churches closed, the effect of which was to create a large partisan underground. One thing more. Hitler interfered with the professional army, overriding commands of the generals and trying to compete with them by creating a rival army with SS troops."

The analysis by the Turkistanis was independently agreed upon by Wehrmacht General Reinhard Gehlen, one of the architects of the invasion into the Soviet Union, who stated that Germany would have won the war if it had been fought against the Russian republic only and not the rest of the Soviet Union, and if Hitler had not interfered with the army or the principles of the nineteenth century theorist von Clausewitz. By wasting resources to destroy the Soviet peoples and Jews instead of wooing them for a common purpose, Germany ensured its own defeat. [1]

CHAPTER 21

GYPSY BLOOD

To authorize for a limited period of time the admission into the United States of certain European *(*author's emphasis*) displaced persons for permanent residence, and for other purposes.....*

"Eligible displaced person" shall also mean a native of Czechoslovakia who has fled as a direct result of persecution or fear of persecution...

-- U.S. Displaced Persons Act of 1948 [1]

Like most refugees, Ilja had no money. He talked to people in the camps who spoke of jobs driving cars for important officials, and others who knew where to sell their meager possessions for the highest price. They said that Americans especially wanted to give jobs to refugees. Ilja had his Czechoslovak license for driving and he applied to exchange it for a German one.

But his need for money could not wait for the formalities of job seeking. He heard from Andrej that smart DP's who obtained cash shopped for their goods in Mohlstrasse, the name of a street in Munich where much trade existed, a place where the majority of people living and doing business were Jews who somehow had survived and formed a market. In Mohlstrasse a man could bring his last possession, a watch or piece of jewelry, and feel certain to fetch a fair price.

Andrej confided, "That is the best place to go for business and exchanging money."

"But I have no money," Ilja complained.

"You have a gold watch," pointed out his friend. "The gold cover is very heavy and can be separated from the mechanical part and sold as precious metal."

Andrej sent Ilja on the train to Mohlstrasse, Munich, where he dropped off Ilja and ran his own errands. It was a crowded affair, with people conducting business from stalls, houses, stores, the sidewalk and even on foot, calling out their intentions as they walked. Remarkably, in a short period of time the street became known as a place to exchange goods and shop for good prices. The stores had won a reputation for delivering a vast array of goods.

Ilja spotted two men hawking jewelry, doing business on their feet in the street and asked them if they wanted to buy a gold watch with heavy chains. The tall one nodded his head in the affirmative. "Follow us," he advised in German.

"To where?"

"We must go to a watchmaker to take out the watch so we can weigh the gold."

They all proceeded to the watchmaker in a small shop a couple of doors down the street, and the value of the gold weighed in at 560 marks. The watch was very heavy.

"I agree," Ilja said to approve the deal.

The money was counted, flipped with professional snaps by the vendor, who rolled out twenty mark notes, and handed them to Ilja. He, in turn, flipped the money over and recounted, agreeing to the count. Satisfied, he put the money in his pocket and turned to walk away.

"Hold on," the trader shouted, "Wait a minute. I think I miscounted."

They stood outside the shop in the street. Ilja brought the money out of his pocket, handed it to the man in the black jacket, and watched. The partner nudged Ilja.

"Do you have any more watches you might like to sell us?" he wondered.

Ilja lost track of the counting. "No."

"Well, how about any of your friends?"

"I don't know. I'll ask around," he promised.

The other man handed back the money to Ilja, folded. Ilja put it back in his pocket.

A minute later, he removed the money to recheck the count, and found that the first bill was a twenty and the remainder, instead of twenties, was switched with one-mark bills. Instead of 560 marks, he now had 38. He whirled around, tried to relocate the men, but they were gone.

He immediately fell into a deep depression. He felt so disgusted, giving up the last valuable thing in his possession, shamed and stupid that he was taken over by two street con artists. He, the businessman and tabilci.

On his return to Murnau he told nobody, such was his shame. But his changed demeanor was noticed by several of his friends.

"What is troubling you?" asked Andrej.

Ilja denied any stress. Andrej persisted and Ilja confessed. The whole kitchen staff admonished him.

The next day, one of the largest men Ilja had seen in the camp, a big Czech, approached him.

"Andrej told me you were cheated at Mohlstrasse. Would you recognize the men who did this?"

Ilja said, "Yes."

"Then take me there and I will get your money back."

The man was a giant and brought a long knife. They took the train back to Munich. He said to Ilja, "When you see them, don't go close, just show me."

Ilja quickly spotted them walking through the crowd with the same chant. He pointed and listened to the big man's instruction.

"Stay put. I will tell you when to come."

A couple of strides and the giant faced the two men.

"Do you want to buy dollars?" he asked.

Before either could answer, he suddenly grabbed the one who had distracted Ilja, closing a meaty hand around his collar. He shouted for Ilja.

When the con man's partner saw Ilja coming he ran away, but the Czech held the other firmly, revealing the knife in his other hand. Ilja froze, having second thoughts about a possible police action and what might end up on his record.

He held his hands in a conciliatory wave. "Please just let him go. I don't want any trouble. We have to have a clean record to emigrate. Just let him go."

But a crowd of men speaking a variety of languages in loud tones accented with waving hands, formed a circle around the action. The big Czech stood firm.

"Stand back," he insisted. "He owes us money."

A leader of the crowd approached the inside of the circle.

"Excuse me," he began. "What are you doing with this man? If there is a problem, perhaps we can help."

Hardly letting go of either the man or the knife, the Czech responded, "This man shortchanged my friend last week. He stole his money."

The jewelry merchant struggled to breathe, but nodded his head in admission. "It wasn't me, it was the one who ran away," he gasped.

The leader held up his hands. "Loosen up on your grip so we can talk."

Free of the strangling hold, the vendor shook his head to test the working of his neck. The leader continued.

"If this is true it isn't right. This must be rectified, and I will make sure you get your money back. We are very concerned about the business that is transacted in this street and want every customer to be satisfied, to know that he will not be cheated. Come back in three hours. In that time I will see to it that they get the money for you."

Before they separated, the big Czech warned the man, "If the money is not returned, maybe not today or tomorrow, but soon, I will have your life. Think about it, 500 marks or your life."

The man's head hung low and he rubbed his neck.

"I guarantee," predicted Ilja, "that they will not show up. Furthermore, we should forget about it, because if the police get involved, we will get a record and never emigrate."

His friend disagreed. "No, No. They will show up, and

we will get the money. This street is known for honesty, and I am here to guarantee it."

After three hours, they returned to the street. With the leader supervising, the culprit returned the money.

The leader checked, "Are you satisfied?"

Ilja shook his head in the affirmative, "Yes."

"Any time that you have a problem here, you can come to me. Tell your friends that this area is one where the business people behave."

They departed with a sense of satisfaction. Ilja decided that when he did have money, he would do his shopping at that location. The leadership of the street achieved something that he had sought when he insisted on proper behavior for his soldiers both in the Wehrmacht and also as partisans.

With his German driver's license issued, he applied for jobs. He heard that many American soldiers were stationed in a certain section of town, so he went there to an office of the American military occupation forces. A week later he was hired to drive a jeep station wagon for an American captain named Jones. The captain was the supply officer for a United States armed forces mess hall. Ilja drove him around on personal errands and business calls, different offices, movies, and basketball games. Most Fridays, Jones told Ilja in perfect German to take the car for the weekend. "I don't need it, but drive carefully."

Some weekends, Jones needed to be driven to his girl friend's house, and other days to bars. The man drank an immense amount of alcohol for a twenty-five-year-old.

"Do you know your way around Munich?" he asked the driver after a month of service.

"Sure," answered Ilja.

"No, I mean the business areas," specified Jones.

"Yes, that too," Ilja responded.

"See if you can sell this," he ordered and handed him twenty pounds of coffee.

Almost every product imaginable stood in short supply in post war Europe. Ilja knew what to do, and immediately headed for Mohlstrasse to wander among the now familiar vendors, smiling at their pitches, showing his American military authorization, and picking out ones to do business with. Quickly establishing stalls that paid the highest prices, he completed the transaction without delay.

The deal pleased Jones and he followed up with more.

The trade grew to include coffee, cigarettes and whiskey. Ilja sold about a hundred marks worth of goods each week, and Jones always demonstrated his pleasure with a twenty-percent tip.

Ilja could soon afford a small room in a German family's house so he could make himself more available to his employer. He carried a hose with him and a five-gallon canister. Gas was in short supply for the Germans, but not for the Americans, and he well knew that five gallons fetched twenty marks.

New escapees arrived almost daily, bloating the rolls. As the true war refugees departed for new homelands, those fleeing from Soviet dominance started to make up the majority. Ilja talked to those escaping from near his Slovak home and they related to him that his family was coping. Some friends sent letters to their families, asking them nonchalantly about the Freidrichs in Hlinik. By 1951, Ilja could write, send money and goods. He received pictures of his family. Eva taught music to bring in a little income, and they still had the house, although the lumber mill had passed out of their control.

Through channels he discovered in the camps, Ilja tried to arrange the escape of his family, but Eva declined. He saved up and paid a man 600 marks to get them out. The guide returned with a letter from Eva saying that things would get better after a few years and she did not want to leave her mother and furniture. This answer shocked Ilja beyond comprehension. Ilja tried to convince her otherwise, telling her the importance of keeping the family together, but her need to hold on to her surroundings was greater than the wish to move to the uncertainty of West Germany. She said that Ilja had no permanent position since his job with the American captain had to end soon, and he could not provide any guarantee of even a place to live.

As the Americans departed, they closed down the mess hall and Jones was transferred, leaving Ilja without a job. The period of unemployment lasted only a short while, as he managed to procure another job at a motor pool that serviced a number of refugee organizations. Throughout the Bavarian area a dozen DP camps requisitioned transportation for various officials, which kept his services in demand.

Then he got an assignment doing the same route each day, between several groups, including: HIAS, (Hebrew Immigration Aid Society), not far from Mohlstrasse; the American Service mail depot; and a route picking up mail or delivering packages.

With time passing, he increasingly became very serious

about emigrating. He avoided his Turkistani friends because if word ever got to the likes of Safi Oraz that someone else entered the U.S. before him, Safi might write something bad in one of his reports.

He solicited means for getting a sponsor to invite a hard worker like himself to America. After refusing a couple of jobs in Australia, he stated a desire to go to Canada, since no plan emerged for the US.

He remembered Martin Suezz, the Jewish lumberman who did business with his father-in-law, and whom he had met in Slovakia. Ilja went to the Jewish organization, HIAS, and asked if they could find the address of Suezz in Canada. They assured him they would try, but would be impeded since Ilja did not even know the name of the town. In one week, they located him in Toronto, even though he had changed his last name to Martin.

Ilja wrote him a letter, reminding him that they had met at his father-in-law's house, and related the unfortunate necessity of his escape. Could he help a person in need? Six weeks later, he was informed that Mr. Martin would sponsor him to live in Canada with a job in a lumber mill. He thanked the Jewish organization profusely for its aid, reflecting on the ways that Jewish organizations and people had helped him after the war both in Czechoslovakia and in West Germany.

As the papers wound their way through the DP process, he received another assignment, driving a Swiss woman on her visits to various camps for interviews with prospective emigrants. One rainy day, he drove her to the city of Rosenheim, where he headed for something hot to drink in the camp cantina (canteen). He started to light a cigarette but discovered he had no matches. Next to him stood a beautiful girl. He asked for a match, which she produced.

"I never saw you before in this camp," she said.

"I do not live here, but am a driver for the Swiss interviewer. Can I buy you a cup of coffee?"

She motioned for him to follow. "I have some good food in my room."

Her room violated all refugee rules: a private room in a refugee camp, stocked with a refrigerator, a nice bed, a radio, drinks and fashionable furniture. She offered Ilja wine, bread, kolbasa and coffee. They talked about emigration, which was the main topic in the camps. He started dating her, taking her to restaurants, making the trip back on weekends to visit her. One day she said they should go to a nightclub.

"I have no money for that," he objected.

"Don't worry, let's go."

Ilja choked when he looked at the prices, and she suggested, "Let's have champagne."

He groaned. "I do not have any money."

"You are not to worry about it."

She ordered the most expensive dishes. When the bill came, she put a 50-mark bill in his pocket, whispering, "I have a German boyfriend who is very wealthy."

He finally told her about his plan to emigrate to Canada because he could not get into the United States, his first choice.

She became concerned, "Why can't you go to the U.S?"

"Because no one will send me sponsorship papers."

"I will help you," she offered.

He brushed her off. "Get out of here. You know how many people promised they would get me a sponsor, even taking my money. After they got to the United States I never heard from them again."

She grew excited. "Wait a minute, I don't want your money. I am your friend, so just give me some information about your camp and where you were born. I have a girlfriend who emigrated a year and a half ago, and I will write to her."

His mind was made up. "No, it's no use. I have something now and don't want to lose it."

She pestered him. "Stall, just five more weeks. You have nothing to lose."

He reluctantly agreed. In six weeks, he received another invitation, this one to come to the United States and be sponsored by an acquaintance of the girlfriend in America.

In preparation for departure, he went through another round of the all too familiar questions. "Where were you born? Give us your life story plus any documents and details."

He spun his lies about a Slovak life, still fearing the American habit of sending people back to Russian torturers against their will. Since many people in the DP camps had no documentation, he swore a declaration in front of a notary that everything was true and this was acceptable to the authorities. He estimated the year and month of his birth since he never had received a birth certificate, calculating a birth in the spring of 1923.

The interviewers called Ilja for a last intensive session before the issuance of visa and immigration papers to the U.S. Three members of a panel questioned him: two Slovaks and one

American. The American did not speak Slovak. In Slovak, one interviewer asked him, "Why are you dark complected while the majority of Slovaks are light? What about the imperfections in your pronunciation? Also, why is your name not Slovak?"

He almost stumbled on that question, but recovered by recalling his early days in Slovakia when, as a German officer, he learned the language in preparation for a possible melting in with transient populations when the war ended. "I am part Gypsy," he coyly admitted.

The interviewers shifted papers.

"Who was your doctor? your school teacher, the chief of police, the butcher?"

These answers he well knew. Three days later, Ilja Narzikul was on the train. He entered the port city of Bremerhaven and boarded a boat, which sailed for the U.S.

He still hoped for a reunion with Eva and his children, but he was helpless, and Eva so reluctant. Out of money and exhausted from always running, he had no choice.

He wrote no notice to the Turkistanis, since he did not want them to know of his emigration, as word might get to Safi Oraz, who was capable of trying to block his departure. His friend Andrej telegrammed a brother in the United States that Ilja Narzikul planned to arrive, instructing the brother to meet the boat.

CHAPTER 22

I AM STILL ALIVE

We hold these truths to be self-evident, that all men are created equal, that they are endowed by their Creator with certain unalienable Rights, that among these are Life, Liberty and the pursuit of Happiness. That to secure these rights, Governments are instituted among Men, deriving their just powers from the consent of the governed.

-- United States Declaration of Independence

The boat of future American residents crossed the ocean in April 1949, and in a few days the ship settled in New York harbor just short of the dock, waiting for the appointed morning crew. On shore, headlights of cars going to work pierced the dim morning light. More cars passed than he had seen in all of Europe. The tall buildings, packed in closely, challenged the sky for space. As the sun rose and gave greater light to the sky, he saw crowds of people scurrying about. Wartime Berlin had reverberated with a pulse of power and purpose, but the activity in New York surpassed even that level.

Andrej's brother met Ilja at the dock, bought him a meal at the Praha restaurant, gave him ten dollars, and put him on the train to Chester, Pennsylvania, where his sponsor welcomed him at the station. The sponsor lived on the first floor in a one-bedroom apartment, so Ilja slept on the couch in the living room while the host family, consisting of husband, wife and two-year-old son, used the bedroom.

He applied for a Social Security card, and found a job with a Ukrainian builder; then he got a job at General Steel in Philadelphia, as a sweeper, cleaning metal chips from the floors. In Jizzakh, Ilja would have welcomed a sweeper job, but that was a long time ago, before he trained as a tabilci, then as a Soviet officer; gained social footing, only to learn defeat; then he had trained a second time as officer and again met defeat; but he gained respect in Czechoslovakia and then found defeat another time. He had to start over once again, and to avoid the embarrassment of his new position, he applied for the late shift. The company granted his request for night work, where he could perform his duties in isolation. Ilja swept floors in Philadelphia and, unknown to each other, his intellectual friend Jurabay swept floors in Jizzakh.

While he worked as a sweeper earning union wages of $1.50 per hour, he practiced English. He watched TV every night and concentrated on the sounds and pronunciations the actors and announcers used and then practiced writing a few new words thirty times each day. Within a short time, he achieved a reading and speaking knowledge of the English language, accented with a smattering of German and Uzbek. But it was not as simple to gain entry into the American way of life. His expertise with a spoon and a fork, love of the theater, and humble manner brought little notice.

"Ilja? What the hell does that mean? I'll call you Jay," decided a fellow worker.

Jay became his name.

He changed jobs after Baldwin Manufacturing Company accepted his application for a helper's position, and after another year, he started to think about machine operation. He picked out a simple machine, the drill press, and asked many probing questions while he watched its motions. His supervisor denied him the position and he withdrew, depressed. In America he could not find a patron. His minority status yielded no benefits, and his knowledge of opera and dancing brought no friends, so he sought solace with the shop steward.

"I am not a born American," Jay explained in slow accented English, "but the drill press is a machine that I now understand. How can someone like me get a chance to prove himself? I come from a country called Uzbekistan, and, if you can help me, I will show you that when an Uzbek is given the opportunity, he can work as well as a Russian or an American."

The shop steward listened intently, sensing the truth of the immigrant's words. While he considered a course of action, he encouraged Jay to continue talking. "Tell me about your homeland," he suggested.

"Uzbekistan is far from here, northwest of India. Before our country was defeated by the Russians, we were a proud, independent people, ruled by leaders whom we called khans or beks," explained Jay, momentarily forgetting his job problem while recounting the past grandeur of his birthplace.

Even though the steward was only half-listening, he perked up upon hearing a point he thought interesting. "Beks," he said. "You were ruled by beks and your people are called Uzbeks. There must be a connection."

"Yes," Jay agreed. "Bek means ruler. Uz is the word for "ourselves." Uzbek means self-rule." [1]

The steward looked at Jay, a defeated man from a defeated country, but recognized that certainly the man would one-day rule himself again. "I will see the company boss today," he promised.

Here, Jay found a champion, not for cultural advancement, but for work and dollar benefits. The agent insisted that Jay had the right to prove himself.

"If Jay fails, you can demote him," he maintained. The supervisor followed the steward's advice.

Jay's performance matched the standards of the factory. The increased pay allowed him to purchase a new Mercury car, which he shortly sold to buy a little triplex in the working man's section of Collingdale. In a couple of years, he opened his eyes to the milling machine. The shop steward intervened on his behalf, repeating again, "Demote him if he can't handle it." He repeated his efforts to learn each new machine until 1957, when he worked as a horizontal boring mill operator, the highest paid machine operator in the plant.

His semblance of stability brought him no peace, as Eva resolutely refused to join him, despite the constant letters and packages he sent. She did not tell him that she had remarried, and he sent the letters addressed to the woman he believed was still his wife.

He missed his old friendships and found difficulty in establishing new ones, so he wrote to the Turkistanis in Germany and discovered that a trickle of them had immigrated to America.

Jay understood this after Safi Oraz moved to Washington, D.C. Safi undertook special assignments, as usual, while the others did tasks such as clipping newspaper articles, translating, and cataloguing. Safi said he worked for the Library of Congress and expressed a great deal of interest in Jay, inquired into the details of his job at the Philadelphia machine shop and invited him to Washington.

"Would you like another job, one that would help our homeland?" Safi asked.

Jay was noncommittal, having just settled into a bit of security and having started to work his way into the American culture. On the other hand, his sense of duty to Turkistan called upon his conscience, and he promised to think about pursuing an undefined mission.

He returned to the second-floor apartment of his house in Collingdale and to the machine factory to punch the Baldwin clock and read papers in the evening.

He answered the bell to his apartment one night. The man who knocked on the door flashed a badge.

"Mr. Narzikul?" he asked.

"Yes. Who are you?"

"I am from the Department of the Army," the man answered.

"What do I have to do with the Army?"

The visitor was patient. " Can I talk to you?"

"Sure, come in," Jay invited.

The man spoke fluent Russian. Later, Safi confirmed that the man was a CIA agent. The officer came for information, or so he said.

"I understand that you graduated from a Red Army military school?" he began.

"Yes, I did," Jay admitted.

"Well, why don't you tell me about it, and about your whole life?"

His stomach curled with the vulnerability of the accused, but he tried another time to submit to another round of interest in his past. "Well, I was born in Slovakia."

The army man interrupted, "No, no, no. We know that you are a Soviet citizen. We knew it when you applied to immigrate, but we let you come anyway. We knew why you lied, but still we said nothing, so your secret is safe with us. So now you can talk. No lies. We are very interested about your life and the Tashkent Military School. Let's start with how you were admitted to Tashkent Military School."

This man started out with heavy artillery, and who knew what he might be holding back. Jay told the truth, about the falsification of his age, school subjects, and training. The Army man wrote everything down. Jay thought the whole act perplexing and could not imagine why they wanted such old information. Fearing that a round of arrests would follow, he began to lose sleep. His dream appeared more frequently. Years of nightmares, and he still ran from Russians in uniforms with guns and still jumped off the bridge.

In three weeks, the man called Jay again, asking him to meet in the Sheraton Hotel in Philadelphia. The man turned on a radio to prevent bugging. After a similar session, he pledged to be in touch again.

Jay started to worry that if anyone found out that he came to America as a Slovak, his immigration might be in jeopardy. Associating with Turkistanis who could identify him might prove as dangerous as moving to Jizzakh. He contacted the International House for advice where a woman lawyer gave a sympathetic ear.

Jay poured out his worries, pointing out that he was just a factory worker trying to establish a home in America.

The woman comforted him. "You are lucky. The government has put an amnesty into effect with regard to cases like yours."

She modified all of his paperwork, making Ilja his middle and Isakjan his first name, and his place of birth, Jizzakh. He became legal. At the end of 1957, he celebrated with a tour of Germany and Turkey, where many of his friends had moved.

Later he was invited to Washington, with all expenses paid by the Army man. Jay accepted and met a couple of Americans who spoke Russian. They hooked him up to a lie detector test. Jay all the time tried to surmise why they were so interested in his past, which couldn't be so significant.

He soon found out. "We need people like you in the Soviet Union. We can train you, give you big money, and plant you back in Uzbekistan."

Jay balked at the suggestion. "That is the one thing I fear the most. If I am ever recognized......" He trailed off, "I can't even guess the penalty."

The man dropped the matter. "Keep it in mind, maybe later, or maybe some other job."

Jay liked that. "I would be happy to accept a job in the Library of Congress."

The interview ended and he retraced his steps to Collingdale.

Safi called. "Come to Washington and visit. There are some people I want you to meet."

Safi threw a dinner party with some Turkistani friends recently called to Washington for jobs, and then requested that Jay come to his office the next day. He met two men who thought he might like to take a trip to Europe.

The offer seemed consistent with Jay's personality changes. He no longer looked to governments in order to satisfy his problems and much preferred his Czechoslovak family life to his earlier one as a zealot. But even with his cynicism regarding political regimes, he still felt a pull to get involved for the sake of his homeland. Jay contacted his friend Shermat who had also immigrated to Washington recently.

Shermat took a cautious attitude. "The State Department does not encourage programs which might lead to national independence for Soviet republics. They do, however, make it possible to gain a little information about the non-Russian peoples of the Soviet Union. See what happens."

The first thing that happened was a medical exam and a session with a psychologist who displayed pictures and asked for stories:

A sad woman with head on hand.

"Maybe someone is far away, or she might have financial troubles." He thought of his mother.

A portrait of flowers:

"It reminds me of when I was young in Tashkent and walked in the parks and between the stalls of beautiful fresh fruits."

Other pictures of dogs, cats, and scenery followed. Then came an invitation.

"There is an International Students Organization meeting in Vienna. We would like to send you and Safi to this conference."

"What do I have to do?" was his obvious question.

"Don't worry about it. Safi knows what to do."

They met one of the men a couple of times. Jay received a false passport, tickets, money and arrangements for a leave of absence at Baldwin.

Jay and Safi flew to Germany and prepared to leave for Vienna, where they called on the same CIA man they had met in Washington. Jay was surprised, ever more convinced he didn't want to know what this game entailed, but he listened as the man instructed them to mingle with the Soviet students.

"The objective is to meet them and see if there is anyone ripe for escape or recruitment."

Jay's reconstructed history was that his mother and father escaped to Afghanistan in the 1930's and eventually got to the U.S. They congregated with the students, especially the Turkistanis, allowing Jay to enjoy himself and the interchanges.

Late each night they rejoined the man from Washington and discussed whom they had talked with that day, planning whom to meet and where to go the next day. Jay loved talking to the people from his old home in the relaxed atmosphere.

After a couple of evenings, at another review, Safi started to tell the CIA representative more and more about one or another student who might want to escape or might be inclined toward recruitment because of disenchantment with the Russian dominance of Turkistan.

Jay was astonished, and cornered Safi afterwards. "No such thing happened, Safi. I was with you the whole time. Those are lies and false information. Why are you telling all of these stories?

Safi tried to calm him down. "Don't worry about these things. That is my job."

Jay was then vexed about how the U.S. got its intelligence to base foreign policy and decisions: from people who give misinformation, have no knowledge, and don't care enough?

Back in Washington, Jay was asked if he wanted to give a report, but declined, since he had already told everything to the CIA man, but Safi filed a thick document. Jay rejected the CIA and such government causes. Between cause and anarchy lies humanity, and that became his option. The righteous path in mass causes had led to naught too often, and he relied more on his own judgment now. Jay concluded that spying was not for him, not professional. He complained to Shermat, "Is this the way the United States conducts its foreign policy?"

Shermat gave him little solace. "First, I do not think that is the way the United States conducts foreign policy. However, this is a great country, but the politicians know so little about Central Asia. I testified before a congressional committee, and spent most of the time explaining where Turkistan is. We are free here, however, and can be thankful to the country which gave us citizenship."

And Jay devoted himself to work, leaving his inclination for politics aside and taking the night shift at Baldwin and a second day job selling used cars for a Hungarian friend. It was just as well that he did not have much time to sleep, as the night dreams still haunted him with pursuing Russian soldiers and leaps from the same bridge. He suffered from the pain of isolation from his family and his history, which caused him to bury his energy in work. After work he drove people around, shined cars and gave sales pitches. He never sold a car, but discovered the disadvantages of a foreign accent. The car lot owner took pity on him and recommended that he try something else.

He needed money also, as he sent regular packages of clothing and household goods to Czechoslovakia for his family. Even though he did not realize that his wife had remarried, he began to realize that he would never be reunited with Eva.

The desire for a stable family life became paramount, and he began to visit Mary, who lived in one of the units of his triplex house with her infant son and worked in a store. Her father didn't have a military rank or entree into exclusive crowds and she could not offer him protection from discrimination or further his pursuit of high culture. She hadn't seen `Hamlet' or `La Traviata.'

Her laugh was enchanting, accented with sparkling Irish eyes and a carefree smile. Some of her friends had warned her that he looked different and therefore could not be trusted.

"Then what do you think I am?"

"I don't know for sure. You have a strange accent with a little German and other things. I think you are Iranian or something like that."

She found something strong in him, something that his correct posture and careful table manners did not reveal. She loved him for his honesty and courage, but most of all for his profound humanity. She found in him all things that he thought were lacking: equality, love, strength, faith and cause. And he, having had access at various times in his life to all levels of society, found that he preferred her innocence and needed the support she so generously gave.

The courtship combined an unusual blend of nationalities and personal habits. He would cook a Turkistani dinner and have it waiting when she arrived home from work, to be shared before he departed for his night shift. They went to the beach and picnics with Mary's son, who looked to Jay as a father.

They were married in a civil ceremony. Two years later, with a church annulment of his Slovak wedding, they married in a symbolic repeat ceremony in the Catholic Church. Religion comprised an important part of their lives, and church attendance was regular. In starting a new marriage, Mary helped him remember the children from the one in Czechoslovakia with assistance in shopping for clothes and goods that were incorporated in the regular package sent East.

They added to their family, first with another son. A second son was born prematurely, weighing two pounds, four ounces. Months passed, but with determination and hope they fought for the child's life using experimental procedures until the boy stabilized. Jay, on the way from Baldwin to a second job, stopped at the hospital with chocolates for the nurses and support for his wife and child every day.

Jay took a job with another couple of friends who owned a small machine shop, calling on factories using machined parts. He spent his days calling on potential customers, and signed up some work after following every lead, pacing and fretting until he pursued it to the end. That was the essence of assimilation in America: work.

Shortly Jay and the two partners who owned the little shop decided to join forces and savings to purchase machines from a retiring shop operator. Jay brought in the work, purchased the materials, and kept the books while his new partners constructed the metal items. All three worked at Baldwin at night, signing tools out when needed to fill certain orders. Even in the machine business, his early guidance in Jizzakh as tabilci and in Slovakia as manager helped him.

The partnership didn't quite flourish. Often discussions on procedure occupied more time than the production itself. The operators didn't respect the specifications of the salesman, sometimes giving a mirror finish when a rough one was called for and other times not conforming to tolerances. One partner required frequent bailouts from drunken sprees. The partnership dissolved, but Jay had tasted the excitement of running a business in the United States and enjoyed it as much as he had in Slovakia.

A lawyer who helped him dissolve the partnership referred him to another machine shop in financial trouble, which allowed him to rent idle machines. Mary answered the phone while he sought orders. He soon hired other Baldwin employees part time to fill his orders while working forty hours a week for Baldwin and forty for himself. He concentrated on office work and sales while hiring men for the production work.

Increasing orders from firms like Mack Truck and Landsdowne Steel allowed him to open his own shop. His technique for landing sales tended to follow a simple process. He returned to potential customers dozens of times until they let him try a small order. He returned those orders quickly and expertly. More orders followed.

Baldwin gave Jay notice that work was slow and he could either get a layoff notice or bump the next operator with less seniority. With business exceeding $500,000 per year at his machine shop, he elected a layoff, and devoted more time to his fledging company. Great success followed.

But he still harbored an empty feeling without seeing his sons in Slovakia. He yearned for his entire family to be together and finally convinced them to visit in 1968. They arrived with an emotional reunion, surprising him with their long hair and news of changes in Czechoslovakia.

"We are making the country our own once again and building for a society without the Russians," they claimed. "Czechoslovakia now is modern and a wonderful place to live, with many reforms being instituted."

But Soviet troops surrounded Prague. Jay begged them to stay, but they did not heed his pleas.

"Don't be silly, the Soviets will leave soon and everything will be fine." They departed. The day after their plane left for Prague, Soviet troops started shooting civilians and tank battles ensued. Contact with Czechoslovakia ceased and Jay thought his sons were doomed to death. After a couple of weeks, a telegram arrived, "Send four tickets." He didn't know how to react. Nevertheless, he sent the tickets. The boys arrived with their girlfriends, having paid off officials to leave. He then had five sons in all.

The girlfriends wore mini-skirts and the boys had long hair. Jay bought them new clothes and sat the boys next to each other in side-by-side chairs at the barbershop. He gave the boys upstairs rooms and the girls accommodations downstairs, with orders that the doors had to be open at all times. They woke up each morning asking for Pepsi Cola.

He planned their weddings, but not without complications. One of the girls was only fifteen at the time and needed parental approval. His lawyer drew papers for a friend to become guardian and then give consent.

The family sat at the dinner table reciting prayers together before dinner. Religion helped hold the family together, and they discussed their beliefs openly and candidly, among themselves and friends, with Jay always reminding his family of the prohibitions regarding prayer in the Soviet Union. The family business became another aspect of the dinner dialogue in a far different manner from what Jay had experienced with his father. Instead of sneaking out to conduct his affairs so that authorities would not discover him, Jay eventually brought four of his sons into his manufacturing business and constructed a large building to house his activities. When his other son expressed an interest in medicine, he encouraged that pursuit.

Jay considered all Turkistanis part of an extended family, so when friends in Washington alerted him that Dr. Karimi, the Uzbek from Tashkent whom they all had known in Berlin, planned to visit Philadelphia, he listened. Karimi had married an Italian girl and lived in Italy since the war. He wanted to study American techniques of orthogeneratology at the Philadelphia General Hospital in order enhance his professional skills and to separate from his wife due to an unsatisfactory marriage. Jay went to visit Karimi in his Philadelphia apartment. Jay visited him weekly. Karimi gave Jay an honorary white medical jacket and brought him along as Karimi visited patients. Jay and Mary often played hosts, treating Karimi to Turkistani meals at their house. Karimi stayed two years, without his wife, preferring the role of a Casanova.

One month Karimi opened an unexpected flurry of letters from his mother in Tashkent, Uzbekistan. She was dying, and her last wish was to see her long-lost son. This affected Karimi very much. He announced intentions to return to Uzbekistan. His visiting status in the United States had expired and he could not bring himself to return to an unsettling marriage in Italy.

Jay minced no words. "Stupid and crazy. They will use you and dig up the past."

But Karimi returned to Tashkent and Jay fell into a deep depression, not only from the departure of Karimi, but also from the sadness that expatriate survivors exhibit, longing to visit the place of their birth and walk the streets and paths that had shaped their lives, but afraid even to speak of it.

Jay also feared that his mother, possibly still living, could suffer when the Communists discovered that he lived in America. But, to his surprise, Karimi received royal treatment. The reason for the friendly welcome soon became obvious as Karimi granted many interviews to Russian and Turkistani journalists, who published stories relating Karimi's love of the Soviet Union and how the Germans had forced his cooperation. Once one of the most fanatical proponents of Turkistani nationalism, Karimi now denounced that cause and wrote of his joy at returning to a Communist Uzbekistan.

Shortly, Jay found a letter from the Soviet Union in his mail. "Greetings from your mother and greetings from your sister."

He never knew he had a surviving sister. Evidently his mother was pregnant when he had last seen her, before his father died and he left for war.

The letter went on: "We didn't know you were alive, but are very happy that we heard from Dr. Karimi that you are well. I and your half-brother looked hard for you, reading and looking at all the lists....."

Jay wrote back, "Yes, I am still alive."

EPILOGUE

In 1971, thirty years after his hasty graduation from military School, the Soviet and United States governments approved an invitation for Jay's mother and sister to come to America. She had never left the Jizzakh area in her life, never traveled on a train, let alone an airplane. Her ways were those of an era long disappeared in the rest of the world.

Jay drove to New York to greet her at Kennedy Airport after her long journey: the train from Tashkent to Moscow and a plane to New York. He grew a beard so that he might resemble his late father and the image of an adult Uzbek. A small wrinkled old woman with receding gum lines in a dark dress stepped fearfully from the plane. She recoiled from the escalator, sitting down on its treads as the moving stairs carried her to the lower floor. She brought a barrel-shaped pot for cooking tea, and other old dirty beat-up pots and pans for food and water, anticipating a necessity to endure the hardships of ancient expeditions.

Jay looked down at her. He had expected to look up, since she had towered over him at last sight. He bent over to embrace her, tears in his eyes.

"What has happened to you? Have you shrunk? You were so strict. When you called, I had to come right away. If you caught me in a lie, you hit me right away. You taught me not to take what doesn't belong to me, and to tell the truth."

His mother talked about the war, about her worries for his sister.

"We tried so hard to find you after the war, but never a sign. Only Jurabay, your friend from grade school and now a drunk, thought you could be alive. Poor Jurabay. He went to Siberia after the war and now just sweeps floors and gets drunk.

"Without a family, obtaining a husband for your sister proved hard. Even wealth does not replace the value of family ties in Uzbek tradition," his mother continued. "She married an orphan who, luckily, turned out to be a hard worker, fixing the house and painting its rooms. Our house is the same and our neighborhood still includes the old families, but with more children and new faces.

"And you, my son, why don't you come home?"

What a question. The woman did not understand.

"If I had come home, the government might have shot me or sent me to Siberia. I would be like Jurabay."

Jay spent from his newly acquired wealth, purchasing dresses, cloth and household goods. His sister gasped at the American miracle of plentiful goods, but his mother showed no interest in any of the materials. The women had come from another era of history, still eating with their hands and remaining totally unfamiliar with appliances.

"Take anything the airline will let you return with," he advised.

They carried more than that, but a generous tip to the redcap eased the problem. His sister visited the United States again and again. Jay started to go to the Globe Parcel Service Company on Walnut Street where he could buy anything for delivery around the world. He bought goods for his family in Uzbekistan, usually Soviet-made goods paid for by American dollars plus taxes, charges, transportation: cloth, raincoats, and refrigerator.

A dress costing six U.S. dollars could be sold in the USSR for sixty dollars equivalent, because those kinds of goods did not exist for the Soviet citizen at any affordable price. Usually in the USSR there was a ten-year wait for a car, but with American currency the automobile he ordered for his family arrived in a few weeks.

By then a number of Turkistanis displaced throughout the world began to discover America and the fact that Isakjan Narzikul would help them, sponsor them, find them jobs, assist them with English and guide them around the Philadelphia area. He and his wife directly sponsored close to forty people and helped another hundred. Many started with jobs in the Narzikul factory and lived in their house or in apartments supplied by them.

When "cultural representatives" and diplomats came to the United States from Turkistan, they often found their way to the Narzikul or Shermat household. Outside by the barbecue they defended the Soviet position against cries and hoots from the Washington Turkistanis, who claimed they were Russian lackeys and Moscow's servants, and did not serve the national interest of Turkistan. Away from the crowd, in the comfort of a quiet living room, they sometimes reviewed the facts of Russian domination and agreed to take the statistics provided by the Soviets and see how the income of the Turkistani republics compared with the budget and the number of Turkistani citizens. They saw that if all the income generated by Turkistan remained within its borders instead of being transferred to Moscow's projects, the people could live well. Also the truth of the Russian conquest and liquidation of Turkistani patriots was studied.

In 1981, Soviet authorities organized a heavy campaign to get Jay to visit Uzbekistan, sending a representative to his home and offering a "guarantee in writing" that he would be their guest and no harm would come. Jay gave vague answers.

"Sure, later on," he hinted.

After the representative departed, Jay received a letter from the Soviet embassy in Washington with an application for visa, already approved, "All you have to do is just fill in the blanks."

Shermat advised him not to return to the Soviet Union, even for a visit. "Perhaps they would arrest you, or perhaps they would treat you well. If they are generous and honored their commitment, they could use your visit later in propaganda to entice others. If they plan a trick, anything could happen."

Jay listened to the experiences of others who returned for visits. He became friendly with a Turkistani family planning to tour Uzbekistan. The family had escaped through Afghanistan and Turkey years before World War II, and thus feared no particular trouble with the Soviets. They visited Tashkent and asked permission from the tourist authority to visit Jizzakh, off limits normally, to see the mother of Isakjan Narsikul.

The day after that, a convoy of trucks brought lumber and concrete to fix the house, followed by another convoy with new furniture. When the friend visited, his mother was told to give a small party, and officials sent five people to attend, including a professor and other community leaders. Even though the kolkhoz workers did not use eating utensils, these instruments were supplied. At the party, quests were served nice drinks and had lively conversation. They did not invite Jurabay, who blundered into the party as town drunk instead of the professor or official he had desired to become.

Jay also listened to one of his old platoon commanders who had given in to a desire to visit his family in Turkistan. During the visit, Soviet agents tried to pressure the man into accepting an assignment for them, and as a result of his refusal, packages sent to his family are now returned.

As part of the campaign to have Jay visit Turkistan, the vice president of the Soviet Uzbek Society corresponded regularly with Jay and wrote that his boss, the president of the society, planned a trip to America and Canada. A phone call came from the Philadelphia Holiday Inn that the president had arrived. The man was a poet and had written

many books. The man said he liked what he saw in the

U.S. and would like to bring his wife for a holiday.

Jay wanted some sort of clearance from an American authority. He called the local FBI office, which sent out a young agent. The man had never heard of Uzbekistan, but advised that in America a person can invite whomever he wishes.

In 1983 the society president wrote that he was leaving in a couple of weeks. When the Uzbek couple arrived and stayed at Jay's house for a few weeks, he escorted them to the sights of Philadelphia, New York and Washington.

Jay believed in talking with the Soviets, saying it could never hurt, that he could learn something, might indoctrinate the other side, or might accomplish something. The Soviet Uzbek Society president claimed that his organization was strictly humanitarian, wanting to preserve the language and keep communication alive among the disparate ethnic members. Jay believed he was KGB and a Communist Party member, so he began to think of a way to challenge him.

The society president wanted Jay to come to Uzbekistan with his American wife, all expenses paid, and the Uzbek Society would guarantee his safety. He presented an invitation written in both Russian and Uzbek to Mr. and Mrs. Narzikul, which declared that the Association had met and voted in favor of the offer.

Jay saw an opening for politics.

"The organization can always be overruled. Do you have anybody higher than you?"

"No," claimed the president. "We are powerful and have enough influence."

Jay retorted, "If you have so much influence, instead of all your preaching, why don't you show that you can work for our community as well as serve your own purposes by helping one of our American-Turkistani families bring out its other members from Uzbekistan. Show some sincerity about helping Uzbeks. Five kids and two adults. Show me how many Jewish people come out and how many Uzbeks come out. Absolutely no Uzbeks have ever officially emigrated from the Soviet Union. If you have such a powerful organization and have influence, show me."

The president promised to consider the proposal and departed for his trip back to the USSR.

A couple of months later, the young FBI man paid a call. "I received a letter complaining that you invited the son of Lenin, with his wife, to the U.S. Why did you do such a thing?"

Jay struggled to conceal his disgust. "If you remember, I just invited an ordinary diplomat from Uzbekistan who is certainly not the son of Lenin, who had no son. I gave him some presents and he brought some tea glasses and other gifts for my family."

The man from the FBI wanted to know where they went and what they did. "Why did you do this if you knew he was a Communist official?"

One year afterward, the Uzbek Society president phoned to say that the Turkistani family would get permission the next day to leave. After a month, the first Uzbek family ever to emigrate officially from the Soviet Union arrived in New York.

The Uzbek Society back in Tashkent then bombarded him with inquiries, letters and phone calls. "When are you going to come?"

Jay kept postponing: school, business, excuses until the Society president retired.

Although he continued to help Turkistanis on a personal level, Jay's past embraces of mass political causes did not produce the results promised and instead placed him in physical and mental jeopardy. While waiting for the realization of his hopes for a free Turkistan and a world immune from chauvinism, he concentrated on personal rather than governmental efforts, both for himself and his homeland. The zealot became a humanist.

Jay did not know what the Soviets would like to have done with him: friend or foe, prisoner or hero; propaganda or discourse. His mother died in the summer of 1987. Afterwards, contacts with USSR officials and his sister dwindled.

He never expected to see the many new buildings, which have been constructed in Jizzakh, especially during the time when his old mentor, Sharaf Rashidov, became first secretary of the Uzbekistan Communist Party. After Sharaf's rise to the presidency of Uzbekistan and mysterious death, the government posthumously found him guilty of practicing a personality cult -- promoting himself more than the Party -- and dismantled statues of him. Rashidov did not bargain well for the sale of natural resources in his country. Uzbekistan's natural gas was piped to Western Europe, and the residents receive rhetoric rather than cash as payment.

In Turkistan, the cotton crop was larger than ever. Fewer men wore traditional clothes. Rumor stated that the resilient Alimov, Jay's former commander, served time in Siberia and thereafter worked his way into a job of responsibility. The son of the cousin promised to Jay in marriage served with the Red Army, stationed in Czechoslovakia, while the husband of his girlfriend in grade school was rehabilitated from his Western exposure during the German liberation effort after only five years in Siberia and the help of an influential family. Jurabay did not receive a promotion, but, then again, he was not sent back to Siberia.

Isakjan worked outside of Philadelphia in a large office, with room for sofas, bookshelves, desk and conference table. One day he read that the United States government wanted bidders for a part his firm already made for private companies. He sold the part for thirty-five dollars when men from Washington were accustomed to paying much more. It took him several months to get on the bid list.

Intrigued, he attempted to obtain names of other parts he might want to bid on. After intense efforts, he found that his company had for years been on thirty or forty potential bidding lists. The government, in an effort to get a wider range of bids, had demanded names of competitive contractors from their usual suppliers. Nobody bothered to inform the Narzikul firm of its right to bid directly to the United States. His efforts resulted in new orders as direct contractor and savings for the government.

His training as tabilci in Jizzakh stood him in good stead.

Isakjan Narzikul started to ease himself out of his businesses. He never lost his peasant inclination, and maintained it by tending his own garden. He never found the ideal society that was so often promised, but life in America came as close as he ever witnessed. The compromises were human, and his children and grandchildren lived near. He kissed them all often, even those grown into men, and advised, "Never be ashamed to show affection to your family." He had no plans to recheck behind the Iron Curtain, but bore no ill will towards the Russian people. He wished that the regime that suppressed his native land would abide by its own teachings.

Isakjan “Jay” Narzikul passed away in the spring of 1989.

PART V

BACKGROUND AND HISTORY

SHARAF RASHIDOV

WRITER, MENTOR, POLITICIAN

The small city of Jizzakh produced a number of people destined to rise through the ranks of Soviet power. Isakjan Narzikul's inspiring grade school mentor combined his political sense with clever authorship to mold a career that led him to become one of the Turkistanis most trusted by Secretary General and President Leonid Breznev. It all started when the son of a kolkhoz leader began writing revolutionary poetry in the Jizzakh paper.

Born in 1917, Rashidov graduated from Jizzakh tekhnikum (vocational middle school) in 1935, and taught students including Isakjan Narzikul and his friend Jurabay. By 1937, his efforts for the Jizzakh paper won him a position in the big city of Samarkand as executive secretary for the larger newspaper "Lenin Yoli (Way of Lenin)," and his first book Border Patrol was published. Recognition of his journalistic abilities brought Rashidov to the attention of Communist Party officials, and they invited him to become a member in 1939. As he progressed to assistant editor and then editor, Rashidov expanded his writing to include fiction, and published the novella Virgin Lands in 1940, followed by Laboring Girls.

The German invasion of the Soviet Union interrupted his career for a brief spell as he entered the army in August of 1941, but an injury in 1942 resulted in an early return home. He picked up his pen once again in Samarkand as an editor, but then his political talents propelled him into a larger arena when in 1944 he ascended to the position of Secretary of the Communist Party of Samarkand.

Dual roles as writer and Party member fed his continuing rise, and in 1947 he became editor of the newspaper "Red Uzbekistan" (later called "Soviet Uzbekistan") in Tashkent. One of the junior editors was the uncle of Isakjan Narzikul, who had aided his nephew's application to technical school in Tashkent in 1939.

By 1949, the Uzbek Writer's Union had chosen Rashidov as chairman, and, in 1950 he became Chairman of the Presidium of the Uzbek Supreme Soviet. During this period, more books by Rashidov were published, including a collection of poetry, Kashmir Song, and a novel called The Victors. In 1959 he became the First Secretary of the Communist Party of Uzbekistan, the highest ranking Uzbek in the Soviet Union.

Rashidov's career did not stop at the borders of his native land, however. In 1961 he entered Soviet national politics with an appointment to the Party Central Committee in Moscow, in 1966 in the Soviet Politburo as a non-voting member, and in 1970 into the Politburo of the Supreme Soviet of the USSR.

His stature brought many important assignments such as leadership of Soviet delegations to states around the world including Cuba, Chile, Mali, Algeria, Indonesia, India, Guinea, North Korea, Italy, Austria, Iraq, Bulgaria, and Egypt. No less a man than Leonid Brezhnev championed his advancement. For his work, Rashidov received the Medal of Lenin eight times plus various other decorations including the prestigious Hero of Socialist Labor Medallion in 1974.

Through all his fame, Rashidov never forgot his writing or his friends. He elevated Jizzakh to the status of oblast (county of the republic), adding many buildings, offices, hospitals, water facilities, and statues of himself. His old city and his old friends prospered and grew wealthy.

In 1983, Rashidov suddenly died. Shortly thereafter, leaders in the government denounced his actions in office with accusations of favoritism, practicing a personality cult, and cheating the government. These charges seem well-founded by many observers. After proclamations that he was an enemy of the people, down came the many statues of him in different poses. Today the phrase "Rashidovism" is synonymous with corruption and bureaucratic waste.

NATIONAL TURKISTANI UNITY COMMITTEE

In the times of the great khans, Mongol rulers controlled Russia. But in the late fifteenth century, Ivan III forged an alliance with some disgruntled tribes and refused to pay tribute or to "kiss the stirrup" of his suzerain, and his successors continued battling Mongol and Turkic regimes until they pushed their domination into Turkistan. Czarist Russian troops captured Tashkent, the largest city in Central Asia, in 1865, and Communist Russian troops retained control after 1917.

For a brief time, during the 1940's, Turkistan had men who proclaimed a government formed without Russian direction. That group functioned as an exile establishment in the City of Berlin under the aegis of wartime Germany, calling itself the Turkistani Unity Committee. They claimed legitimacy from several factors. First, the man who conceived and formed the organization, Mustafa Chokay, had been elected president of the ineffectual Turkistan Moslem council which then declared autonomy from the Soviets and subsequently was vanquished by the Red Army. Secondly, the exile government conducted an election among well over a hundred thousand Turkistani citizens who had quit the Red Army in favor of the German Army. And finally, the stated purpose of the government consisted of securing freedom for Turkistan in order to conduct elections and begin a national policy. The major activity of the Committee consisted of the formation of an army which numbered over 200,000 and fought with Germany.

The Committee's legitimacy was never ratified by any segment of either population or organizations in Turkistan and it never gained any base of operation there. In fact, the Committee was a creation of Germany. The leaders may very well have seized an unusual opportunity to plan for the liberation of their homeland and thereby continue a widely popular desire for independence. Thus they can warrant a place in history to show that all Axis troops were not Fascist or racist, but pursued commendable goals in a war that gave no ground to subtle cross-currents and no reprieve to those who fought with Germany. They were not, however, a government that controlled any land.

The exiles operated as a committee with various departments:

Executive	President Veli Kayum-kahn
Military	Baymirza Hayit
	Ramazon Kurjan
Secretary General	Said Karimi
Ideology	Ergash Shermat (and radio)
Information	Kurban
Press	Majit (literary journal)
	Ahmat Jan Umarhan (magazine, "National Turkistan)
	Abul Zavqi (newspaper, "New Turkistan")
Science	Ahad Salimi
Chief of Staff	Alman Bet

These men met in sub-committees and as directors of different operations. They coordinated with the German government representatives: Dr. Benzing from the Department of State, Major Luderzen from the Wehrmacht, Professor von Mende from the East Ministry, Doer from the Propaganda Ministry, and Professor Oslo from the SS. They set up offices and cooperated with similar exiles from places like Armenia, Georgia, Russia, Crimea, the Ukraine, Azerbaijan, the Tatar region, and others.

As the German army advanced across the Soviet Union, they could see reality in their dreams of independence for their homeland. Then came the defeat of the Wehrmacht at Stalingrad and subsequent retreat. Still they labored, holding a Turkistani Congress in Vienna in 1944 which presaged the Prague Congress at which the Russian defector General Vlasov proclaimed the formation of a liberation army to end the Soviet Union.

In 1944, the Turkistani Unity Committee no longer envisioned a German-led victory and liberation of their country, but rather an Allied victory. With this anticipated end to the war, the committee exerted its efforts towards moving their troops away from the Eastern front, where an angry Soviet Army would wreak havoc and death on their forces. They hoped to station the men on the Western front. Here they planned to seek refuge with the American and British forces and negotiate for permission to continue efforts directed at their fight for freedom. That negotiation never took place, as the English-speaking forces hunted down the members of the Eastern Army and returned them to the Soviet Union for imprisonment or execution. A very few lucky ones managed to survive and remain in the West where they eventually gained employment by Western governments or in private firms.

NOTES FROM TURKISTAN

Historically, groups of Central Asians have been called by different names including Cimmerians, Scythians, Bulgars or Kalmyks. Not all of these were Turkic, as peoples of other stock, including Iranian, traversed the great plains of the area. Those of the Altaic people, which include various mixtures of Turkic, Mongol, Tungus and Manchurian, have contributed the largest population over the last two millennia. They founded the countries of Turkey, Hungary, and Bulgaria, plus many governments which have now superseded central Asian Soviet republics. Whatever the name, they followed the trails to the Orient, the Occident and the Indus, sometimes bringing items of trade and sometimes riding as hordes of militia.

The names of the thousands of faceless caravan drivers lie buried in the sands that now cover the ancient highways, but those of the martial leaders still inspire a fearsome respect, including Tamerlane and his descendant Babur (who established the Mughal Empire in India.) Although not from Turkistan, Attila the Hun, Genghiz Khan, and the long-lasting Ottoman empire rulers came from Turkic or Mongol stock. Turks and Mongols are often referred to separately, but they frequently mixed armies. These erupting armies often followed the totem of a wolf, traveling from their bleak harsh lands to gaze longingly at the rich foods and materials of the farming communities. The hunters struck and the massacres which followed totally destroyed the will for resistance, but afterwards the conqueror set himself up as khan, emperor or sultan, and the agriculture continued.

The sons and grandsons of the subjugators settled down into a life of luxury. But then new hordes of undomesticated horsemen would eventually challenge those sons and grandsons. Thus a cycle was completed when the conquerers became the vanquished. Once ensconced in the life of new subjects, former "barbarians" inevitably became rulers and protectors of their adoptive civilizations and did their best to enforce and continue the history and goals of their new subjects.

The horse was the vehicle of the steppes and the engine of military superiority. Together with cavalry, arrow and lasso, a fierce heritage combined to weld mighty armies. Men of the steppes wore pants and vests, garments suited to mounted action -- a trait shortly imitated by the defending civilizations accustomed to donning robes.

The history of Central Asia should not be traced only by its military ascendancy, but also by its resources and trade, especially along the many fingers of the Silk Road. In passing along this greatest of all ancient roads, leaving ancient China, travelers crossed Eastern Turkistan, now Sinkiang of modern China, and made their way into a land of fabulous wealth and splendor, yesterday's Soviet Turkistan.

By 3000 B.C., domesticated animals had enabled traders to organize regular trading practices, as Turkistan supplied gems, jade, timber, horses, two-humped camels, copper, and tin, which flowed from the region to the Middle East, China, and India. These other trading societies returned with wine, spices, cotton, silk, grain, rice and fruit seeds.

The West learned of printing through the Silk Road; and other developments in science, engineering, religion and weapons were transferred along with the business. Grand cities like Samarkand grew to 500,000 people in very early years. Spotted along the heavily traveled road were miles of lush gardens, complex canals delivering water to houses, and huge trading markets.

A culture thrived, rivaling that which rose in Europe hundreds of years later as measured by engineering, weaving, architecture, literature, clothing and knowledge of the world. Over the years traditions of art in ceramics, jewelry, painting, medicine and minstrel prospered. Buildings constructed a thousand years ago still survive today and are known as many of the most beautiful and imposing in the world. Paintings from the area depict an extensive culture replete with the accouterments found in highest civilizations. Chinese and Indians from the East and Persians and Greeks from the West stabilized the route, but it was always subject to brigands and more serious raids by wild tribes of the north.[1]

The power of Turkic-Mongolian rulers dwindled as the result of leadership squabbles, skillfully exploited by men like Ivan III, who liberated Russia in the late fifteenth century and started a reverse conquest process that eventually had Russians controlling their old lords and inheriting an empire. China and Persia revolted successfully from Turkic-Mongol dominance, but China reverted to the rule of the Manchus, an Altaic group which ruled until 1912. [2]

A pattern evolved which amounted to steady erosion of independence for Central Asia as a result of Russian imperialism. The Russians and British fought Afghan wars to determine preeminence in the area, with the resultant buffer state of Afghanistan separating the two empires. The Red revolution and the establishment of the Soviet Union extended the suppression of Turkistani independence.

After taking power by their revolution, Russian Communists separated Soviet Turkistan into separate Republics. Soviet authorities and their czarist predecessors always brutally reacted to any sign of regional cooperation or nationalistic tendencies.

One of the last pre-revolutionary rebellions against the czar started in the small city of Jizzakh in 1916, in response to an order from the czar for forced labor. Riots in Jizzakh gathered momentum and grew to a revolt which spread to the rest of Turkistan. Soldiers of the crown ruthlessly suppressed this uprising, increasing the anti-Russian sentiment of the people. The czars ruled the area as colonialists, and did not attempt to learn or adapt to the language, customs, and religion of the Turks.

The Russian Communists, in their struggle for control, curried favor from Turkic leaders. However, both in conferences of all the Moslem provinces in the Russian empire, and also in a Turkistan Moslem Council with Mustafa Chokay as president, independence from Russia was voted. In every instance, the Soviets combined guile, control of rails, local Russians, and strong military tactics to unseat the Moslem regimes.

New ways and new cities worked to the disadvantage of the peasants as the Russians guided them more into a one-crop cotton economy. Peasants lost their land to taxes, water disputes, and debts. Peasants often found themselves worse off than before; the Russians earned the enmity of the mullahs by persecuting religious followers, confiscating property of the mosques, and imprisoning the faithful. As in the rest of the Soviet Union, both prosperous and middle-class peasants had their lands confiscated and were either liquidated or exiled to other lands. [3] Even the character of the bazaar changed, with the kolkhoz (collective farm) opening stands and forcing others to withdraw from commerce.

These actions, coupled with extreme isolation from news

sources of world events outside the Soviet Union, combined to contribute to partial success in the effort to eradicate a regional and national identity in Turkistan. However, right from the beginning of the Communist revolution, efforts on the part of individuals in Turkistan to maintain their unique history and culture persisted. Resistance to Soviet domination came in the form of open rebellion against the early Marxist regime in what is called the Basmachi movement.

As a survivor of these rebellions, Mustafa Chokay fled to Paris and also established a base in Warsaw. Poland proved a reliable supporter of many Soviet liberation organizations, much to the dismay of Moscow, and in Warsaw these groups cooperated under an umbrella called Proatee, named after a bird of freedom.

Without support from Western powers and with the collapse of Poland from external aggression by Germany and the Soviet Union in the beginning of World War II, Chokay moved to Berlin and received an offer of cooperation from the Nazi government in exchange for a hope of liberation of his country from the Soviets. In Berlin he discovered a well-established community of Soviet exiles, rivaling the Paris, London and Warsaw groups in both size and intellectual production.

His ideas were well received by the East Ministry and the German Army, which resulted in the formation of the Turkistani legions, comprised of Turkistani soldiers in the Red Army who, upon surrender and capture during World War II, joined the Wehrmacht. Chokay died of typhus contracted while recruiting in POW camps, but his idea of a Turkistani legion was realized as over 200,000 of his countrymen fought in the Wehrmacht with hopes of eventually liberating their homeland. An entire exile committee functioned in Berlin, where their cause was welcomed. This legion was started with "Operation Tiger B," six Turkistani and one Azerbaidzhani companies joined to the Wehrmacht in 1941 with Isakjan Narzikul as one of the officers. The Tiger B battalion saw action as "Infantry Battalion Number 450." [4]

Central Asia no longer holds any sort of monopoly on either trading routes or military supremacy. However, within the confines of these lands in general and Turkistan in particular, natural resources of every sort abound, including gold, petroleum, natural gas, extensive minerals and metals. The pasture lands are among the largest in the world and the quantity of cotton, called "white gold," rivals any other region. Although large and fierce deserts lace the territory, fertile valleys, oases, and irrigation supply agricultural products from melons to cereal grains and support many kinds of livestock.

A 1968 appeal to Islamic representatives of the United Nations, requesting them to propose that the U.N. supervise free elections to determine the sincerity of Khrushchev's assertion that the Islamic republics could secede from the USSR if they so desired, fell on deaf ears.

One part of Turkistan recently and actively fought Russian control, and that part lies in northern Afghanistan, where Turkic Mujahedin participated in the revolt against the Soviet occupation.

With the break-up of the Soviet Union, Soviet Turkistan today consists of the countries of Kazakstan, Uzbekistan, Tajikstan, Kyrgyz Republic, and Turkmenistan. Even though the countries are free from their old master, freedom in the sense of Western politics, religion and economics has not arrived. The 1999 Index of Economic Freedom has listed all of these countries as among the most repressive in the world.

FOOTNOTES

SURVIVOR FROM AN UNKNOWN WAR

Chapter 1 footnotes

[1] Andropov, Yuri V., "The USSR is Sixty Years Old," report to Soviet special session, reprinted from the Soviet press in Nations & Peoples: the Soviet Experience, Marilyn Bechtel, and Daniel Rosenberg, editors (New York: NWR Publications, Inc., 1984) p.13.

[2] Jizzakh is spelled following English usage, but elsewhere Dzhizak and Dzizak are used.

[3]Catherine Andreyev, V*lasov and the Russian Liberation Movement.* (Cambridge: Cambridge University Press, 1987), pp. 175-187. Also, Aleksandr I. Solzhenitsyn, The Gulag Archipelago I-II. (New York: Harper & Row, 1974), p.24, 174.

[4] A series of paths and routes connecting China, India, Turkistan, and the Mediterranean area.

Chapter 2 footnotes

[1] V.I. Lenin, "Speech to Eleventh Congress of the Russian Communist Party, March 27, 1922," Collected Works vol 33, Moscow: Progress Publishers, 1966.

Chapter 3 footnotes

[1] Joseph Stalin, "The Policy of the Soviet Government on the National Question in Russia," in Marxism and the National Question, Selected Writings and Speeches, (U.S.A., International Publishers Co., Inc., 1942), p. 84.

[2] USSR constitution of 1924 as in Aryeh L. Unger, Constitutional Development in the USSR. (London: Methuen & Co.), 1981, pp. 59-76.

[3] Ibid.

Chapter 4 footnotes

[1] Aleksandr I. Solzhenitsyn, The Gulag Archipelago I-II. (New York: Harper & Row, 1974), p. 243.

Chapter 5 footnotes

[1] Combination of two speeches and one telegram in J. Stalin, Works (Moscow: Foreign Language Publishers House, 1955), pp. 67, 211-213, and N. S. Khrushchev, The anatomy of Terror (Washington: Public Affairs Press, 1956) p. 42-43.

[2] This series of rebellions continued into the early 1930's. Turkistanis called them the Kurbashi (officer's) or Beklar (self-rule) Movement, while Russian Soviets referred to it as the Basmachi (bandit or robber) Movement. Likewise, today in Afghanistan those who fought the Soviets are called Mujahedin, while Russian Communists refer to them as basmach.

Chapter 6 footnotes

[1] Boevoi Ustav Pekhoty vol. 2, 1942-1945, p.28, italicized and in capitals, and Warriors of the Red Army Do Not Become Prisoners, Leningrad: 1940, as translated by Raymond L. Garthoff, in How Russia Makes War, London: Ruskin House, 1954), pp. 250-151.

[2] Jurgen, Thorwald, The Illusion: Soviet Soldiers in Hitler's Armies translated by Richard and Clara Winston, (New York and London 1975), p.83. Many studies assert that Stalin completely ignored warnings from many sources regarding the Nazi plan to attack the USSR. The experience of Narzikul suggests that, at least a week or two before the invasion, he did take some action.

[3] Bryan Perrett, A history of Blitzkrieg, (New York: Stein and Day, 1983), pp. 60-61, 125.

[4]Actually the Soviets signed a separate peace after Lenin unilaterally issued his Soviet order number 1, namely for all soldiers to lay down their arms and leave

Chapter 7 footnotes

[1] Jurgen Thorwald, *The Illusion: Soviet Soldiers in Hitler's Armies,* translated by Richard and Clara Winston (New York and London: Harcourt Brace Jovanovich, 1975), p. 12, 33, 38, 44

[2] Catherine Andreyev, *Vlasov and the Russian Liberation Movement* (Cambridge: Cambridge University Press, 1987), p. 153-5.

Chapter 8 footnotes

[1] Catherine Andreyev, Vlasov and the Russian Liberation Movement. (Cambridge: Cambridge University Press, 1987), p. 153-5.

[1] Baymirza Hayit lives in West Germany today where he obtained a doctorate degree, has written numerous books and articles on Turkistan and remains an outspoken critic of Russia and the USSR.

Chapter 9 footnotes

[1] Alexander Dallin, German Rule in Russia 1941-1945: A study in Occupation Policies. 2nd revised edition (Boulder, Colorado: Westview Press, 1981) p. 54.

[2] Hans Von Herwarth, with S Frederick Starr, Against Two Evils. New York: Rawson, Wade Publishers, Inc., 1981, pp. 197-204.

[3]Nikolai Tolstoy, Stalin's Secret War. (New York: Holt, Rinehart and Winston), 1981, pp 3-285.

[4] Jurgen Thorwald, The Illusion: Soviet Soldiers in Hitlers's Armies. translated by Richard and Clara Winston, (New York and London: Harcourt Brace Jovanovich, 1975), pp. 9-50.

[5]Rene Grousset, The Empire of the Steps. (New Brunswick, New Jersey: Rutgers University Press, 1970), p. 395.

[6] WE, Inc., Tank Data - Aberdeen Proving Grounds Series. (Old Greenwich, Conn.: WE, Inc., n.d.), p 57.

[7]In a little village outside of the city lived the future Soviet leader, Mikhail Gorbachev. Donald Morrison, editor, Mikhail S. Gorbachev (New York: Time Incorporated, 1988), pp.36-39.

[8] Bryan Perrett, A History of Blitzkrieg (New York: Stein and Day, 1983), pp. 121-221.

Chapter 10 footnotes

[1] Werner Keller, East Minus West = Zero, translated by Constantine Fitzgibbon (New York: C.P. Putnam's Sons, 1962) p. 241-245.

[2] Marvin D. Bernstein, and Francis L. Lowenheim, "Aid to Russia: The First Year," as shown in Harold Stein, editor, American Civil - Military Decisions, (Birmingham: 1963), pp. 97-152.

[3]George C. Jr. Herring, Aid to Russia 1941-1946 (New York and London: Cloumbia University Press, 1973) pp. 60-109.

[4]V. Kayum-Khan, "Turkestan." The Eastern Quarterly, October 1950, p. 39.

[5] Kayum-Khan, "The 8th Anniversary of the National Congress," in Milli Turkistan. June-July 1952, pp. 3 - 5.

[6] Adolph Hitler, Mein Kampf. (New York: Reynal and Hitchcock, 1939) pp. 389-457, 636, 932-969.

[7]Himmler

[8]German Armed Forces High Command, Grundlagen der Propaganda gegen Wehrmacht und Voelker der Sowjetunion, 23.III.42., as translated by Edgar Howell in Heeresgruppe Nord, Propaganda Befehle. 75131/104.

[9] Heinz Hohne, The order of the Death's Head. translated by Richard Barry, (New York: Coward - Mc Cann, 1970) pp.293-323.

[10] Edgar M. Howell, The Soviet Partisan Movement: 1941 - 1944, (Washington, D.C.: Department of the Army, 1956) pp. 97-115.

Chapter 11 footnotes

[1] Harold Lamb, Tamerlane, (New York: Robert M. McBride & Co., 1928)

[2]H. Ikram, "God with Us (III)," Milli Turkistan, English edition. October-December 1953, pp. 11-13.

[3] Catherine Andreyev, Vlasov and the Russian Liberation Movement. (Cambridge: Cambridge University Press), 1987, p.3,7. Also, Alexander R. Alexiev, and . Enders S. Wimbush, Ethnic minorities in the Red Army, (Boulder and London: Westview Press), p. 4.

[4]Baymirza Hayit, Turkestan im xx Jahrhundert. (Darmstadt, Germany: C.W. Leske Verlag), 1956, pp. 342-346.

[5] Cornelius Ryan, The Last Battle (New York: Simon and Schuster, 1966) p. 52.

Chapter 12 footnotes

[1] Antoni Chrusciel, (`Monter'), Powstanie Warszawskie (London: 1948), p. 15, as translated by Jan M. Ciechanowski, in The Warsaw Uprising of 1944 (Cambridge: Cambridge University Press, 1974) p. 269.

[2]N Bethell, The Last Secret. (N.Y., Basic Books, Inc.), 1974, p.4.

[3] Richard C. Lukas, The Forgotten Holocaust (Lexington, Kentucky: University Press of Kentucky, 1986) pp. 182-219.

Chapter 13 footnotes

[1] Hermann Rauschning, The Voice of Destruction, New York: G.P. Putnam's Sons, 1940, pp. 30-43.

[2] Helmut Krausnick, Hans Buchheim, Martin Broszat, and Hans-Adolf Jacobsen, Anatomy of the SS State, (New York: Walker and Company, translated by Richard Barry, Marian Jackson, and Dorothy Long, 1968), p. 523.

[3] Jurgen Thorwald, The Illusion: Soviet Soldiers in Hitlers's Armies (translated by Richard and Clara Winston, New York and London: Harcourt Brace Jovanovich, 1975), pp. 12, 33, 38, 44.

[4] Jurgen Thorwald, The Illusion: Soviet Soldiers in Hitlers's Armies. translated by Richard and Clara Winston, (New York and London: Harcourt Brace Jovanovich, 1975.) pp.184-238. Thorwald is incorrect in assuming that efforts to form a Turkistani SS unit were not successful.

[5] Cornelius Ryan, The Last Battle (New York: Simon and Schuster, 1966), pp. 71-104.

Chapter 14 footnotes

[1] Winston S. Churchill, Triumph and Tragedy, Boston: Houghton Mifflin Company, 1953, pp.534-538.

[2] Edward Taborsky, President Edvard Benes Between East and West 1938-1948 (Stanford, California, Hoover Institution Press, 1981) pp. 117-118.

[3]Churchill, Truimph and Tragedy, pp. 440-537.

Chapter 15 footnotes

[1] "United Family," Soviet Uzbekistan, English edition, May, 1985, p. 1.

Chapter 16 footnotes

[1] Department of State, Executive Agreement, Series No 505, released to the press March 8, 1946.

[2] Jurgen Thorwald, The Illusion: Soviet Soldiers in Hitlers's Armies. translated by Richard and Clara Winston, (New York and London: Harcourt Brace Jovanovich, 1975), pp. 294-316.

[3] United States Army, by Command of Lieutenant General Keyes, U.S. Army Procedures for the Forcible Repatriation of Soviet Nationals. Headquarters Third United States Army: January 22, 1946. in the United Nations (UNRRA) Archives, New York. PAG-4/3.0.11.0.1.4:3, "Repatriations."

[4] Catherine Andreyev, Vlasov and the Russian Liberation Movement. (Cambridge: Cambridge University Press), 1987, p. 79.

[5] Aleksandr I. Solzhenitsyn, The Gulag Archipelago I-II. (New York: Harper & Row, 1974) pp. 78-83.

[6] Cornelius Ryan, The Last Battle, (New York: Simon and Schuster, 1966), pp. 26-130.

Chapter 17 footnotes

[1] Jefferson Caffery, airgram to the Secretary of State, Dec. 19-25, 1946; Airgram, Paris, Sept. 9, 1946, as by Yeshayahu Jelinek in The Lust for Power, N.Y.: Columbia University Press, 1983.

Chapter 18 footnotes

[1] United Nations, Laws Concerning Nationality, (N.Y.: United Nations, 1954), p. 567.

[2] A. I. Romanov, Nights are Longest There: Smersh from the Inside. (London, 1972) pp. 169-74.

[3] Nikolai Tolstoy, Victims of Yalta. (London, 1978), p. 104.

Chapter 19 footnotes

[1] William Bullit, "How We Won the War and Lost the Peace," Life, (August 30, 1948), p. 94.

[2] Edward Taborsky, President Edvard Benes Between East and West 1938-1948 (Stanford, California, Hoover Institution Press, 1981) p. 206.

Chapter 20 footnotes

[1] Reinhard Gehlen, The Service. translated by David Irving, (New York: Word Publishing, 1972)

Chapter 21 footnotes

[1] United States Public Law 774, passed June 25, 1948.

Chapter 22 footnotes

[1] Uzbek is also the name of the man who is credited with founding the Uzbek tribe.

Notes from Turkistan

[1] Irene M. Frank, and David M. Brownstone, The Silk Road. (New York: Facts on File Publications, 1986) pp.2-229.

[2] Renee Grossest, The Empire of the Steps. (New Brunswick, New Jersey: Reuters University Press, 1970) pp. 199-530.

[3] Elizabeth Bacon, Central Asians under Russian Rule, (Ithaca and London: Corneal University Press, 1968),

[4] Hoffman, Die Ostlegionen, pp. 28-029.

BIBLIOGRAPHY

INTERVIEWS AND UNPUBLISHED DOCUMENTS

Hayit, Baymirza, conversations with Stephen L. Crane, 1988-1989.

Narzikul, Isakjan, interviews with Stephen L. Crane, 1986-1988.

Shermat, Ergash, interviews with Stephen L. Crane, 1987-1989.

Rogozinski, Letter to Dr. Hayit and Dr. Shermat, 12 January, 1946.

PUBLISHED MEMOIRS, AUTOBIOGRAPHIES AND DOCUMENTS

Churchill, Winston S., Closing the Ring, Boston: Houghton Mifflin Company, 1951.

Churchill, Winston S., The Hinge of Fate, Boston: Houghton Mifflin Company, 1950.

Churchill, Winston S., Triumph and Tragedy, Boston: Houghton Mifflin Company, 1953.

The Conferences at Malta and Yalta, Foreign Relations of the United States Diplomatic Papers, Westport, Connecticut: Greenwood Press, 1945.

Committee on Un-American Activities, House of Representatives, 86th Congress, The Crimes of Khrushchev Part 6. Washington: U.S. Government Printing Office, 1960.

Gehlen, Reinhard The Service, translated by David Irving, New York: Word Publishing, 1972.

Hitler, Adolph. Mein Kampf. New York: Reynal and Hitchcock, 1939, edited and translated by Chamberlain, John, Fay, Sidney, and others.

Himmler - Der Untermensch - degeneration of Slavs.

International Military Tribunal, Trial of The Major War Criminals. Nuremberg, Germany: International Military Tribunal, 1947.

Khrushchev, The Anatomy of Terror, Washington: Public Affairs Press, 1956.

Kovtum, George J., The Czechoslovak Declaration of Independence, Washington: Library of Congress, 1985.

Lanb, Harold, Tamerlane, New York: Robert M. Mc Bride & Co., 1928.

Lenin, V.I., Collected Works, Moscow: Progress Publishers, 1966.

Stalin, Joseph, Marxism and the National Question, Selected Writings and Speeches, U.S.A., International Publishers Co., Inc., 1942,

Stalin, Joseph, Works vol. 1-13, Moscow: Foreign Language Publishers House, 1955.

United States Army, by Command of Lieutenant General Keyes, U.S. Army Procedures for the Forcible Repatriation of Soviet Nationals. Headquarters Third United States Army: January 22, 1946. in the United Nations (UNRRA) Archives, New York. PAG-4/3.0.11.0.1.4:3, "Repatriations."

United States Government, Trials of War Criminals before the Nurenberg Military Tribunals. Washington, D.C.: U.S. Government Printing Office: 1946-49.

United States Public Law 774, approved June 25, 1948.

PUBLISHED BOOKS AND ARTICLES

Alexiev, Alexander R., and Wimbush, S. Enders, Ethnic Minorities in the Red Army, Boulder and London: Westview Press.

Andreyev, Catherine, Vlasov and the Russian Liberation Movement, Cambridge: Cambridge University Press, 1987.

Andropov, Yuri V., "The USSR is Sixty Years Old," report to Soviet special session, reprinted from the Soviet Press in Nations & Peoples: the Soviet Experience, Bechtel, Marilyn, and Rosenberg, Daniel, editors, New York: NWR Publications, Inc., 1984.

Armstrong, J. A. Ukrainian Nationalism. 2nd ed. New York: Columbia University Press, 1963

Basi, Bulaq. "The National Government of Kokand and the Alash Orda." Millij Turkistan, vol 70-71B, March 1951. pp13-20.

Bethell, N. The Last Secret, N.Y., Basic Books, Inc., 1974.

Boshyk, Yury, ed. Ukraine During World War II. Edmonton: University of Alberta, 1986.

Bullit, William, "How We Won the War and Lost the Peace," Life, August 30, 1948.

Caffery, Jefferson, Airgram to the Secretary of State, 860F.00/a-746, Summary No. 377, Dec. 19-25, 1946; 860f.00/9-546, Airgram No. A-1254, Paris, Sept. 9, 1946, as researched by Jelinek in The Lust for Power.

Carroll, W. "It Takes a Russian to Beat a Russian: Life. NY Dec 19, 1949.

Chiaromonte, Nicola, The Paradox of History. Philadelphia: University of Pennsylvania Press, 1985.

Ciechanowski, Jan M., The Warsaw Uprising of 1944, Cambridge: Cambridge University Press, 1974.

Conquest, Robert, editor, The Last Empire, Stanford, California: Hoover Institution Press, 1986.

Cookridge, E.H., Gehlen, Spy of the Century. N.Y.: Random House, 1971.

Craven, Wesley Frank, and Cate, James Lea, editors, The Army Air Forces in World War II, Volume Three, Chicago: University of Chicago Press, 1951.

Dallin, Alexander, German Rule in Russia 1941-1945: A Study in Occupation Policies. 2nd revised edition, Boulder, Colorado: Westview Press, 1981.

Dawson, Raymond H., The Decision to Aid Russia, 1941, Chapel Hill, North Carolina: University of North Carolina Press, 1959.

Dicks, Henry V., Licensed Mass Murder, New York: Basic Books, Inc., 1972.

Divine, Robert A., Roosevelt and World War II, Baltimore, Maryland: Johns Hopkins, 1969.

Epstein, Julius, Operation Keelhaul, Old Greenwich: The Devin-Adair Company, 1973.

Fischer, George. Soviet Opposition to Stalin. Westport, Connecticut: Greenwood Press, 1970.

Frank, Irene M., and Brownstone, David M., The Silk Road. New York: Facts on File Publications, New York, 1986.

Garthoff, Raymond L., How Russia Makes War, London: Ruskin House, 1954.

Grousset, Rene, The Empire of the Steps. New Brunswick, New Jersey: Rutgers University Press, 1970.

Hayit, Baymirza, Turkestan im xx Jahrhundert. Darmstadt, Germany: C.W. Leske Verlag, 1956.

Herring, George C. Jr., Aid to Russia 1941-1946, New York and London: Cloumbia University Press, 1973.

Hoffman, Die Ostlegionen,

Hohne, Heinz. The Order of the Death's Head. Translated by Richard Barry, New York: Coward - Mc Cann, 1970.

Howell, Edgar M., The Soviet Partisan Movement: 1941 - 1944, Washington, D.C.: Department of the Army, 1956.

Ikram, H., "God with Us (III)," Milli Turkistan. October-December 1953, pp. 11-13.

Jelinek, Yeshayahu A., The Lust for Power: Nationalism, Slovakia, and the Communists 1918-1948, New York: Columbia University Press, 1983.

Johnson, Walter, editor, Roosevelt and the Russians, Garden City, New York: Doubleday & Co., 1949.

Kajum-Kahn, Veli, editor, "The 8th Anniversary of the National Congress," Milli Turkistan. June-July 1952.

Kajum-Kahn, Veli, "Turkestan." The Eastern Quarterly, October 1950. pp. 35-39.

Kajum-Kahn, Veli. "A Turkistan Tragedy." Millij Turkistan, vol. 72-73B, April-July 1951.

Kajum-Kahn, Veli, "Recollection of the last years of Mustafa Chokai." Millij Turkistan, vol. 70-71B, March 1951, pp. 21-23.

Keller, Werner, East Minus West = Zero, translated by Constantine Fitzgibbon, New York: C.P. Putnam's Sons, 1962.

Krausnick, Helmut, Buchheim, Hans, Broszat, Martin, and Jacobsen, Hans-Adolf, Anatomy of the SS State, New York: Walker and Company, Translated by Richard Barry, Marian Jackson, and Dorothy Long, 1968.

Kunanbayev, Abai, Selected Poems. Moscow: Progress Publishers, 1970.

League for the Liberation of the Peoples of the USSR, Captive Nations in the USSR, Munich: League for the Liberation of the Peoples of the USSR, 1963.

Lewis, Ronald, Hitler's Mistakes, New York: William Morrow & Co., 1984.

Littlejohn, D., The Patriotic Traitors: A History of Collaboration in German Occupied Europe 1940-1945. London: Heinemann, 1972.

Lorimer, Sister M. Madeline, America's Response to Europe's Displaced Persons, 1945-1952, Ann Arbor, Michigan: St. Louis University, 1964.

Lubin, Nancy, Assimilation and Retention of Ethnic Identity in Uzbekistan, IREX, 1980.

Luckett, R. "A Million Russians Fight for Hitler" London Sunday Times 14 May 1972

Lukas, Richard C., The Forgotten Holocaust, Lexington, Kentucky: University Press of Kentucky, 1986.

Lyons, Graham, The Russian Version of the Second World War, New York: Facts on File, Inc., 1976.

Maenchen-Helfen, Otto J., The World of the Huns, Berkeley, Los Angeles, California: University of California Press, 1973.

Mitcham, Samuel W. Jr., Hitler's Legions. New York: Stein and Day, 1985.

Donald Morrison, editor, Mikhail S. Gorbachev, New York: Time Incorporated, 1988.

National - Liberation Revolutionary Organizations of the Islamic Peoples of the U.S.S.R., Appeal, New York: National Centers for the Islamic Emigration from the Soviet Union, undated.

Pipes, Richard, The Formation of the Soviet Union, Cambridge, Massachusetts: Harvard University Press, 1954.

Perrett, Bryan, A History of Blitzkrieg, New York: Stein and Day, 1983.

Popov, V.I., Ovsyany, I.D., and Nikhamin, V.P., editors, A Study of Soviet Foreign Policy, Moscow: Progress Publishers, 1975.

"Portrait of a Traitor." Article. Izvestia. 29 September, 1968.

Poulton, Robin and Michelle, "A Recent Visit to Bukhara and Samarkand," Royal Geographic Society, 1976, pp. 299-310.

Proudfoot, Malcolm J., European Refugees: 1939-1952. London, 1957,

"Rachidov, Sharaf." Uzbek Soviet Encyclopaedia. Published in Tashkent by the Academy of Science of Uzbekistan, 1977.

Rauschning, Hermann, The Voice of Destruction, New York: G.P. Putnam's Sons, 1940.

Riasanovsky, Nicholas V., "The Emergence of Eurasianism," California Slavic Studies Volume IV. Berkeley and Los Angeles: University of California Press, 1967.

Romanov, A.I., Nights are Longest There: Smersh from the Inside. London, 1972.

Ryan, Cornelius, The Last Battle, New York: Simon and Schuster, 1966.

Scott, John, Behind the Urals, Cambridge: Houghton Mifflin Co., 1942.

Shipler, David K., Russia, United States of America: Penguin Books, 1986.

Shub, Boris. The Choice. New York: Duell, Sloan, and Pearce, 1950

Snell, John L., editor, The Meaning of Yalta, Baton Rouge: Louisiana State University Press, 1970.

Solzhenitsyn, Aleksandr I., The Gulag Archipelago I-II. Translated by Thomas P. Whitney, New York: Harper & Row, 1974.

Solzhenitsyn, Aleksandr I., The Gulag Archipelago III-IV. Translated by Thomas P. Whitney, New York: Harper & Row, 1975.

Solzhenitsyn, Aleksandr I., The Gulag Archipelago V-VI. Translated by Harry Willetts, New York: Harper & Row, 1978.

Stein, Harold, editor, American Civil - Military Decisions, Birmingham: University of Alabama, 1963.

Strong, Anna Louise. Red Star in Samarkand. New York: Coward-McCann, Inc., 1929.

Taborsky, Edward, President Edvard Benes Between East and West 1938-1948, Stanford, California, Hoover Institution Press, 1981.

Tenenbaum, Joseph, Race and Reich, New York: Twayne Publishers, 1956.

Thompson, E.A., A History of Atilla and the Huns, Oxford: Claredon Press, 1948.

Thorwald, Jurgen, The Illusion: Soviet Soldiers in Hitler's Armies. translated by Richard and Clara Winston, New York and London: Harcourt Brace Jovanovich, 1975.

Tolstoy, Nikolai, Stalin's Secret War. New York: Holt, Rinehart and Winston, 1981.

Unger, Aryeh L., Constitutional Development in the USSR. London: Methuen & Co., 1981.

United Nations, Laws Concerning Nationality, N.Y.: United Nations, 1954.

Uzbek Society for Friendship and Cultural Relations with Foreign Countries, Soviet Uzbekistan, 3/85, 5/85, 10/85, 11/86, 12/86, 2/87, 7/87.

Uzbek Society for Friendship and Cultural Relations with Foreign Countries, Soviet Uzbekistan: Past, Present, Future. Tashkent, 1983.

Whaley, Baston, Codeword Barbarossa, Cambridge, Massachusetts: MIT Press, 1973.

Wheeler-Bennet, J. The Nemesis of Power: The German Army in Politics 1918-1945 London, 1953

Von Herwarth, Hans, with Starr, S. Frederick, Against Two Evils. New York: Rawson, Wade Publishers, Inc., 1981.

WE, Inc., Tank Data - Aberdeen Proving Grounds Series. Old Greenwich, Conn.: WE, Inc., undated.

Williams, Robert C., Culture in Exile, Ithaca and London: Cornell University Press, 1972.

Wixman, Ronald, The Peoples of the USSR, Armonk, New York: M. E. Sharpe Inc., 1984.

Zavki, A. and Tolqun, I. "The Poet Cholpan." Millij Turkistan. December 1951 - January 1952, pp. 18-22.

INDEX

INDEX

Notes

Notes

Notes

Notes

Notes